Pearson's Canal Com[panion]
SEVERN & AV[ON]

Published by Wayzgoose
Staffordshire DE13 9RS
email:enquiries@jmpearson.co.uk
www.jmpearson.co.uk

WAYZGOOSE

Eighth Edition 2020
ISBN 978 0 9928492 6 9

Upper Lode, Tewkesbury, R. Severn

O N the rare occasions I unguardedly let slip that I've earned my living writing about the inland waterways for over forty years, jaws have a tendency to drop. Not, I imagine, in shock that the subject matter is capable of sustaining a literary output of such lengthy duration, more that my outward appearance belies four decades of Sisyphean toil. 'You must have started very young!' they gasp. Indeed I did. The first Pearson guide rolled off the presses at the tender age of ten. Well, 'rolled' is poetic licence, because I was using a toy John Bull printing set at the time. But there, nevertheless I was, demonstratively 'in print', and *Scenic Haunts of Needwood Forest* could be obtained, for the not unreasonable sum of threepence, from 'all good book shops'. Though, more authentically, by knocking discreetly on the playroom door, nerve centre of the nascent Pearson publishing empire.

Publishing's raw materials were never in short supply in our household. My father - co-founder, let it never be forgotten, of this series of guides, thirty-nine years ago - managed a printworks with a stationers cum bookshop fronting on to the High Street. Dickensian would not do it justice. I doubt if it had changed significantly since Disraeli popped in, surreptitiously rearranging his novels advantageously, a time-honoured authorial ploy. In February 1916, a passing Zeppelin dropped a bomb which reduced the shop front window to smithereens, leaving a jagged tear at the top left-hand edge of Ian Hay's 1914 lightweight romantic romp *A Knight on Wheels*. Saved for posterity, its resides on our bookshelves to this day ... still unread.

Sadly - and there are Burtonians who have never recovered emotionally from its demise - the shop was a victim of the print-works' move to new purpose-built premises on the outskirts of town in 1964. Wearing his trademark paterfamilial beam, my father presented me with a display case of Esterbrook fountain pen nibs. 'Surplus to requirements,' he announced,

Jackie Pearson

Lock-wheeling

a phrase which has disquieted me ever since.

But I digress - an occupational hazard where guidebook compilers are concerned. One day Father came home with a copy of British Railways *Holiday Haunts*, a five hundred page vade-mecum to the attractions of Southern England from Kent to Cornwall. For a child raised on Jennings and Just William, it was a revelation. How avidly I devoured its contents. Beguiled by the photogravure, motorcar-absent images of cathedral closes, market squares, and promenades perambulated by gents in sports jackets and womenfolk with dresses so billowy they'd double as windbreaks. I absorbed the gazetteer's subliminal descriptions, quickly learning to read between the lines: 'panoramic sea views' (five miles inland); 'invigorating climate' (above average rainfall); 'handy for exploring Dartmoor' (damn all to do). Even the advertisements enthralled me, with their exhortations to send for an illustrated brochure. Needless to say, the Town Clerks of Southern England were systematically bombarded with urgent requests. 'More brochures, Master Michael,' our elderly postman would teasingly grumble, struggling up the path to our front door with the latest sackful.

Next off the press came *Through the Window: Burton-on-Trent to Ashby de-la Zouch*, a description of the dubious delights to be seen on my six days a week train ride to school: 'Emerging from Gresley's dankly sulphureous tunnel the train enters a smoky landscape of sanitaryware works and collieries. As we approach Moira, there are tantalising glimpses of Overseal engine shed and the silted remains of the Ashby Canal.' The die was cast. My life mapped out. Hence my disarmingly youthful demeanour. I could afford to by-pass the messy business of growing up. Yet something of an hiatus ensued, for I was summarily dispatched to boarding school. My parents thought my outlook required broadening. Hindsight has proven otherwise. It was my imagination that needed curbing.

Hawford, Droitwich Canals

Bidford Bridge, River Avon

Contents

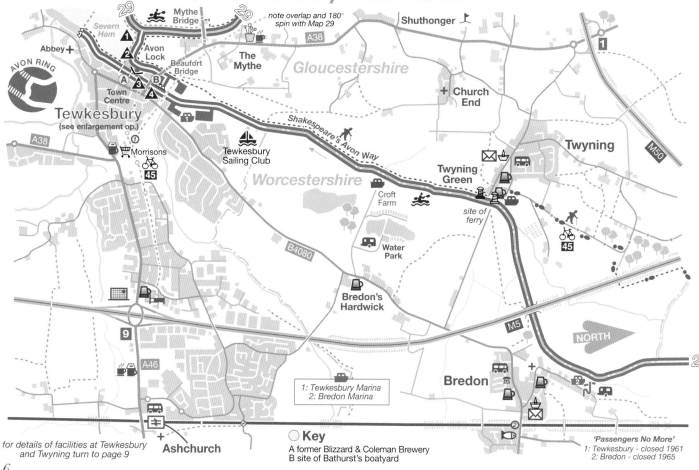

AVON NAVIGATION Tewkesbury 4mls/11k/1hr

note overlap and 180° spin with Map 29

Mythe Bridge

Severn Ham

Abbey

Avon Lock

Beaufort Bridge

The Mythe

Shuthonger

Gloucestershire

Church End

AVON RING

Town Centre

Tewkesbury
(see enlargement op.)

Morrisons

Tewkesbury Sailing Club

Shakespeare's Avon Way

Worcestershire

Croft Farm

Twyning Green

Twyning

site of ferry

Water Park

Bredon's Hardwick

NORTH

Ashchurch

Bredon

'Passengers No More'
1: Tewkesbury - closed 1961
2: Bredon - closed 1965

1: Tewkesbury Marina
2: Bredon Marina

○ **Key**
A former Blizzard & Coleman Brewery
B site of Bathurst's boatyard

for details of facilities at Tewkesbury
and Twyning turn to page 9

6

T O the uninitiated, Tewkesbury's waterways may appear complex; for instead of being content with one confluence with the Severn, the Avon branches into two channels. The main navigation passes through Avon Lock and meets the Severn below Mythe Bridge, whilst the 'Mill Avon' flows between the back of the town and the open pastures of Severn Ham, being navigable as far as the ancient and picturesque Abbey Mill.

As far as visiting boaters are concerned, however, Avon Lock serves as the 'gateway to the river'. During working hours it is manned, and operated by representatives of the Avon Navigation Trust, who are normally prepared to dispense liberal quantities of local information and advice; they will certainly help you find a mooring (the best facilities being located on the Mill Avon between King John's Bridge and Borough Mills) and may even try and sell you something from their range of souvenirs. ANT deserve your support, for without them there would be *no* navigable Avon.

Tewkesbury's waterfront is a delight. So many scenes catch the eye: the ancient arches of King John's Bridge; the quiet backwaters of the mill stream reflecting half-timbered houses and the town's towering abbey. Solely the abandoned Borough Mills introduce a sombre sense of melancholy. Long term Canal Companion users will recall when Healings barges, *Tirley and Chaceley*, would arrive here gunwale-deep with grain transhipped at Avonmouth. A nearby bench commemorates

⚠ Advice for Boaters

1. Entering or leaving the Avon from or for the Severn it is important to avoid the sandbar. Give this a wide berth by keeping over towards the southern bank as you turn into the Avon, and by making sure that Mythe Bridge is in view before turning upstream into the Severn.
2. Traffic lights control access into Avon Lock for upstream travellers. Green denotes the chamber is clear to use, red that you should 'stand off' or moor on the adjacent pontoon and ascertain the situation.
3. Travelling downstream you may have to wait until Avon Lock is free for your use. Try to avoid being taken past the lock entrance by the current.
4. Use the largest arch only at King John's Bridge, and proceed carefully for visibility of oncoming craft is restricted.

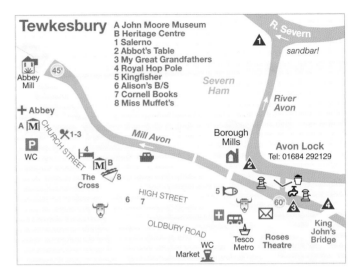

Tewkesbury
A John Moore Museum
B Heritage Centre
1 Salerno
2 Abbot's Table
3 My Great Grandfathers
4 Royal Hop Pole
5 Kingfisher
6 Alison's B/S
7 Cornell Books
8 Miss Muffet's

Abbey Mill — 45'
Abbey
Church Street
WC
The Cross
HIGH STREET
OLDBURY ROAD
WC
Market
Tesco Metro
Roses Theatre
R. Severn
sandbar!
Severn Ham
River Avon
Borough Mills
Avon Lock
Tel: 01684 292129
60'
King John's Bridge

William John (or 'Jack') Hitchman, one of Healings former skippers.

Demure and, for the most part, dreamy these days, the Avon can trace its navigable status farther back than most. Canals hadn't even been thought of when a certain Mr Sandys (pronounced 'Sands') of Fladbury sought Letters Patent to render the river commercially navigable in the 1630s. A resident of Fladbury (Map 4), William Sandys came from a wealthy family and was educated at Oxford where he came under the influence of John Hawley who was involved with upgrading the Thames. Sandys grasped that an Avon, made navigable in the manner of the Thames, would boost trade in the Vale of Evesham's rich agricultural hinterland; connect the by no means unimportant town of Warwick with the sea; and provide a means of carriage for the emerging coalfields in the vicinity of Coventry. Naturally not everyone shared his outlook, let alone his enthusiasm. Landowners were horrified at the thought of a towing path traversing their hitherto peaceful riparian

Avon Lock and Borough Mills

meadows. Millers baulked at the adverse effect on water levels the passage of craft might have. But the industrious Mr Sandys, as he was dubbed by a contemporary historian, by sheer perseverance (and possibly also a bribe to King Charles I) overcame such obstacles and the river was complete as a trading route by 1639. Decades of uninterrupted prosperity might have been Sandys' well-deserved dividend, but for the onset of the Civil War.

Leaving Tewkesbury - however reluctantly - in your wake, you soon find yourself lost in a timeless landscape of lush water-meadows. The M5 motorway intrudes briefly, and noisily, into the river's secret world, before disappearing as rapidly as it arrived. And how delightfully intimate and cosy the Avon seems if you have come off the mighty Severn. How elevated your view of things, now that there are no high banks to hide the outside world. Sailors and canoeists share your enjoyment of the river beneath the broad flank of Bredon Hill. The riverside villages of Twyning and Bredon - the latter well nigh impossible to visit by boat - are in different counties because this reach of the Avon forms the boundary between Gloucestershire and Worcestershire.

Upstream from Tewkesbury

Tewkesbury

Map 1

The radiant abbey of St Mary's looms maternally over the tumbling roofs of tight-knit streets, alleyways and courtyards which lead, at dizzy intervals, to tantalizing glimpses of boats moored on the Mill Avon: when the bells ring out for evensong it is easy to imagine that the centuries have rolled back to more god-fearing times. Tewkesbury was the fictional 'Elmbury' of John Moore's *Brensham Trilogy*, glorious post-war portraits of a Gloucestershire market town and its hinterland. When (and *if*) you've exhausted the charms of the town itself, there are some bracing walks to be enjoyed around the Severn Ham.

Eating & Drinking

ABBOT'S TABLE - Church Street. Tel: 01684 297878. Open Tue-Sat from 6pm and Sun lunch. Modern menu with a European twist. GL20 5RX

KINGFISHER - Quay Street. Tel: 01684 293220. Splendid fish & chip shop/cafe. GL20 5BE

MY GREAT GRANDFATHERS - Church Street. Tel: 01684 292687. Traditional English restaurant offering lunches and dinners (ex Thur lunch and Sun). GL20 5RX

ROYAL HOP POLE - Church Street. Tel: 01684 274039/278670. Well-loved Tewkesbury watering hole, which Dickens had Mr Pickwick visit. Now a Wetherspoon lodge. GL20 5RS

SALERNO - Church Street. Tel: 01684 850614. Italian open for dinner from 5pm Mon-Sat and lunchtimes Wed-Sun from noon. GL20 5RX

Shopping

A lovely town to shop in, but do beware the narrow pavements and traffic which appears reluctant to take prisoners. Miss Muffet's is an admirable delicatessen by The Cross. Food for the brain can be sourced at three bookshops: Alison's on High Street is an excellent example of how an independent bookseller (new) can thrive, and they have a nice line in classical music as well. Almost next door is Cornell Books (alongside Barclays Bank) who are especially strong on s/h topography and old OS mapping, whilst also on High Street is Bookworms (s/h). But if it's more mundane merchandise that you're seeking, there are small Tesco and Co-op supermarkets and a larger Morrisons on the eastern outskirts. Market days are Wednesday and Saturday, and there's a Farmers Market on the second Saturday in the month.

Things to Do

TOURIST INFORMATION & HERITAGE CENTRE - Church Street. Tel: 01684 855040. Local history displays housed in former hat shop. Particularly good section devoted to the town's two rivers. GL20 5AB

BOAT TRIPS - Back of Avon. Tel: 01684 593112. Short duration round trips and 'ferry' to Twyning operated by Severn Leisure Cruises. GL20 5AQ

JOHN MOORE COUNTRYSIDE MUSEUM - Church Street. Tel: 01684 297174. Small admission charge. Open Tue-Sat Apr-Oct plus Bank Holidays and Saturdays and school holidays in winter. Timber-framed 15th century town house devoted to interpretations of natural history and the literary output of John Moore, a number of whose books are on sale. Admission fee also provides access to neighbouring Merchant's House, cottage garden, and Old Baptist Chapel. GL20 5SN

TEWKESBURY ABBEY - Church Street. Tel: 01684 850959. Open daily. The visitor's centre features displays and exhibitions, as well as a refectory overlooking the abbey grounds. Ascents of the tower (212 steps) may be booked in advance. GL20 5RZ

Connections

BUSES - Stagecoach service 41 operates at 20 minute intervals (hourly Sun) to/from Cheltenham and provides a useful link with Ashchurch railway station. 42 and 43 provide additional hourly links with Cheltenham. Service 351 operates Mon-Sat to/from Upton and Gloucester, whilst service 71 operates a faster, daily link to/from Gloucester. 540 runs to/from Evesham via Bredon. Tel: 0871 200 2233.

TRAINS - Ashchurch (for Tewkesbury) station lies two miles east of the town centre. Great Western Railway services operate bi-hourly to/from Worcester and Gloucester. Tel: 0345 700 0125.

TAXIS - Avonside. Tel: 01684 293916.

Twyning

Map 1

Extensive, yet peaceful Gloucestershire village jutting into Worcestershire. Pronounced as 'twinning'. A 'ferry' operates to/from Tewkesbury during the summer months calling additionally at Croft Farm on the Worcestershire bank of the river. See 'Boat Trips' under Tewkesbury.

Eating & Drinking

FLEET INN - Fleet Lane. Tel: 01684 274020. Extensive riverside inn serving Wadworth (of Devizes, Wiltshire) ales. Mooring pontoon in association with Avon Navigation Trust. Lunch served 12-3pm daily, dinner from 6pm (3pm at weekends). GL20 6FL

VILLAGE INN - Fleet Lane. Tel: 01684 293500. Traditional local overlooking village green. Open from 5pm Mon-Thur and from noon Fri-Sun. Wye Valley HPA plus guests. GL20 6DF

Shopping

Spar convenience store and post office. Open 7am-8pm daily (from 8am Sun).

Bredon

Map 1

'Uncommonly enjoyable' according to Pevsner. All the more frustrating, then, that this well endowed Worcestershire village is to all intents and purposes 'out of bounds' to boaters and SAW walkers alike.

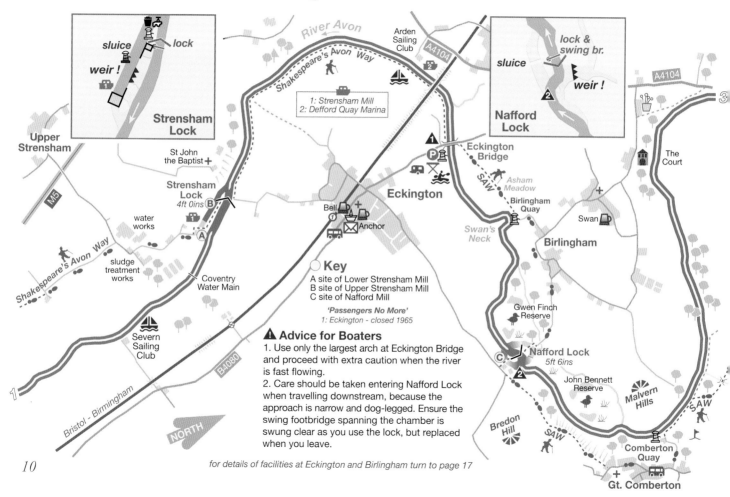

2 AVON NAVIGATION Eckington & Comberton 6mls/2lks/2hrs

Strensham Lock (inset)

sluice
lock
weir !
Strensham Lock

Nafford Lock (inset)

sluice
lock & swing br.
weir !
Nafford Lock

River Avon
Shakespeare's Avon Way
Arden Sailing Club
A4104

1: Strensham Mill
2: Defford Quay Marina

Upper Strensham
M5
St John the Baptist +
Strensham Lock
4ft 0ins
water works
Shakespeare's Avon Way
sludge treatment works
Coventry Water Main
Severn Sailing Club
B4080
Bristol - Birmingham

Eckington Bridge
Eckington
Bell
Anchor
Asham Meadow
Birlingham Quay
SAW
Swan's Neck
Birlingham
Swan
A4104
The Court

Gwen Finch Reserve
Nafford Lock
5ft 6ins
John Bennett Reserve
Malvern Hills
Bredon Hill
SAW
Comberton Quay
Gt. Comberton
SAW

⭘ Key

A site of Lower Strensham Mill
B site of Upper Strensham Mill
C site of Nafford Mill

'Passengers No More'
1: Eckington - closed 1965

⚠ Advice for Boaters

1. Use only the largest arch at Eckington Bridge and proceed with extra caution when the river is fast flowing.
2. Care should be taken entering Nafford Lock when travelling downstream, because the approach is narrow and dog-legged. Ensure the swing footbridge spanning the chamber is swung clear as you use the lock, but replaced when you leave.

NORTH

for details of facilities at Eckington and Birlingham turn to page 17

INFATUATED by Bredon Hill, the Avon hardly lets it out of its sight, as if fascinated by the summit's constantly changing shape. Half wooded, half bare, like mottled baize, it forms an island between the Cotswold Edge and the distant serrated outline of the Malvern Hills. Because, at 961ft, its peak narrowly falls short of a thousand feet, John Parsons, an 18th century MP and squire of Kemerton Court (on the southern flank of the hill) erected a folly tower on its top so that he could fancifully claim to stand that high above sea level. Still intact, and clearly visible from the river, the tower is somewhat ignominiously employed to boost mobile telephone signals nowadays. An open-air church service is held every Good Friday alongside it.

Bredon features - in one thousand, seven hundred and forty-first place - in the list of 'Marilyn' hills compiled by Alan Dawson in 1992; Marilyn, of course, being homophonously and humorously related to the better known 3000ft and above Munros of Scotland. A distinctive feature of Bredon Hill is its Iron Age fort, said to date from 200BC or earlier. The hill also plays host to a number of standing stones, of which perhaps the best known is the Banbury Stone, said to resemble a kneeling elephant.

Second only to the Thames in the amount of writing it has inspired, this stretch of the Avon is particularly rich in literary associations. Every guidebook quotes A. E. Housman's poem *In Summertime on Bredon* (an odd geographical aberration for a set of poems entitled *A Shropshire Lad*), but a better poem was written by Sir Arthur Quiller-Couch about Eckington Bridge. 'Q' had canoed the river as a young man in 1890, and had been inspired to compose a magnificent ode to the bridge which speaks of 'eloquent grooves worn

into the sandstone by labouring bargemen'. Jamie Davies, in his insightful 1996 book *Shakespeare's Avon: the History of a Navigation*, succinctly describes the process by which the hauling gangs negotiated a bridge when travelling upstream: 'a coil of rope would be carried up onto the bridge ... a log would be tied to one of its ends and dropped over the upstream parapet ... when the log had floated down to the waiting boat ... the boat could be pulled through'.

Quiller-Couch also employed the river in his adventurous tale *True Tilda*, painting an especially evocative scene of the bustling barges and steam tugs at Tewkesbury. Following his own journey down the river in 1910, Temple Thurston (Map 10) used Nafford Mill (destroyed by fire in 1909) as the setting for his Richard Furlong trilogy (*The Antagonists*, *Richard Furlong* and *The Achievement*), now long-forgotten and out of print, but still enjoyable reading if you can find them (as it is reasonably easy to do) second-hand. Other literary associations include the local writer John Moore who called it 'Brensham Hill' and the children's author Ursula Moray Williams who lived the latter part of her life at Beckford

Strensham Lock

on the south-west side of the hill. It is not difficult to see why such writers were moved to capture the spirit of this quintessentially English landscape. It would constitute one of life's missed opportunities, were you not to moor - at Eckington Bridge or Comberton Quay - make a not too gruelling ascent of Bredon Hill, and see for yourself Housman's 'coloured counties' and what you have come to think of as *your* river, meandering through this peerless panorama like some wandering minstrel.

continued overleaf:

continued from page 11:

The Severn Sailing Club was formed in 1936 and originally sailed on the Severn at Tewkesbury until World War II intervened. Their present location dates from the 1960s. Equally confusing, is the location of the Avon Sailing Club at Chaceley Stock on the River Severn (see Map 29).

Say Strensham to most people, and they'll recognise it as a stereotypically ubiquitous service area on the M5. But an older, wiser Strensham lies within a stone's throw of what Simon Jenkins referred to in *England's Thousand Best Churches*

Eckington Bridge

as the 'throbbing, roaring, hissing' motorway. He was on his way to visit St John the Baptist, of which more anon.

At the site of Lower Strensham Mill, burnt down in 1958, the former millstream is used for moorings by Strensham Mill boatyard. Upper Strensham Mill, which stood alongside the lock chamber, was demolished in the early 1920s. Photographs of both appear in Josephine Jeremiah's *The River Avon - A Pictorial History*, a delightful trawl through archive photographs. Several charming pen & ink drawings of river scenes in the neighbourhood of Strensham were drawn by Charles Showell for his 1901 book *Shakespeare's Avon: from Source to Severn*. Showell kept his houseboat at the lower mill, or did until a change of miller resulted in relations being not quite so cordial. Indeed, the new incumbent went as far as causing the author's boat to sink. Was it something Showell said!

Tantalisingly inaccessible, the church of St John the Baptist basks piously on the brow of a wooded hill to the west of the river, its lime-washed tower looking as though it might be made of cheese. Lamentably, there is no legal way of approaching it directly on foot from the riverbank. Yet, if ever a church cried out to be visited, this is one. Isolated now, half a mile to the west lie the moated remains of Strensham Castle, and once there was a village between them. Not surprisingly there are no regular services, but under the loving care of the Churches Conservation Trust the church is open to visitors. Amongst many interior features of interest are 15th century floor tiles, elaborate monuments to the local Russell family, a barrel roof, box and family pews, and a painted rood screen supporting a gallery illustrating Christ flanked by apostles, prelates and saints. Make a holy vow to go back by road one day, you will be well rewarded.

Either side of Strensham the river roams attractively past shallow banks of reeds and lily-pads, rutted by cattle and sheep intent on quenching their thirst. In a reach plied by sailing craft from the Arden club, the busy Bristol-Derby line crosses the river by way of a not ungraceful iron span resting on stone piers. It comes as something of a surprise to learn that Herbert Spencer, the influential Victorian philosopher (and plausible inventor of the 'slip coach') was instrumental in its design during a youthful sojourn in the engineering offices of the Birmingham & Gloucester Railway.

The present bridge at Eckington dates from the 16th century. The neighbouring wharf is popular with picnickers and boaters. Asham Meadow opposite is maintained as a traditional Lammas meadow where hay is grown between spring and summer, then, following harvesting, cattle and sheep are allowed to graze. Frequently flooded in winter, the meadow is a conducive habitat for waders such as redshank and curlew. The river coils itself in knots at the Swan's Neck and there are idyllic moorings at Birlingham Quay.

Temple Thurston described the melancholy ruins of Nafford Mill in *The Flower of Gloster* thus: 'the four pink-washed walls of it still stand with their sightless windows facing the evening sun like a palace built upon a Venetian canal ... the charred beams have been left to rot upon the ground; the great iron wheels and shafts, distorted into wild shapes by the fierce flames that embraced them, are lying now in a debris of bricks and mortar ... the roof is an open vault to heaven ... the heavy mill-wheel is quite still, water trickles over its slimy plates ... the chains are rusted and broken and it will never revolve again.' Photographs of the mill prior to its conflagration can be accessed on the Mills Archive website, a useful resource for mill-lovers.

Two wetland nature reserves adjoin the north bank of the river at Nafford Lock. The Gwen Finch Reserve is cared for by the Worcestershire Wildlife Trust but is deemed so sensitive that there is no public access other than on special open days. There is, however a hide, open for visitors on the neighbouring John Bennett Wetland Reserve where one might confidently expect to encounter skylarks, herons, and a variety of warblers.

Flanked by swathes of fertile arable farmland, the Avon proceeds pensively between Great Comberton and Pershore as if lost in its own thoughts; such introspection proves highly infectious. Boaters have the river to themselves as walkers are diverted via farmland to the north.

Swan's Neck & Bredon Hill

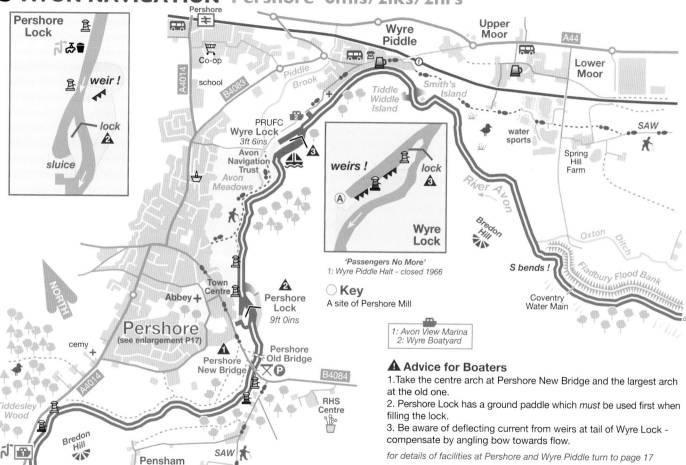

Pershore Lock

weir !

lock

sluice

Pershore

Wyre Piddle

Upper Moor

Lower Moor

A44

Co-op

school

A4014

B4083

Piddle Brook

Tiddle Widdle Island

Smith's Island

water sports

SAW

Spring Hill Farm

PRUFC
Wyre Lock
3ft 6ins

Avon Navigation Trust

Avon Meadows

weirs !

lock

Wyre Lock

'Passengers No More'
1: Wyre Piddle Halt - closed 1966

River Avon

Bredon Hill

S bends !

Oxton Ditch

Fladbury Flood Bank

Coventry Water Main

○ **Key**
A site of Pershore Mill

1: Avon View Marina
2: Wyre Boatyard

Pershore
(see enlargement P17)

cemy

Abbey

Town Centre

Pershore Lock
9ft 0ins

Pershore New Bridge

Pershore Old Bridge

B4084

RHS Centre

Tiddesley Wood

Bredon Hill

Pensham

Pensham Fields Farm

SAW

NORTH

A4014

14
2

⚠ Advice for Boaters

1. Take the centre arch at Pershore New Bridge and the largest arch at the old one.
2. Pershore Lock has a ground paddle which *must* be used first when filling the lock.
3. Be aware of deflecting current from weirs at tail of Wyre Lock - compensate by angling bow towards flow.

for details of facilities at Pershore and Wyre Piddle turn to page 17

ENTRENCHED in the Vale of Evesham, the Avon makes its stately way past Tiddesley Wood, where the famous Pershore 'Egg' plum was discovered growing wild in 1833. Pollarded willows and swaying poplars betray the river's course as it meanders towards the sturdy tower of Pershore Abbey.

Pershore Old Bridge, being strategically located on the London to Aberystwyth road, was destroyed during the Civil War. Half-heartedly, at first, by the Cavaliers, then entirely by the Roundheads who, as history records, were puritanically much better at demolishing things. William Sandys, of Royalist persuasion, lost control of the river to an anti-royalist called William Say. Bridges at Evesham and Stratford were similarly ill-treated and the navigation fell into disuse. Infrastructure, and by implication civilisation, are invariably casualties of war, past, present or future. Following the Restoration of the Monarchy, Say, one of the men who'd added his signature to Charles I's death warrant, was stripped of his estates, including the river, and sought exile in Switzerland. Pershore Bridge was rebuilt and fulfilled its role for a further three centuries until the motor age dawned, demanding construction of a wider, flatter span. Erected in 1928, its successor was hailed as the first concrete bridge in Worcestershire, though perhaps sadly not the last. For years it bore the brunt of the A44's increasing traffic until that in turn was diverted away to the north of Pershore. Now in its dotage, even the upstart evinces a curious post-concrete charm.

Pershore Mill was destroyed by fire in 1971, the fate of so many mills. It had been the last mill on the Avon in commercial use, and was also the river's last source of traffic. A little barge, with the biblical name of *Pisgah*,

Pershore Old Bridge

traded to and from the mill until the end, then happily escaped (like Charles II) to France where, after a period of use as a hotel boat, it is now apparently to be found in private use on the Canal du Midi.

Pershore presents a smiling face to its riverfront. There is something of a seaside air, with playing fields stretching to the rear of the High Street successfully masking any sense of urbanisation. In the early years of the 20th century Pershore enjoyed a halcyon era of pleasure steamer cruising, operated for the most part by Bathursts of Tewkesbury. Pershore Football Club play in the West Midlands Regional League where their opponents include a goodly number of Black Country teams from less bucolic locales such as Dudley, Wednesfield, Smethwick and Bilston: but who are the bigger bruisers? Meanwhile the east bank is entirely agricultural, stretching flatly across the Avon's broad fruit and vegetable growing valley.

Wyre Lock is diamond shaped: many of the original Avon locks were of unusual configuration to reduce erosion of the chambers by the force of water from the sluices. The Avon Navigation Trust have offices and workshops located in the old mill at Wyre. Desirable residences create an enviable riverside environment for the villagers of Wyre Piddle, but upstream the river soon loses itself amongst the fruit fields and orchards of this fertile valley. Herons and kingfishers abound. Shakespeare's Avon Way loses touch with the river again. Time hangs motionlessly over the landscape like the cobwebby pendulum of an unwound grandfather clock. Fladbury flood bank dates from 1881. Four feet high, it has sluice valves built into its bank to protect the farmlands from the ravages of the river. The flood bank hasn't always been up to its task, as several high water marks in Fladbury village (Map 4) testify.

Cropthorne

Birlingham
Map 2

Isolated village accessible both to walkers on Shakespeare's Avon Way, and also boaters who can most efficaciously moor at the Swan's Neck.

Eating & Drinking

SWAN INN - Church Street. Tel: 01386 750485. Half a millennium old, this welcoming thatched and half-timbered pub serves food Tue-Sat 12-3pm and 6-9pm and Sunday lunchtimes from noon. WR10 3AQ

Eckington
Map 2

Worcestershire village idyllically located on the pleated hem of Bredon Hill but prone to flooding when the Avon bursts its banks. The church contains a monument to John Hanford of Woollas Hall, his wife and their *thirteen* children.

Eating & Drinking

THE ANCHOR - Cotheridge Lane. Tel: 01386 750356. Cosy 17th century village pub. Open 10am-3pm and from 6pm daily. Food served Tue-Sat 12-3pm and 6-9pm plus Sun 12-3pm. Real ales include Prescott, Hobsons and Hook Norton. WR10 3BA
THE BELL - Church Street. Tel: 01386 750033. Refurbished country pub offering accommodation. Food served Mon-Fri lunchtimes and evenings (from 6pm) and throughout the day from noon at Weekends. WR10 3AN

Shopping

Post office stores open from 6am daily. Closes 6.30pm Mon-Fri, 6pm Sat and 1pm Sun.

Great Comberton
Map 2

Shopless and publess but possessed of a book exchange telephone kiosk. The parish church of St Michael is honey coloured, surrounded by yews, and inviting, but not, apparently, as trusting as the telephone kiosk, for it is usually locked.

Pershore
Map 3

Balconies blossoming from Georgian houses lend a holiday feel, an inherent *joie de vivre* to Pershore, best known nowadays, not for pears as the name implies, but for rich, ruby red plums. Asparagus (or 'gras') is another local delicacy, widely available between March and June. The Abbey, only slightly less imposing than Tewkesbury's, was only partially demolished following the Dissolution of the Monasteries. John Betjeman wrote of the abbey bells being rung for evensong in a poem called *Pershore Station*. Tourist Information is available from the library on Church Street. The Town Hall (High Street) contains a first floor Heritage Centre: open Wed-Sat, Apr-Sep.

Eating & Drinking

THE ANGEL- High Street. Tel: 01386 552046. Historic Pershore hotel. Breakfasts daily from 8am, lunches from noon, dinner from 6pm. WR10 1AF
PICKLED PLUM - High Street. Tel: 01386 556645. Gastropub at the north end of High Street. Open daily from noon. Food served 12-3pm and from 6pm weekdays (from 5pm Fri) and from noon throughout

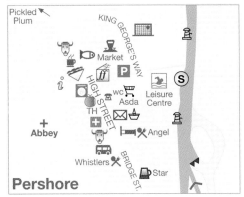

Pershore

at weekends. *Good Beer Guide* listed. WR10 1EQ
STAR INN - Bridge Street. Tel: 01386 561356. Former 15th century coaching inn with garden running down to the riverbank. Bar lunches Mon-Sat and dinner from 5pm. Sunday roasts noon to 4pm. WR10 1AJ
WHISTLERS - Royal Arcade. Tel: 01386 556900 Amiable first floor wine bar overlooking the sweep of Broad Street. Balcony tables. Open 10am-2.30pm Mon-Sat and from 7pm Mon-Thur, 5.30 Fri & Sat. WR10 1AG

Shopping

Retailers tend to be in for the long haul here: Elts have been selling shoes since 1872, and Browns ironmongery since 1913. The indoor retail market operates Wednesday through Saturday. The Post Office is housed in Tesco Express on the High Street, where you will also come across the excellent Sedgeberrow Books who always seem to have a good selection of inland waterways titles, and indeed transport generally.

Connections

BUSES - First Worcestershire X50 links Pershore with Worcester and Evesham hourly Mon-Sat. Some services connect with the rather 'out of town' railway station but in a pattern too obstuse to elucidate here. Tel: 0871 200 2233.
TRAINS - Cotswold Line services provided by the Great Western Railway. Connections to Worcester, Evesham, Oxford and London Paddington. Tel: 0345 700 0125.
TAXIS - Pershore Taxis. Tel: 0779 947 7571.

Wyre Piddle
Map 3

One of those comically named English villages which tickle the vulgar fancy. Pershore Rugby Club play at Piddle Park; cue for much ribaldry from visiting teams.

Eating & Drinking

ANCHOR INN - Tel: 01386 556059. Much refurbished after a period of closure, but still providing moorings for patrons. Pleasant decking overlooking the river and Bredon Hill. Open from noon daily, food served throughout until 9pm (6pm Sun). WR10 2JB

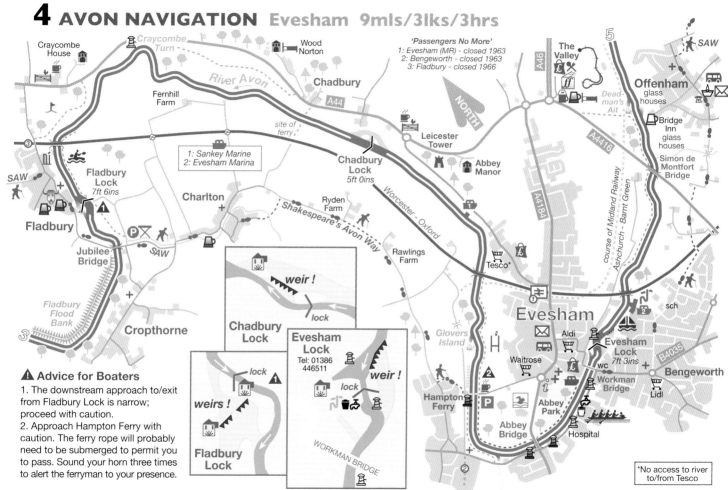

4 AVON NAVIGATION Evesham 9mls/3lks/3hrs

Craycombe House

Craycombe Turn

River Avon

Wood Norton

Chadbury

A44

'Passengers No More'
1: Evesham (MR) - closed 1963
2: Bengeworth - closed 1963
3: Fladbury - closed 1966

Fernhill Farm

site of ferry

NORTH

The Valley

A46

SAW

Offenham
glass houses

A4416

Bridge Inn glass houses

Dead-man's Ait

course of Midland Railway Ashchurch – Barnt Green

Simon de Montfort Bridge

Leicester Tower

Abbey Manor

1: Sankey Marine
2: Evesham Marina

Chadbury Lock
5ft 0ins

SAW

Fladbury Lock
7ft 6ins

Charlton

Ryden Farm

Shakespeare's Avon Way

Worcester - Oxford

A4184

Fladbury

Jubilee Bridge

SAW

Rawlings Farm

Tesco*

Cropthorne

Fladbury Flood Bank

Chadbury Lock

weir !

lock

Evesham Lock
Tel: 01386 446511

weir !

lock

Glovers Island

Evesham

Aldi

Evesham Lock
7ft 3ins

B4036

Bengeworth

Lidl

Waitrose

wc

Workman Bridge

weirs !

Fladbury Lock

lock

WORKMAN BRIDGE

Hampton Ferry

Abbey Park

Abbey Bridge

Hospital

⚠ Advice for Boaters

1. The downstream approach to/exit from Fladbury Lock is narrow; proceed with caution.
2. Approach Hampton Ferry with caution. The ferry rope will probably need to be submerged to permit you to pass. Sound your horn three times to alert the ferryman to your presence.

*No access to river to/from Tesco

for details of facilities at Fladbury and Evesham turn to page 21

BETWEEN Cropthorne and Offenham the river practically boxes the compass on its gorgeous meanderings through the fecund vale. In the 19th century the only way to cross the river at Cropthorne was to ford it. But in Queen Victoria's Jubilee year a bridge was built to span the river here, so that Fladbury lads could go courting Cropthorne lasses without necessarily getting their feet wet.

One of the river's last working water-gates occupied the reach below Jubilee Bridge. These were devices for altering water levels without adversely affecting supplies to the mills. A conventional lock here would have lowered the water level to the detriment of the mill at Wyre. The water-gate provided a simple alternative. It consisted of a gate fitted with sluices set into a weir. In normal circumstances the gate would remain open until a boat passed through on its way upstream. Then the gate would be closed while the boat waited for a sufficient level of water to be built up to enable it to navigate up to Fladbury Lock. On the way back the sluices would be drawn on reaching the gate, and there a boat would wait until the levels had equalised and the gate could be opened. L. T. C. Rolt described its use in *Landscape With Machines*. He and his fiancee, Angela, had hired a cabin cruiser called *Miranda* from a boatyard at Wyre Piddle in 1938 in order to 'test the water' prior to plunging into full-time life afloat with *Cressy* as related in his timeless classic *Narrow Boat*.

The Avon at Fladbury is the stuff of dreams. Once there were two mills, that beside the lock being known as Cropthorne Mill in deference to its position. It is linked to the outside world by a private rope ferry. The other, quite naturally, was called Fladbury Mill and in its working heyday ground corn and made cider. Late in the 19th century a pair of Armfield 25hp turbines were installed to provide the village with electricity. Grandiosely known as the Fladbury Electric Light & Power Co., they charged ten shillings per light per annum to householders in the district, and erected seven street lights. Now in private use, the owners still derive electricity from the river. Altruistically, they grant 'permissive access' to the riverbank downstream of the mill, where can be found an interesting interpretive board and a bench conducive to watching the world go by.

The rhyming locks at Fladbury and Chadbury deserve a poem about them. Certainly there is plenty of inspiration in the landscape as the river winds past the orcharded flanks of Craycombe and Wood Norton. Craycombe House - guarded by a tall cedar - was built for George Perrott, an 18th century owner of the navigation. The novelist Francis Brett Young lived in it during the Thirties. Wood Norton Hall was ostentatiously erected in 1897 for the Prince Philippe (1869-1926) Duke of Orleans, exiled pretender to the French throne. His family had resided in England since his great-grandfather's abdication and banishment in 1848. An adventurer, on many levels, he could equally be described as a soldier, mountaineer, yachtsman, explorer, hunter and philanderer: famously enjoying a dalliance with the Australian opera singer Nellie Melba. If one can't be king, what else is there to do!

At the onset of the Second World War, Wood Norton was acquired by the British Broadcasting Corporation. Many of their wartime transmissions emanated from here, especially broadcasts to the resistance movements throughout occupied Europe. The monitoring of enemy broadcasts was another discipline. Quite possibly, Adolf Hitler's death was first learned of here. During the Cold War a nuclear bunker was constructed in the grounds. We can be thankful that it never fulfilled its true function, though, appropriately enough, it was used as a set for an episode of *Doctor Who*. Still employed as a BBC training centre, it is also a country house hotel; and very comfortable they made us on a research trip for this edition. Chadbury Lock, formerly diamond-shaped, was the first to be rebuilt by the Lower Avon Navigation Trust in 1953. Much of the work was done by the Royal Engineers, a pioneering use of military resources on a civilian project.

Above the treetops bordering the next reach stands the Leicester Tower, built in 1840 as a memorial to Simon de Montfort, the Earl of Leicester, who came a cropper at the Battle of Evesham in 1265. The monks of Evesham Abbey planted vineyards on these south-facing slopes in the Middle Ages. Round the corner two railway bridges spanned the river. One remains, carrying the highly scenic Cotswolds & Malverns line. The other - a client of the ferroequinological firm of undertakers, Beeching & Marples - carried the Midland Railway route from Redditch to Ashchurch near Tewkesbury. If it had remained open north of Evesham at least, it might have been more than a little useful as a commuter link with Birmingham today. A mere sixteen miles of railway permanently lost through dubiously reached and short-sighted, accountancy-led thinking, and far too expensive to reinstall now. The abandoned abutments of the vanished bridge retain a latent dignity as exemplified by their ochre-coloured corner stones.

A video called *Steam in the Vale of Evesham 1963* can be found on YouTube Six minutes in, it nostalgically depicts a steam train running down the Midland line past Hampton Ferry. Tap in 'Hampton Ferry' on your search machine and you'll come upon a fascinating site compiled by the Huxley family who have operated the river crossing since 1929. Ernie and Eileen Huxley ran the ferry, grew asparagus and kept racing pigeons. The latter were requisitioned during the Second World War and trained to bring back messages from occupied Europe. Nearby Hampton House was taken over by a branch of the BBC who would mendaciously broadcast the 'News from London' notwithstanding that they were actually in Evesham.

The present ferry was launched in 1986. This is one of only two public ferries still in existence on the Avon. It provides a popular short cut for the inhabitants of the growing suburb of Hampton, together with Huxley's static caravan site, to reach Evesham's shops. There is an aesthetic pleasure in its to-ing and fro-ing which makes you sad that not more of the river's ferries have survived. Local authorities, one feels, might have done more to preserve such operations, if only to maintain the integrity of public rights of way.

A stately bridge, named after one of the town's Victorian mayors, spans the Avon in the centre of Evesham, and recreation grounds, bordered by an avenue of limes, create a gracious riverside environment. On hot days, with Evesham *en fête*, you might be reminded of Seurat's pointillistic masterpiece *A Sunday Afternoon on the Island of La Grande Jatte*. Rowing sculls, 'fours' and 'eights', trip boats et al add to the general sense of busyness

here throughout the summer months, and there will be occasions when the passing boater finds it difficult to either manoeuvre or moor. Such activities hark back to an Edwardian heyday when steamers regularly plied the river. Workman Bridge dates from 1856, having replaced a crumbling medieval bridge of eight arches. A typically 'go-ahead' Victorian, Henry Workman also endowed the town with its riverside park, or 'pleasure grounds' as originally known.

Evesham marked the frontier between what used to be known as the Lower and Upper navigable sections of the River Avon, restored and administered by separate trusts but now under the aegis of one combined body. Following decades of disuse, the Lower Avon was re-opened to navigation in 1962, the Upper in 1974; blithe dates which do scant justice to the monies raised and volunteer labour involved in restoring the river to the state that so many people enjoy today.

Evesham Lock is the highest upstream on the Lower Avon. A triangular-shaped lock-keeper's house spans the original, long since disused chamber, though recently the building has been deemed unstable and is now - for the time being at least - sadly uninhabited.

Between Evesham and Offenham the river is left pretty much to its own devices. The railway and the by-pass cross the Avon but leave little impression on it. Beyond the watermeadows, and the likelihood of floods, the countryside is thick with regimented fruit trees and the ubiquitous green houses in which Evesham's reputation as a centre for the cultivation of tomato plants is forged.

Deadman's Ait was the scene of heavy fighting during the Battle of Evesham. Many Welshmen were slaughtered in the vicinity, and large quantities of human remains were unearthed during the eighteenth century. The peace we associate with the English landscape had to be fought for. Offenham is known throughout the district for its annual 'wake', a week of fun and frivolity at the beginning of June. Notwithstanding signposts in the village, the ferry, apparently, ceased operating in the early Sixties, though you have to go back a couple of centuries earlier to find the bridge which gave the pub its name.

Fladbury
Map 4

Alas and alack, the absence for many years of suitable moorings has rendered the pretty village of Fladbury effectively beyond the reach of boaters. Slim wonder it is no longer capable of sustaining a general store. Temple Thurston would feel betrayed and Mrs Izod aghast that the ferry no longer operates for the benefit of the public and radish pickers. The railway station is another victim of the passage of time; ditto the bus service. Once the railway's goods yard 'reeked with fruit', local plums went all the way to a jam factory in Lancashire, and savoy cabbages spilled on to the rails they were stacked so high.

Eating & Drinking
ANCHOR INN - village green. Tel: 01386 860391. Welcoming village local offering B&B. WR10 2PY.
CHEQUERS INN - Tel: 01386 861854. Refurbished country pub with rooms. WR10 2PZ
CRAYCOMBE CAFE - Craycombe Farm (A44). Tel: 01386 860732. Accessible from Craycombe Turn ANT moorings but take care of traffic. WR10 2QS

Shopping
Fladbury Pies & Sausages make the mouth water, and their little emporium opposite the church is open Tue-Sat, EC Thur & Sat. Tel: 01386 860228.

Evesham
Map 4

Iron Curtain accents proliferate in Evesham, cynosure of its fruity vale. The by-pass and pedestrianisation between them seem to have created a semblance of calm that has been absent since the invention of the motor car. Highlights include the Bell Tower, all that's left of an abbey demolished following the Dissolution. Compare its fate with Pershore, losing only its nave and Tewkesbury, surviving virtually intact. Time your visit to hear the tower's carillon - playing *Linden Lea* when we last paused, rapt, to listen. Standing alongside is St Lawrence's, cared for by those paragons, the Churches Conservation Trust. Some of its stained glass is the work of Frederick Preedy, born in Offenham in 1820, and a prolific designer of church architecture and glass throughout the Vale of Evesham and beyond. Indeed examples of his windows can be found in the cathedrals of Worcester, Gloucester, Ely and Lincoln. On the Bengeworth side of the river, The Regal is a fine example of Art Deco cinema architecture and includes a good cafe.

Eating & Drinking
CASA - Vine Street. Tel: 01386 48509. Italian restaurant open for lunch and dinner (from 5pm) Mon to Fri and from noon throughout at weekends. WR11 4RE
RAPHAEL'S - Boat Lane. Tel: 01386 442458. Riverside cafe overlooking Hampton Ferry. Open from 10am daily (9am at weekends) until 5pm (3pm on Mon) and 6pm at weekends. WR11 4BP
RED LION - Market Place. Tel: 01386 761688. *Good Beer Guide* listed town centre pub. WR11 4RE
ROYAL OAK - Vine Street. Tel: 01386 442465. Half-timbered town centre inn offering accommodation. Breakfast 9.30-11.30am. Food served thereafter from noon throughout. Hogs Back & Purity ales. WR11 4RE

Shopping
Bridge Street and High Street are the principal shopping thoroughfares, along with the River Side indoor shopping centre, the latter being the site for many of the well known chain stores. Waitrose opened a supermarket on Merstow Green in 2018. It opens from 8am to 8pm daily except for Sunday 10am-4pm. Bengeworth, east of the river, boasts a bike shop, launderette, pharmacy, a plethora of East European food stores, heaps of takeaways, and a Lidl. Regrettably, the large Tesco which overlooks the river on the western edge of town is inaccessible therefrom.

Things to Do
TOURIST INFORMATION - The Almonry, Abbey Gate. Tel: 01386 446944. WR11 4BG
ALMONRY HERITAGE CENTRE - Abbey Gate. Tel: 01386 446944. Open Mon-Sat 10am-5pm and Suns (Mar-Oct) 2-5pm. Small admission charge. The former home of the Abbey Almoner today houses a heritage centre detailing the history of the town. WR11 4BG
THE VALLEY - Twyford. Tel: 01386 298026. Countrified retail complex on the northern outskirts of town. Farm shop, garden centre, cafe/restaurant etc. Again, no direct access from river, unfortunately! WR11 4TP
EVESHAM VALE LIGHT RAILWAY - Twyford. Tel: 01386 422282. Integral attaction to the above, this mile long, 15 inch gauge railway is open every weekend throughout the year. WR11 4DS
AVON LEISURE CRUISES - Tel: 0777 465 3112.

Connections
BUSES - First Worcestershire service X50 links Evesham with Pershore and Worcester hourly Mon-Sat. Service 540, operated by Astons of Kempsey, runs hourly Mon-Sat to/from Tewkesbury offering a magical mystery tour of Bredon Hill in the process. For Stratford via Bidford catch Johnsons service X18. Tel: 0871 200 2233.
TRAINS - Great Western Railway Cotswold & Malvern Line services to/from Worcester via Pershore and London Paddington via Oxford. Tel: 0345 700 0125.
TAXIS - BR Taxis. Tel: 0771 656 6829.

Offenham
Maps 4/5

Market gardening village with maypole. Church unusually co-dedicated to St Milburga, an 8th century abbess.

Eating & Drinking
FISH & ANCHOR - Offenham Lock (Map 5). Boater access. Tel: 01386 40374. Riverside pub open from noon daily. Lunches and dinners (from 5pm) weekdays. Food 12-8.30pm Sat and 12-5.30pm Sun. WR11 8QT

5 AVON NAVIGATION Harvington 5mls/3lks/2hrs

⚠ Advice for Boaters

1. Cruising upstream keep left on leaving the lock and accelerate past the weir. Cruising downstream keep right to counter the draw of the weir and beware dog-leg approach to chamber.

2. Keep left, away from the weir channel, as you approach Marlcliff/IWA lock from upstream. The lock channel is very narrow and tightly angled, proceed with due care.

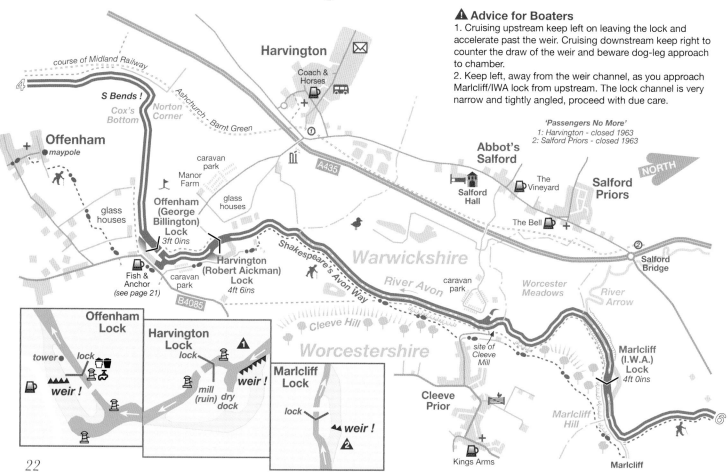

course of Midland Railway

Ashchurch - Barnt Green

Harvington

Coach & Horses

Offenham
maypole

S Bends !

Cox's Bottom

Norton Corner

caravan park

Manor Farm

glass houses

glass houses

Offenham (George Billington) Lock
3ft 0ins

Fish & Anchor
(see page 21)

caravan park

Harvington (Robert Aickman) Lock
4ft 6ins

B4085

Shakespeare's Avon Way

Warwickshire

River Avon

'Passengers No More'
1: Harvington - closed 1963
2: Salford Priors - closed 1963

Abbot's Salford

Salford Hall

The Vineyard

Salford Priors

NORTH

The Bell

Salford Bridge

River Arrow

caravan park

Worcester Meadows

River Arrow

Cleeve Hill

Worcestershire

site of Cleeve Mill

Marlcliff (I.W.A.) Lock
4ft 0ins

Marlcliff Hill

Cleeve Prior

Kings Arms

Marlcliff

Offenham Lock
tower
lock
weir !

Harvington Lock
lock
mill (ruin)
dry dock
weir !

Marlcliff Lock
lock
weir !

22

DRIFTING through time and space, the Avon wends its secluded way between Evesham and Bidford. Hitherto, boaters have more or less enjoyed exclusive access to these reaches of the river, but with the development of *Shakespeare's Avon Way* ramblers have acquired a more robust route, albeit one frequently out of sight of the river: reasonably well-signposted, reasonably well-maintained; but prone, here and there in high summer, to over-abundant nettles, brambles and crops grown without consideration for rights of way. With determination, however - and calves impervious to nettle rash - it can be walked the whole eighty-eight miles from Tewkesbury to the Avon's source at Naseby in Northamptonshire.

Substantially different in character to the lower river, the Upper Avon has a wilder feel to it, akin perhaps to the uppermost reaches of the River Thames between Oxford and Lechlade. It was appropriate, therefore, that second-hand paddle gear from Thames locks was used in the restoration of the Upper Avon. And what a mammoth undertaking it was, costing more than six times as much as the Lower Avon restoration project.

All the Upper Avon locks are dual-named after individuals or groups associated with the restoration of the river. The work at Offenham/George Billington Lock was completed in just six weeks so that its donor, who was terminally ill in his thirties, might observe the effect of his benefaction before he died. Harvington/Robert Aickman Lock commemorates one of the most influential figures of the post war inland waterways renaissance. Aickman founded the Inland Waterways Association in 1946 and crusaded for the waterways cause for a further twenty years. Returning navigation to the Avon was dear to his heart, and he was on the council of both Trusts. A memorial plaque, set in an attractive sweep of brickwork, graces the lockside, paying homage to his achievements and determination.

More practically, the boater is thankful for the provision of free overnight moorings on most lock cuts, many located in blissfully remote rural surroundings. From Offenham Lock it's a pleasant mile's walk along Anchor Lane to Harvington with its distinctive copper-spired church. The late David Hutchings, who masterminded restoration of the Upper Avon, lived here in a house he'd built out of an old railway bridge. The moorings at Harvington Lock provide access to the village as well, whilst you can also view the ruins of an old water mill which hasn't worked in a century.

Sir Arthur Quiller-Couch wrote of 'clouds of sweet-smelling flour' issuing from the doorway of Cleeve Mill, but virtually all trace of the lock, weir and mill at Cleeve has vanished. Up until the Second World War this was a popular venue for picnics. Below the weir the Avon was shallow enough to be forded by hay carts at harvest time. A correspondent from Canada wrote to tell us that his great uncle once lived in the mill, commuting from Salford Priors station to Birmingham, where he was the conductor of the symphony orchestra and on personal terms with Tchaikovsky: what interesting people the *Canal Companion* users are!

Downstream of the Marlcliff/I.W.A. Lock, the River Arrow has its confluence with the Avon. Consideration was given to making this navigable in the 17th century, but nothing materialised. The Arrow rises on the Lickey Hills and passes through the lower reservoir at Bittell (Map 16) beside the Worcester & Birmingham Canal, so you may well see it again. Likewise its tributary, the Alne, which follows the Stratford Canal for a while in the vicinity of Preston Bagot.

Marlcliff is aptly named, for the Trust had considerable problems during the construction of the lock, due to the unyielding quality of the substrata. ANT's excellent handbook (worth acquiring to boost their coffers) describes many of the difficulties overcome during the restoration in a matter of fact way, a modesty which fails to disguise the vast amount of work they undertook - and continue to undertake - on our behalf.

Like an airlock in a sluice, a memory bubbles to the surface of bumping, at breakneck speed, along a pot-holed lane, in David Hutching's battered Landrover, a golden retriever, with a tongue like emery paper, licking Lock-wheeler's neck. We're off to deal with a troublesome weir. Meat and drink to the man beside me. Glancing sideways at his determined profile, I am irresistably reminded of another David ... Hemmings, in *The Charge of the Light Brigade*.

6 AVON NAVIGATION Bidford & Welford 6mls/3lks/2½hrs

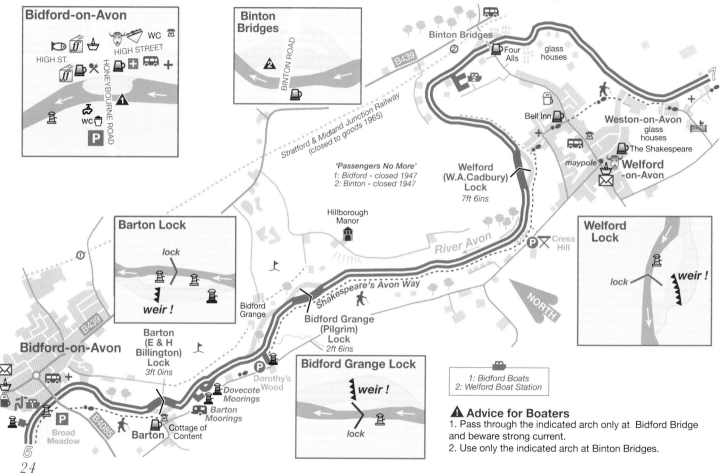

Bidford-on-Avon
HIGH ST. HIGH STREET WC
Honeybourne Road
WC
P

Binton Bridges
BINTON ROAD
2

Binton Bridges
B439
Four Alls
glass houses
Bell Inn
Weston-on-Avon
glass houses
maypole
The Shakespeare
Welford-on-Avon

Stratford & Midland Junction Railway
(closed to goods 1965)

'Passengers No More'
1: Bidford - closed 1947
2: Binton - closed 1947

Welford (W.A.Cadbury) Lock
7ft 6ins

Hillborough Manor

River Avon

Shakespeare's Avon Way

Cress Hill
P
NORTH

Barton Lock
lock
weir !

Welford Lock
lock
weir !

Bidford Grange

Bidford Grange (Pilgrim) Lock
2ft 6ins

Barton (E & H Billington) Lock
3ft 0ins

Bidford Grange Lock
weir !
lock

Dorothy's Wood
P
Dovecote Moorings
Barton Moorings
Bidford-on-Avon
B439
B4085
Broad Meadow
Barton
Cottage of Content

1: Bidford Boats
2: Welford Boat Station

⚠ **Advice for Boaters**
1. Pass through the indicated arch only at Bidford Bridge and beware strong current.
2. Use only the indicated arch at Binton Bridges.

5

24

NARROW and winding - rather after the fashion of life itself - the Upper Avon is at its loveliest between Bidford and Weston. Like dividends from a sagaciously garnered investment portfolio, the locks - not always situated in exact accordance with those on the original navigation - come at satisfying intervals, but the rest of the time you have every justification for just sitting back and watching the peaceful landscape slip uneventfully astern, grateful that there were believers enough to restore navigability to the river. Reflect that the attitudes of landowners, local and water authorities influenced the final shape of restoration. Sometimes such individuals and bodies were extraordinarily helpful, whilst others seemed determined to stop the scheme in its tracks. Inexplicably, as Robert Aickman put it, the restorers were not always seen to be on the side of the angels.

Bidford positively bristles with boats, coming in to moor with varying degrees of proficiency, or threading their way gingerly through the eye of a needle navigation arch of the 15th Century bridge. The Romans elected to cross the Avon at Bidford. Their Ryknild Street forded the river here on its way to the town of Alcester. Later the road was known as Buckle Street, and it was the monks of Alcester who erected the present bridge which dates from 1482. None of its seven arches are alike in size or shape.

The official moorings at Bidford provide sufficient space for only three or four narrowboats alongside the Recreation Ground. If there are no spaces left you could see if Bidford Boats have any spare room. Or try Barton/E&H Billington Lock, which is linked by a pleasant footpath across the meadows to Bidford, a quarter of an hour's walk away.

Five leisurely miles upstream of Bidford, the river splits into several channels - only one of which is navigable - to pass beneath the ancient arches of Binton Bridges. Nearby lies the trackbed of the old Stratford & Midland Junction Railway, one of those endearingly independent cross-country lines which seemed to lead from nowhere to nowhere. At plum-picking time as many as twenty wagons a day were loaded with fruit in the tiny siding at Binton. Amongst the line's best remembered trains were the banana specials operated by the Midland Railway between Avonmouth Docks and London; a somewhat elongated route, designed perhaps to give the bananas time to ripen. Binton church - half a mile to the north - is worth a detour. One of its stained glass windows commemorates Captain Scott's polar expedition. The connection being that the rector's sister, Kathleen, was the explorer's wife, a well-known sculptress and, of course, the mother of naturalist, painter and early inland waterway activist, Peter Scott - see Map 34.

Bidford-on-Avon   Map 6

There is a resort-like air about Bidford. Day-trippers pour on to the riverside recreation ground (known locally as Broad Meadow) but rarely stray further than the local pubs and fast food outlets. Shakespeare came here to debauch himself too, immortalising the place in one of his poems as 'drunken Bidford'.

Eating & Drinking

THE BRIDGE - High Street. Tel: 01789 773700. Stylish 'eaterie'. Riverside decking. Open lunchtimes daily, and for dinner (from 6.30pm) Mon-Sat. B50 4BG
COTTAGE OF CONTENT - Barton (reached by footpath from Bidford Bridge). Tel: 01789 772279.

Country pub offering B&B. Food served 12-2pm and from 6pm Mon-Sat, 12-4pm and 6-8pm Sun. B50 4NP

Shopping

More shops than most villages of this size can sustain: butcher, baker, pharmacy, convenience store (with cash machine), newsagent, and even a Budgens supermarket (with post office) on the main road.

Connections

BUSES - Stagecoach service 28 runs half-hourly Mon-Sat to/from Evesham and Stratford. Tel: 0871 200 2233.

Welford-on-Avon   Map 6

Lack of public moorings (though they can usually be arranged at Welford Boat Station - Tel: 01789 750878) hampers exploration of this pretty village complete with maypole and many thatched cottages.

Eating & Drinking

FOUR ALLS - Binton Bridges. Tel: 01789 332184 Limited customer moorings. Smart waterside pub. Open daily from 9am, food throughout. CV37 8PW
There are two other pubs, more handy for walkers, in the village: THE BELL (Tel: 01789 750353 - CV37 8EB) and THE SHAKESPEARE (Tel: 01789 750443 - CV37 8PX).

Shopping

Convenience store (with post office) and excellent butcher/deli (Maypole Butchers - Tel: 01789 750213).

7 AVON NAVIGATION Stratford-on-Avon 4mls/3lks/1½hrs*

⚠ Advice for Boaters

1. Picking up and setting down crew members at the entrance to Bancroft Basin is not easy and it may be advisable to take the long way round by Tramway Bridge.

2. Whilst the statutory head of navigation is at Alveston, 3 miles upstream of Stratford, in practice it is inadvisable for deep-draughted craft to proceed beyond Cliffe Cottage, whilst the average narrow boat will find even the Old Bathing Place potentially shallow.

Stratford Waterways Information Centre is based on a boat in Bancroft Basin. A fund of local boating knowledge, it is open daily, Apr-Oct, 9.30am-6pm. Tel: 0758 408 6321.

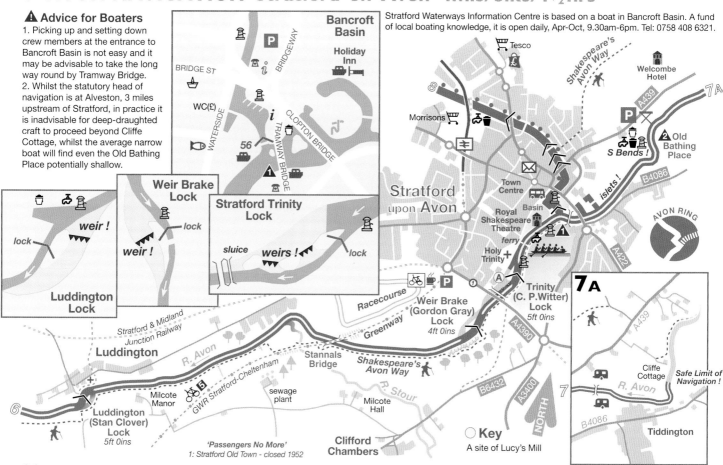

Bancroft Basin

Holiday Inn

BRIDGE ST

BRIDGEWAY

WC(£)

WATERSIDE

CLOPTON BRIDGE

TRAMWAY BRIDGE

56

Weir Brake Lock

lock

weir !

lock

Stratford Trinity Lock

sluice

weirs !

lock

Luddington Lock

lock

weir !

lock

Tesco

Morrisons

Shakespeare's Avon Way

Welcombe Hotel

A439

7A

P

S Bends !

Old Bathing Place

B4086

islets !

AVON RING

Stratford upon Avon

Town Centre

Basin

Royal Shakespeare Theatre

ferry

Holy Trinity

A site of Lucy's Mill

Racecourse

Greenway

Shakespeare's Avon Way

Weir Brake (Gordon Gray) Lock
4ft 0ins

Trinity (C. P. Witter) Lock
5ft 0ins

A4390

A422

7A

Cliffe Cottage

Safe Limit of Navigation !

A439

R. Avon

B4086

Tiddington

7

NORTH

A3400

B6432

Stratford & Midland Junction Railway

Luddington

R. Avon

GWR Stratford-Cheltenham

Stannals Bridge

sewage plant

Shakespeare's Avon Way

R. Stour

Milcote Manor

Milcote Hall

6

Luddington (Stan Clover) Lock
5ft 0ins

'Passengers No More'
1: Stratford Old Town - closed 1952

Clifford Chambers

○ **Key**
A site of Lucy's Mill

26

*Time refers to Luddington to Stratford and the lock count does not include access to Bancroft Basin.

BOATERS have three river locks to contend with (plus a fourth if they are moving on to or off the canal at Stratford) as the Avon winds from Luddington, past Stratford, to the present head of navigation at Alveston Weir. Luddington Lock's alternative name honours one of the former Upper Avon Navigation Trust's loyal supporters. Boosted by the Stour, whose source lies near the brewery town of Hook Norton, the Avon widens perceptibly after the narrow reaches in the vicinity of Bidford. Above the confluence a large steel girder bridge carries the trackbed of the old Great Western Railway's Stratford-Cheltenham line. Now known as 'The Greenway', it stretches from Stratford to Long Marston, a useful escape route from the busy tourist town for walkers, cyclists and horse-riders. The indefatigable Andrew Yarranton proposed rendering the Stour navigable in the 17th Century.

Weir Brake Lock (built in just thirty-eight days by Borstal boys back in the early Seventies) commemorates Gordon Gray, a previously anonymous donor who made his fortune in the diamond mines of South Africa. Shakespeare's Avon Way offers a panoramic view from high above the lock. The Queen Mother travelled from here to the next lock up by narrowboat during the opening ceremony of June 1st 1974, as celebrated in the poem *Inland Waterway* by Sir John Betjeman.

The short reach separating Weir Brake and Stratford Trinity locks is spanned by the Stratford & Midland Junction Railway bridge which was converted to carry road traffic. One of the last trains to cross over the river was the Royal Train, carrying the Queen Mother to officiate at the reopening of the Stratford Canal in 1964. Her Royal Highness obviously had a soft spot for Stratford and its inland waterways. A footbridge also crosses the river at this point, making it easy for pedestrians to enjoy a circular walk beside the Avon. Blocks of highly desirable flats occupy the site of Lucy's Mill, which stood here for hundreds of years and was an important customer of the river barges until the advent of the railway. They employed a steam vessel to import Irish corn from Bristol docks.

Stratford Trinity Lock is also known as Colin P. Witter Lock. Indeed, his name appears on the massive steel frames which protect the chamber from collapse threatened by high ground pressures. The Witter family were early canal stalwarts, and well known manufacturers of towbars based in Chester. The bold steeple of Holy Trinity Church (Shakespeare's burial place) overlooks the lock, above which Stratford's passenger ferry boat, built in 1937 and given the suitably Shakespearean name of *Malvolio*

Stratford Trinity Lock

after a character in *Twelfth Night*, operates by means of a submerged chain fed through a winch on the pontoon wound by the ferryman.

Stratford's riverfront is familiar to people from all over the world, though it has subtly altered since the multi-million pound refurbishment of the Royal Shakespeare Theatre, completed in 2010. Originally erected in 1932, to the vaguely Cubist designs of Elizabeth Scott (cousin of Sir Giles), the theatre was itself a replacement for the Shakespeare Memorial Theatre of 1879, gutted by fire in 1926.

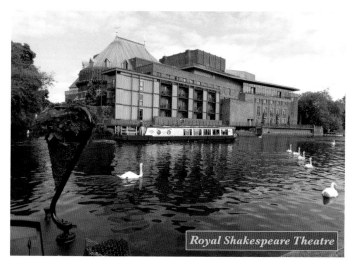

Royal Shakespeare Theatre

Construction of the new theatre came at the expense of a number of wharves and warehouses adjoining Bancroft Basin.

As a boater, you have your own cameo role to play - just don't make too much of a performance of it! The world and his wife seem determined to get afloat, and barnacle-encrusted navigators of the Avon Ring have to keep a weather-eye peeled for sudden unexpected and unpremeditated lurches to port or starboard; moreover the reach is additionally a training ground for the more accomplished performers of Stratford Rowing Club. A long river bank, backed by a recreation ground, excellent for mooring alongside, extends beyond the lock. A fee is payable between April and October, though its collection doesn't appear to be rigorously enforced.

Upstream of the entrance lock to the Stratford Canal and Bancroft Basin the river is spanned by the Tramway Bridge, a redbrick structure built in 1826 to carry the Stratford & Moreton Horse Tramway, one of whose wagons is on display nearby. The bridge itself is now the preserve of pedestrians ... large numbers of them. In contrast, the stone arches of Clopton Bridge date back to 1480, deriving its name eponymously from a local merchant who went on to become a Lord Mayor of London. Four centuries apart, the two bridges harmonise well with their shared environment, as though the age gap was just a twinkling ripple in the timespan of the river which flows beneath them.

Beyond Stratford it is feasible for most craft to voyage a further mile or so to the Old Bathing Place, a picnic site provided with boating facilities, albeit on the shallow side for narrowboaters. The Stratford & Warwick Waterways Trust advocate a bold scheme to extend navigation up to a junction with the Grand Union Canal at Warwick. Six locks and a lift seem modest by the standards of many inland waterway project proposals, and the boost to tourism and the benefits of improved flood control are manifest, but the concept has so far foundered on the reactionary response of riparian landowners. Meanwhile, thanks to the continued work of ANT and its volunteers, boaters have fifty miles of gorgeous river to play with. Attitudes and personalities change - the river can bide its time.

Clopton Bridge

Stratford-on-Avon Maps 7 & 8

That Stratford-on-Avon is second only to London in the esteem of foreign visitors, serves to emphasise the charisma surrounding Shakespeare. Without his omnipresence, one imagines Stratford's position in the league table of tourism would be academic. And yet, subtract the Shakespeare factor, and you are still left with an attractive town with a generous helping of good architecture, its setting enhanced by the proximity of the Avon; and there is a hair-down demeanour about the people in the streets which becomes infectious. All those earnest foreign crocodiles! Contriving a dramatic analogy, Stratford delivers its lines and plays its part with its integrity and dignity intact, really being the rather nice place to visit as extolled by the tourist propaganda.

Eating & Drinking

To eat aboard or not to eat aboard? That is the question! Sometimes Stratford's culinary options can be a tad overwhelming and it's a relief to retreat to your boat and raise the gang-plank. On the other, Hamletian hand, your crew may feel they deserve a treat, and in the time-honoured Pearson spirit of helpfulness, we offer the following subjective choice:

CARLUCCIO'S - Waterside. Tel: 01789 267424. Italian cafe/restaurant/deli overlooking basin. CV37 6BA
COUNTESS OF EVESHAM - Bancroft Basin. Tel: 0783 676 9499. Lunch and dinner cruises on the Avon. CV37 6BA
HATHAWAY TEA ROOMS - High Street. Tel: 01789 264022. Delightfully old-fashioned breakfasts, lunches and teas in half-timbered town centre setting. CV37 6AU
LA MARINA - Clopton Bridge. Tel: 01789 299921. Tapas bar/restaurant overlooking Avon backwater. CV37 6YY
LOXLEYS - Sheep Street. Tel: 01789 292128. Restaurant and wine bar. Food served from noon throughout daily, plus breakfasts from 9.30-11.30am Fri-Sun. CV37 6EF
No.9 CHURCH STREET - Church Street. Tel: 01789

Stratford Ferry

415522. *Good Food Guide* listed restaurant located in the heart of Stratford's 'Old Town'. Lunch Tue-Sat, dinner Tue-Sat from 5pm. Plus 3rd Sun monthly for lunch. CV37 6HB
OPPOSITION BISTRO - Sheep Street. Tel: 01789 269980. 'The Oppo', as its regulars call it, does lunches Mon-Sat 12-2pm and dinner on those days from 5pm. CV37 6EF
ROOFTOP - Royal Shakespeare Theatre. Tel: 01789 403449. Open daily from 10.30am for lunch, drinks and dinner. CV37 6BB
SALT - Church Street. Tel: 01789 263566. Paul Foster's *Good Food Guide* listed restaurant. Lunches Wed-Sun, dinner (from 6.30pm) Wed-Sat. CV37 6HB

Shopping

Market day is Friday and a good one it is too. 'Upmarket' features craft and food stalls and is held on Waterside on Sundays and Bank Holiday Mondays throughout the year. Elsewhere the town bristles with quality shops engaged in the hectic business of emptying the bank accounts of visitors. But many of these shops have such character that you don't resent being plunged into the red. On the northern outskirts of town, within easy reach of Bridge 65 on the Stratford Canal, lies Maybird Shopping Park.

Things to Do

TOURIST INFORMATION - Bridgefoot. Tel: 01789 264293. 9am-5pm (10am-4pm Suns). CV37 6GW
ROYAL SHAKESPEARE THEATRE - Waterside. Tel: 01789 403493. Whatever else you do in Stratford, try to catch a performance at the RST. CV37 6BB
SHAKESPEARE'S BIRTHPLACE - Henley Street. Tel: 01789 204016. S's childhood home. Additionally the custodians of four other properties in the district. CV37 6QW
CITY SIGHTSEEING - Open top bus tours providing a good introduction to the town. Tel: 01604 676060.
VINTAGE TRAINS - Tel: 0121 708 4960. The Bard's favourite means of transport - steam hauled trains to Birmingham and back on selected Sundays July-mid Sep.
AVON-BOATING - Swan's Nest. Tel: 01789 267073. Skiff, punt and motor-boat hire, plus river trips. CV37 7LS

Connections

BUSES - useful downriver links with Bidford-on-Avon and Evesham (Stagecoach X18) and up-canal connections with Wootton Wawen, Hockley Heath, Shirley et al (Johnson's Excelbus X20). Tel: 0871 200 2233.
TRAINS - half-hourly West Midland services to Birmingham. Less frequent but useful direct link with London Marylebone by Chiltern Trains. Parkway station adjacent Stratford Canal Bridge 63. Tel: 0345 748 4950.
TAXIS - 007 Stratford's Taxis. Tel: 01789 414007.

8 STRATFORD CANAL Wilmcote & Stratford-on-Avon 4mls/17lks/4hrs

VISITING Stratford with his parents in the 1930s, a moodily adolescent Robert Aickman took himself off for a walk along the towpath of the Stratford Canal to visit Mary Arden's house at Wilmcote. The canal he encountered was in an advanced state of decay: 'Wild vegetation abounded; the water was shallow; the locks were leaking and crumbling, many with gates either flapping or jammed.' Were he somehow transported back to see it now, a fully functioning canal once more, his life's work - or at least that part of it pertaining to the inland waterways, as opposed to 'strange stories' - would be spectacularly vindicated. It doesn't fall to many people to make so positive a difference. Contrast Aickman's approach with that of the authorities who would have had the Stratford erased from the map in the late 1950s.

Small wonder, then, that the Stratford upon Avon Canal holds a special place in the affection of a generation of canal enthusiasts, its southern section being the first great restoration success of the post-war canal movement, an about-turn victory in the face of years of official neglect: 'Instead of expecting canals to get worse and worse and fewer and fewer, we suddenly saw that they might get

better and better and more and more extensive,' enthused John Gagg, doyen of a generation of canal authors who came to prominence on the back of the inland waterways reinvention as a leisure industry.

One only has to lean nonchalantly on the footbridge spanning the tail of Lock 56, looking down on all the fun-packed activity of Bancroft Basin to see how far the Stratford Canal has travelled from its nadir. The coal, lime and timber wharves of the past have been transmogrified into an aquatic caravanserai of trip boats, restaurant boats, ice cream boats, food boats et al. Here also are fishbone pontoons offering 48 hour visitor moorings - perhaps too centre stage for shrinking violets - together with a floating Information Centre, jointly sponsored by ANT and CRT. Perched atop the Gower Memorial, Shakespeare, surrounded by a quartet of his immortal characters, turns his back on the basin, as if finding the unremitting traffic on the neighbouring road more conducive to his muse. Exit *right*, pursued by a bear, might be stage direction he has in mind.

Canals are renowned for quick scene changes, for as soon as you have negotiated the narrow

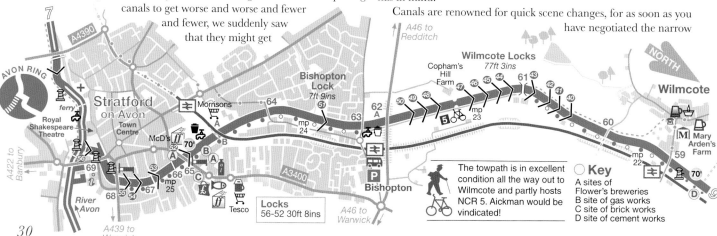

30

Lock 54

Lock 52

confines of Bridge 69, the mood changes abruptly, and you find yourself embalmed in a quiet residential zone, where notices encourage you, politely, not to run your engines noisily. Almost immediately the canal commences its climb out of the Avon valley. The environs are exceedingly pleasant. Hollyhocks thrive by lock chambers. Quite a few towns could usefully take a leaf out of Stratford's book. We witnessed a party of jocularly altruistic senior citizens, *Last of the Summer Wine* look-alikes and act-alikes, journeying up the flight on a diminutive outboard powered dinghy, bagging litter as they went, merrily on their way.

Bridge 65 carries Birmingham Road over the canal. Lock 52 is framed by a McDonald's fast food outlet and a Premier Inn travel lodge. One hopes the canal rubs off on their respective clientele: 'People have the oddest ideas about what canals are and where they go,' Robert Aickman wrote half a century ago, and despite the best efforts of sundry television celebrities, it still rings largely true. Ah, but would we aficionados want

it any other way? Don't we rather relish the secrecy the inland waterways bestow? Transparency would come at a price.

Briefly the canal changes character, like a small cloud obscuring the sun. Hereabouts stood Flower's brewery and a brickworks, a goods yard and a gas works. In their place, business premises offering little hint of what it is they do. Though tucked away in buildings adjacent to the towpath side of Bridge 64 are Ragdoll Productions, a television company once famous for the canal boat puppets Rosie & Jim. Whilst backing onto the off-side of the canal are Pashley, makers of traditionally styled bicycles.

Two railway bridges span the canal by the site of a hire base; though there remains access to water and Elsan disposal facilities. Bridge 64B is trackless, leaving 64A to carry trains into Stratford station, a terminus now, but once part of the old GWR through route from the Midlands to the West Country. Scheduled steam excursions operate on summer Sundays evoking memories of when *The Cornishman* once puffed proudly this way:

Wilmcote Locks

9am off Wolverhampton Low Level, 6.10pm into Penzance!

Bridge 62A carries Stratford's northern by-pass around the edge of the town. The road is the A46 which, as originally designated, connected Bath with Grimsby; though it would be difficult to imagine anyone willingly driving from the former to the latter. The bridge - the ugliest you'll encounter until you reach the M40 on Map 10 - is known - officially at least - as Chaly Beate Bridge. To understand why, retrace your steps to Bridge 63, alongside which a group of local entrepreneurs opened a spa in 1837. Sadly, from their perspective, it didn't become popular enough to make it pay, but some of the associated buildings remain, not least Bishopton (aka Victoria Spa) Lodge, an upmarket B&B

these days, with a spring still bubbling in its basement, and bearing a blue plaque commemorating the fact that Bruce Bairnsfather, the First World War cartoonist, lived here. Six weeks prior to becoming Queen, Princess Victoria ceremoniously opened the spa and overnighted at the Lodge.

Wilmcote Locks come thick and fast, though there are often CRT volunteers on hand to lighten the workload. Urban Stratford has been left astern, to be replaced by the sort of Warwickshire countryside that will unostentatiously accompany you all the way to the outskirts of Birmingham.

Wilmcote

turned a significant corner. Mercurially led by the same David Hutchings who subsequently masterminded restoration of the Upper Avon, teams of volunteers, boy scouts, military and prison labour succeeded in restoring the canal to full navigable status within five years at a cost of £56,000 against the cost of £119,000 quoted for its closure. Hutchings famously uttered: 'Fortunately none of us were experts, or we should have known it was impossible.' Initially the restored canal came under the aegis of the National Trust. But being more versed in the care of country houses, they were never totally comfortable with the day to day operation of a fully functioning canal, and ownership passed to British Waterways (who subsequently became known as the Canal & River Trust) in 1988. It seemed to make a lot of sense for the southern section of the Stratford Canal (below Kingswood) to be brought under the same management as the northern section, but did it lose its individuality in the process?

Everything would appear peaceful, but not so in Andy Griffee's crime caper *Canal Pushers*, the first murder of which occurs at Wilmcote, continuing with chilling regularity all the way to Worcester; great bedtime reading for boaters!

It was Warwickshire County Council's application to lower the road at Bridge 59 across the bed of the canal in 1958 that kick-started the campaign to 'Save the Stratford'. Road traffic, the weight and frequency of which, far exceeding the five tons limit it had been built to withstand, had rendered it dangerously unstable. Permission would undoubtedly have been granted had the fledgling Stratford-on-Avon Canal Society not been able to produce a pair of valid canoe licences, effectively demonstrating that the canal was still, however sporadically, being used for navigational purposes. As far as the Ministry of Transport was concerned, the County Council had to prove that the canal hadn't been used for at least three years. Their application to abandon the canal was denied, and the Stratford Canal's fortunes had

Wilmcote   Map 8

The church may, or may not, be the work of Butterfield, the vicarage and school certainly are. Strong connections with the Catholic revival in the Church of England. Rows of former quarrymen's cottages built from local stone.

Eating & Drinking
MARY ARDEN INN - The Green. Tel: 01789 267030. A Greene King inn offering accommodation. Breakfast served daily 8.30-11.30am. Meals served at lunchtimes and evenings (from 6pm) Mon-Sat. Roasts on Sun 12-4pm. CV37 9XJ
MASON'S ARMS - Aston Cantlow Road. *'For Sale'* as we went to press.

Shopping
Convenience store with 'outreach' post office service.

Things to Do
MARY ARDEN'S FARM - Tel: 01789 204016. Childhood home of Shakespeare's mother preserved as a working Tudor farm operated by the Shakespeare Birthplace Trust. Open daily from 10am. Gift shop and cafe. CV37 9UN

Connections
TRAINS - West Midlands services (from a felicitously well-preserved GWR country station) hourly to/from Stratford and Birmingham; plus bi-hourly Chiltern Railways service to/from Stratford and Leamington. Tel: 0345 748 4950.

9 STRATFORD CANAL Wootton Wawen 5mls/11k/2hrs

BESIDES being so long in the building - see Map 11 - the Stratford Canal never attracted as much trade as its dewy-eyed promoters envisaged. Lacking a hinterland of heavy industry, its main traffic might have been manufactured goods from Birmingham and the Black Country destined for export from Bristol, but the Avon was ponderous in comparison with the virile Severn, so most of that business went down the Worcester & Birmingham. Volume peaked in 1838 at 180,000 tons, and within twenty years the canal had been sold to one of the fledgling railway companies, the Oxford, Worcester & Wolverhampton, itself absorbed by the Great Western in 1865, hence the lozenge weight-restriction notices still encountered (where not 'museum-ed' or stolen) as you make your way along the canal.

Bearley (or rather more romantically, Odd) Lock separates two lengthy and delightfully remote pounds between the

locks at Wilmcote and Preston Bagot. The Warwickshire countryside is at its loveliest and the canal offers wide vistas over rolling hills. Edstone Aqueduct is, without question, the Stratford Canal's most dramatic engineering feature. It consists of an iron trough resting on thirteen tapering brick piers. At 28 feet high and 158 yards long: the longest in England as a Transport Trust plaque helpfully points out. The sunken towpath offers walkers a strange, fish-eye lens view of passing boaters. The aqueduct spans a by-road, a

North of Wilmcote (Map 8) the towpath iis largely unsurfaced, but still comfortably walkable (in single file) and cyclable with determination.

B4089 to Alcester

crse of Alcester Railway

Pennyford Hall

Wootton Wawen

Newnham

Edstone Aqueduct

River Alne

Wootton Pool

mp 19

54

Yew Tree Farm

aq.

57

56 55

39 70'

Bearley or Odd Lock
5ft 10ins

mp 20

53

A3400

52 51

mp 18

58

70'

70'

mp 21

Austy Manor

1: Hill Farm Marina
2: Anglo-Welsh

50

1 = Monarch's Way

Preston Hill Farm

Bearley

Bearley Cross

NORTH

8

10

34

tributary of the River Alne, and the twin tracks of the Birmingham & North Warwickshire Railway. Those with a highly-developed railway eye will notice an overgrown trackbed curving away from beneath the aqueduct across the countryside in a north-westerly direction. This was the Great Western Railway's Alcester branch, an ill-fated and relatively shortlived line which had its track lifted as an economy measure during the First World War, re-opened in 1923, then closed again at the beginning of the Second World War, apart from a cloak and dagger service operated for employees at a motor works evacuated from Coventry. A Heath Robinson-esque arrangement of pipes and valves enabled steam locomotives on the branch to take on canal water directly beneath the aqueduct. Visit *warwickshirerailways.com* to view a delightful period photograph of a tank engine simmering beneath the aqueduct while its fireman perches precariously on a ladder to control the flow of water into the locomotive's tanks. Bearley station is useful launch pad for towpath walkers.

Wootton Wawen introduces a sense of humanity absent from much of the Stratford Canal's southern section, but it is more a sense of fragility that the village's aqueduct evinces in the face of thunderous traffic on the A3400. Seeking abandonment of the canal in 1958, in order to facilitate a number of road 'improvements', Warwickshire County Council wished to widen the road at this point and replace the aqueduct with a pipe to carry residual drainage. Sixty years on, one can only be grateful they didn't get their myopic way. A busy hire base briefly adds activity to the canal, but it soon reverts to its dreamy default setting.

The majority of bridges on this section of the canal are of the deceptively delicate split-cantilever design peculiar to the Stratford. The narrow gap between the two cast-iron arches was designed to permit the tow-rope to pass. Compatriot and friend of Rachmaninov, the exiled composer, Nikolai Medtner (1880 -1951) and his wife lived on the western outskirts of Wootton Wawen during the Second World War as guests of the pianist, Edna Iles and her parents. Inspired by the local countryside - and who's not to say the Stratford's bosky towpath - his Third Piano concerto was completed here and premiered at The Proms in 1943.

Edstone Aqueduct

Wootton Wawen
Map 9

A village full of interest. Wootton Hall (4979 to GWR fans) is a 17th century mansion which once belonged to Maria Fitzherbert, the *secret* wife of George IV. The parish church is of Saxon origin and considered one of Warwickshire's finest. A large old paper mill has been converted into apartments.

Eating & Drinking
NAVIGATION INN - Stratford Road (canalside by the aqueduct). Tel: 01564 792676. Food lunchtimes and evenings (from 6pm) Mon-Fri and from noon at weekends. Regular meeting place of the Stratford on Avon Canal Society. B95 6BZ *See also Bulls Head at the west end of the village - Tel: 01564 795803.*

Shopping
Convenience store on the main road. Post office in the hall grounds.

Things to Do
YEW TREE FARM - Tel: 01564 792701. Barns and byres transformed into a 'contemporary shopping village'. Farm shop & Cowshed Cafe. B95 6BY

Connections
BUSES - Johnsons X20 runs hourly to/from Birmingham via Hockley Heath and Stratford. Tel: 0871 200 2233.
TRAINS - request stop on West Midlands hourly service (ex Suns) to/from Birmingham and Stratford. Tel: 0345 748 4950.

10 STRATFORD CANAL Preston Bagot & Lowsonford 4mls/14lks/4hrs

PLOTTING a lonely course, the canal gives every appearance of revelling in its sense of isolation, like someone who enjoys their own company above almost anyone else's. Woods border the canal, birdsong fills the air, the scent of wildflowers is intoxicating. Temple Thurston (see Map 2) was equally taken with this part of the Stratford Canal. In 1910 he hired a narrowboat known as *The Flower of Gloster*, its captain Eynsham Harry, together with a horse called Fanny, and set off on a journey of discovery which has remained a titular 'desert island' favourite of many canal enthusiasts ever since. Temple Thurston described the Stratford Canal as being 'right out of the track of the world'. He climbed the hillside to a farm at Yarningale for fresh milk, whilst Eynsham Harry bought beer from the wife of a lock-keeper. Reading *The Flower of Gloster* as you travel along the canal today depressingly leads to a feeling of lost innocence.

Travelling northwards, you encounter the first of the Stratford Canal's characteristic barrel-roofed cottages, a design said to have been brought about by the use of the same wooden frames used in the construction of the brick bridges which span the canal. A footpath runs westwards from Bridge 46 to Preston Bagot's remote little church where a brass memorial dated 1637 marks the resting place of Elisabeth Randoll - five centuries in the blink of an eye!

Yarningale Aqueduct lies cheek by jowl with Lock 34. As at Lock 37, the barrel-roofed cottage has been incorporated into a modern extension, but those by locks 28 and 31 remain largely unspoilt. The latter belongs now to the Landmark Trust (see also Map 17) and is available for holiday hire. The previous tenant, Ned Taylor, had been born in the cottage in 1921 - one of eleven children - and didn't leave until 2006.

The abutments of a former railway bridge frame the canal near Lowsonford. The bridge carried a branch-line to Henley-in-Arden, closed when the route was made obsolete by the opening of the North Warwickshire Railway. Legend has it that the track was despatched to The Front during the Great War but ended up at the bottom of the English Channel.

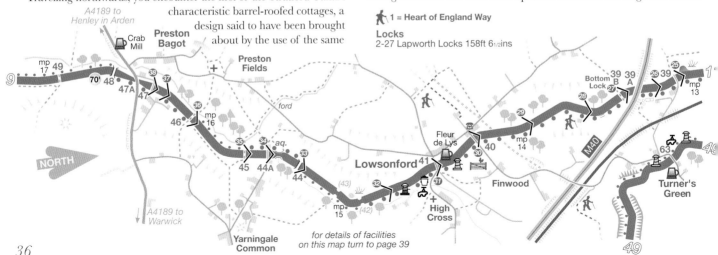

1 = Heart of England Way

Locks
2-27 Lapworth Locks 158ft 6½ins

for details of facilities
on this map turn to page 39

The woeful condition of the bottom lock of the Lapworth flight (No.27) prior to restoration was described by Guy Johnson in *Save the Stratford Canal!*. 'Trees were growing in profusion from the lock walls, water was pouring through the top gate and the balance beam had rotted and broken off. The bottom gate had long since fallen over and was lodged at an angle.' It was by no means unique in its dereliction. Fortunately it was discovered that a good deal of money could be saved using volunteer labour. Salute them as you sail blithely through today.

Temporarily puncturing the spell, the M40 motorway vaults across the canal by means of a charmless concrete span. Lock 25 is graced by another barrel-roofed cottage, home, for many years, of Doug Smith, celebrated cartographer of the canals, whose meticulously drawn 'Lockmaster' pen & ink maps of the system adorn many an enthusiast's wall. Doug was a ferroequinologist too, and relished the propinquity of both transport modes to his home. A wooden bench by Bridge 39 fittingly commemorates his contribution to the canals. What better memorial could one have?

WHETHER you arrive by boat, by bike, or on foot - and however many times you have been there before - Kingswood Junction never fails to captivate. Either side of the junction, the Stratford Canal's unremitting locks can tax the boater, so there is every motive for pausing here, and soaking up the scene. Certainly there is much to see, and the configuration of the two briefly parallel canals, together with the connecting arm, provides plenty of opportunities for circular or figure-of-eight strolls. A car park and picnic area, well masked by pine trees, encourage the non-boat-owning or hiring public to come to the junction, whilst the proximity of Lapworth railway station is serendipitously advantageous for those environmentally conscientious enough to favour the use of public transport.

A short branch canal was built between the Warwick & Birmingham Canal (as the Grand Union was previously called) and the Stratford-on-Avon Canal in 1802. It became a bone of contention between the two companies, jealous of each other's traffics and water supplies. Such emnities are long forgotten, and now the branch provides a strategic link between two popular cruising routes. The lower of two small reservoirs has been adapted for long term moorings, the upper is used by anglers. Hail them with a hearty 'well done', they look like they are only fishing for compliments.

The most dramatic section of the Lapworth flight lies between bridges 32 and 33, beyond Kingswood Junction on the northern section of the Stratford Canal. Here there are seven chambers in close proximity, presenting a spectacular view irrespective of whether you are looking up or down. Leaving Kingswood for King's Norton there are eighteen locks to negotiate before reaching the summit. The top lock is numbered '2'

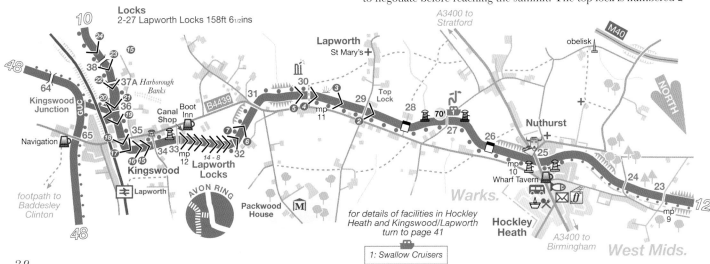

Locks
2-27 Lapworth Locks 158ft 6½ins

for details of facilities in Hockley Heath and Kingswood/Lapworth turn to page 41

1: Swallow Cruisers

because the guillotine stop lock at King's Norton (Map 13) was considered to be No.1.

Alongside Lock 5 lies Lapworth Cricket Club's idyllic ground. They are members of the mellifluously named Cotswold Hills Cricket League, along with such poetically disposed elevens as Ashton under Hill, Chipping Campden and Kenilworth Wardens Thirds. Neville Cardus, John Arlott and Brian Johnson would have been in raptures.

Just to add variety, bridges 26 and 28 are lifting structures: the former of Llangollen pattern; the latter reminiscent of those found in profusion on the Oxford Canal ... both are windlass-operated. A winding-hole by Bridge 27 marks the temporary terminus of the canal between 1796 and 1800, an hiatus brought about by lack of capital. It took so long to build this canal that it averaged little more than a mile a year. The engineer was Josiah Clowes, not one of the more famous canal engineers, though he could list work on the Chester Canal (from which he was dismissed for 'slackness'), the Thames & Severn, Dudley, Shrewsbury and Herefordshire & Gloucestershire canals on his curriculum vitae.

From the visitor moorings at Hockley Heath by Bridge 25, you can make your way past an imposing Victorian Baptist church (built of blue lias) to the Nuthurst obelisk raised in 1749 by Thomas Archer - architect of St Philip's Cathedral in Birmingham - to modestly mark his elevation to the peerage.

Preston Bagot — Map 10

Eating & Drinking
CRAB MILL - Warwick Road (access from Bridge 47A). Tel: 01926 843342. Three centuries old former cider mill, now a well appointed gastro-pub belonging to the reliable Brunning & Price group. Open from 10.30am daily, food served throughout from noon. Nice outdoor eating area. B95 5EE

Lowsonford — Map 10

Eating & Drinking
FLEUR DE LYS - Lapworth Street, Lowsonford (access from either bridge 40 or 41). Tel: 01564 782431. Charming canalside country pub which once inspired a range of commercially produced pies and which can still boast eight varieties on the menu. Open from 11am (12pm on Sun). Greene King ales. B95 5HJ

Shopping
FINWOOD HILL FARM SHOP - Mill Lane, Lowsonford (short walk east of Bridge 40). Tel: 0789 992 3075. Lovely little farm shop specialising in Dexter beef, Gloucester Old Spot pork and a wide choice of eggs. Ostensibly open only Tue & Sat but happy to serve if you ring ahead and they're in. B95 5HH

Kingswood

Lapworth — Map 11

St Mary's church, reached by a field path from Bridge 30 or along the road from Bridge 29, is a gem, curiously equipped with a detached tower and a chantry atop an open archway. Inside there is a stained glass window dedicated to a victim of the First World War, and a memorial tablet by Eric Gill. The churchyard contains a tomb belonging to the Catesby family, of whom Robert Catesby was implicated in the Gunpowder Plot of 1605.

Eating & Drinking
THE BOOT - Old Warwick Road (adjacent Bridge 33). Tel: 01564 782464. Elegant country pub open lunchtime and dinner (from 6.30pm) daily ex Sun dinner. B94 6JU

Shopping
Village shop by railway bridge between the canals. Off licence/post office near Bridge 65 (Grand Union). Gifts, and canalia (not to mention home made cakes, and an array of potted plants) from the Briar Cottage canal shop by Bridge 33 - Tel: 01564 782379.

Things to Do
PACKWOOD HOUSE - Packwood Lane. Tel: 01564 782024. Sublime Tudor (National Trust) property remodelled by Graham Baron Ash (whose industrialist father was a director of Fellows Morton & Clayton) in the Twenties & Thirties. Famous for clipped yews resembling Sermon on the Mount. Open daily ex Winter Mons. Shop and cafe/restaurant. B94 6AT

Connections
TRAINS - approx bi-hourly Chiltern Railways service linking with Warwick, Leamington, Birmingham Moor Street/Snow Hill and Marylebone. Tel: 0345 748 4950.

12 STRATFORD CANAL Earlswood 5mls/0lks/2hrs

MUCH of the canal is tree-lined. Oak, alder, hazel and willow predominate, creating a soothing, sylvan quality which, however beautiful, is apt to become soporific after a while. When you do catch glimpses of the surrounding countryside, it reminds you of the Home Counties, exuding an air of affluence epitomised by large detached houses, and horsey people, trotting down dappled lanes on dappled steeds.

The winding hole by Bridge 22 marks the site of a wharf once linked by tramway to the limestone quarries of Tanworth-in-Arden. Originally a branch canal had been planned to cater for this traffic. Near Bridge 19 the extensive, but private miniature railway of the Birmingham Society

of Model Engineers stands close to the canal, though hidden by a cutting. It does, however, open to the public on selected dates.

St Patrick's Church by Bridge 17 at Salter Street, was built with money paid by the canal company in compensation for acquiring common land on which to built Earlswood Reservoirs. An embankment carries the canal over the River Blythe and a feeder enters the canal from the reservoirs which lie to the south-west. These days they are a popular amenity, attracting ramblers, anglers, bird watchers and interpretive board collectors. The old engine house, to which narrowboats carried coal up the feeder until 1936, looks a bit sorry for itself these days. Just the sort of project the Landmark Trust could wave their wonderful wand over.

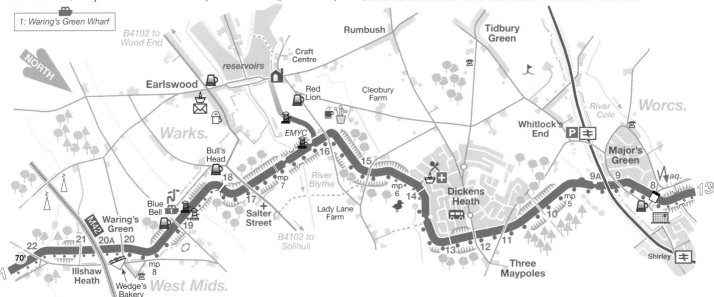

1: Waring's Green Wharf

40

Billed as a 'village for the 21st Century', anything less like a village than Dickens Heath would be difficult to imagine. Balconied apartments - which wouldn't look out of place in Fuerteventura - overlook the nonplussed canal. And whilst there are shops and restaurants in there (somewhere!) we would not advise you to go too far in search of them, lest you get irretrievably stranded in the future; and what true canal traveller could bear the thought of that?

The canal passes beneath the North Warwickshire railway line, opened belatedly in the Edwardian era by the Great Western Railway as an alternative route to Stratford and the West Country. British Railways, the nationalised body vested with operating the country's railway network in 1948, attempted to close the line in the late Sixties and mid Eighties, but were twice thwarted by the strength of public opinion. Nowadays it is a flourishing commuter route. Which just goes to show how life's 'closer-downers' should never be allowed to get away with their corporate negativity. The canal could have gone exactly the same way in the face of official malpractice.

Shirley Drawbridge is an electrified lift bridge on a busyish by-road, necessitating the use of barriers, a control panel (accessed with a Canal & River Trust Yale key), and a mollifying way with motorists. Nearby a high embankment carries the canal above the River Cole, a twenty-five mile long tributary of the Tame. Three miles to the north stands Sarehole Mill, a preserved watermill which has associations with Matthew Boulton, who leased it in the mid-18th century, and J. R. R. Tolkien, who lived across the road. Wake Green Amateurs' precipitous football pitches defy opponents' calls for a level playing field.

Hockley Heath
Map 11

Commuterland strung out along what used to be the A34 linking Southampton with Manchester. The War Memorial is poignantly inscribed: "The days short, the work great, their time passed like a shadow".

Eating & Drinking
MILLER & CARTER - Stratford Road. Tel: 01564 784137. Steak bar open from noon daily. B94 6NL
TAGORE - Stratford Road. Tel: 01564 784800. Indian restaurant open from 5.30pm daily. B94 6NL
WHARF TAVERN - Stratford Road (Bridge 25). Tel: 01564 782075. Greene King canalside pub open from noon daily. Food served throughout. B94 6QT
There's also a fish & chip shop and Chinese takeaway,

Shopping
Convenience store and post office on one side of Bridge 25, baker and butcher on the other.

Connections
BUSES - Johnsons X20 usefully links Hockley Heath hourly Mon-Sat with Birmingham, Henley-in-Arden and Stratford-on-Avon. Tel: 0871 200 2233.

Illshaw Heath
Map 12

Wedge's sublime bakery (Tel: 01564 702542 - B94 6RP) flourishes in its unlikely rural setting in the shadow of the M42. Fresh bread, sandwiches made to order, pies in profusion, mouthwatering cakes and puddings and a vegetable stall make it difficult for passing canaller's to resist. Outdoor tables beneath a canopy encourage immediate consumption.

Earlswood
Map 12

Eating & Drinking
BLUE BELL - Warings Green Road (Bridge 19). Tel: 01564 702328. Canalside cider house and home brew pub. Breakfast served from 9am Mon-Sat and 8am Sun. Main menu Wed-Sun. B94 6BP
BULL'S HEAD - Lime Kiln Lane. Access from Bridge 17. Tel: 01564 700368. Thwaites pub serving food from 10am daily. B94 6BU
RED LION - Lady Lane (west of Bridge 16). Tel: 01564 702946. Vintage Inns pub/restaurant open daily from 11am. B94 6AQ

RESERVOIR - The Common (adjacent reservoirs). Tel: 01564 702220. 'Hungry Horse' (Greene King) pub/restaurant open daily from 11am. B94 5SL

Shopping
Co-op convenience store (7am-10pm daily) and post office quarter of an hour's walk south of Bridge 17.

Things to Do
EARLSWOOD LAKES CRAFT CENTRE - Wood Lane. Tel: 01564 702729. B94 5JH

Major's Green
Map 12

THE DRAWBRIDGE - Drawbridge Road (Bridge 8). Tel: 0121 474 5904. Flaming Grill (Greene King) pub/restaurant open from 11am daily. B90 1DD

Connections
TRAINS - frequent West Midlands services to/from Whitlocks End station (near Bridge 9) make it a handy railhead for towpath walks. Tel: 0345 748 4950.

Warstock
Map 13

Access from Bridge 5 to a range of facilities including: Co-op convenience store, pharmacy, post office etc.

13 STRATFORD CANAL Warstock & King's Norton 4mls/0lks/1½hrs

ALTHOUGH the map emphasises how built-up these south-western suburbs of Birmingham are, the canal seems oblivious to the proximity of so many houses and people, retaining an aloof quality, like a recluse in a crowd. There was a time when a goodly percentage of waterside properties had boats moored at the bottom of their gardens and one was forever throttling down. But this no longer seems to be the case. Perhaps those boats are all in marinas now. Quietly forgotten; old amusements no longer of interest.

Tantalisingly, for enthusiasts of ecclesiastical architecture, there is no access from Bridge 6 to Christ Church, a Grade II listed mid 19th century structure of considerable charm approached through a sagging lych-gate considerably at odds with its suburban setting. Inside there are 17th century carvings brought here from St Bartholomew's, Birmingham destroyed by bombing in the Second World War. Lovers of bus depot architecture, on the other hand, are more fortunate, for Bridge 5 provides easy access to the impressive premises of Yardley Wood Bus Garage, originally built for

Birmingham City Transport in 1938. Their coat of arms appears in bas-relief above the office entrance, but the vehicles inside are adorned in National Express livery these days, Brum's 'blueberry and cream' buses of yore being a distant memory.

By Bridge 3 a side bridge crosses an arm which led to a dock serving lime-kilns. To the rear lies Cocks Moors Woods golf course, threaded by Chinn Brook, a tributary of the River Cole. Wool-gathering between sonnets, Shakespeare looks inscrutably down from the western portal of Brandwood Tunnel. Brandwood was built without a towpath, so horses were led over the top while boats were worked through by the simple expedient of boatmen pulling on a handrail set into the tunnel lining. The horse path still provides walkers with a right of way and also offers access to some useful suburban shops. Sometimes it's good to go 'over the top'.

Between the tunnel and King's Norton Junction stood a bridge with a history, a *cause celebre* in the embryonic days of the Inland Waterways Association. It was originally a lift bridge and, during the Second World

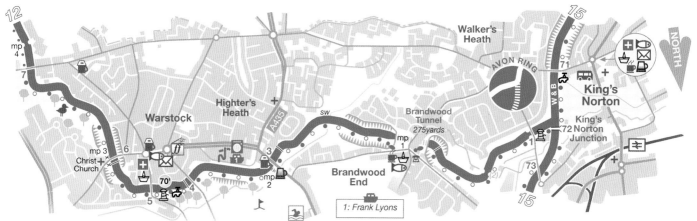

1: Frank Lyons

War the Great Western Railway, who owned the canal at that time, clamped down the platform following damage by a lorry. Commercial traffic had ceased on the canal, but the IWA maintained that a right of navigation still applied. The GWR claimed, somewhat disingenuously, that they would be only too happy to jack up the bridge to permit boats to pass as required, little realising that the IWA intended to organise as many boat passages as would be necessary to have the bridge fully repaired. On 9th May 1947, Tom Rolt's *Cressy* set off from Kingswood with Robert Aickman aboard. Aickman, it emerged, had alerted the press to achieve maximum publicity for the fledgling IWA. Publicity was anathema to Rolt. Already the differences in their character and outlook were causing fault lines in the pair's relationship.

Eager to appear in a good light, the GWR had sent a formidably crewed work boat ahead to anticipate any difficulties. It was the Grand Union Canal Carrying Company 'Town' class motor *Bilster* which has survived into preservation. As a curious aside, and as Williams and Sylvester point out in their book *Historic Working Narrowboats Today*, there is no town called 'Bilster' in Britain, speculating that the boat was meant to be named *Bilston*.

Unsurprisingly, *Bilster* found the heavily silted canal hard going, at one point having to be dragged through a bridge-hole by a Fordson tractor which had been serendipitously ploughing a neighbouring field. Eventually the vanguard, aground for the umpteenth time, was ignominiously abandoned. *Cressy* overtook it and pressed on. Emerging from Brandwood Tunnel, the participants were greeted to the kind of roar Robert Aickman associated with the Cup Final at Wembley: 'We made statements. We posed for photographs. We signed autographs. We accepted cups of tea' he recalled in *The River Runs Uphill*. Rolt, in *Landscape with Canals*, remarked upon how relieved he was to 'plunge like a rabbit' into Wast Hill Tunnel.

Lest the GWR felt they could rest on their laurels, further campaign cruises ensued, but it was not until Nationalisation that a fully operable swing bridge was installed, and even that is now defunct. Often erroneously referred to as Lifford Lane Bridge, Bridge 2 was, in fact on, Tunnel Lane. Long disused, but reasonably well preserved, the 'guillotine' stop lock at Bridge 1 was, as previously noted, officially Lock No.1. It's nice to see it still in situ, albeit frequently disfigured by graffiti. Shame it can't be made to operate automatically, French Revolution style.

Guillotine Lock '1'

14 WORCESTER & BIRMINGHAM CANAL Edgbaston 4mls/0lks/1½hrs

OLD TURN JUNCTION might well be described as the pivotal point of the inland waterways network. Overlooked by Arena Birmingham and the National Sea Life Centre, it symbolises the massive changes which have overtaken the canals generally - and those of Birmingham and the Black Country in particular - during the last three decades. They rang the church bells all day when the canal reached Birmingham, and wild celebrations continued well into the night. The first section, completed in 1769, linked Birmingham with the mines at Wednesbury, and the price of coal is said to have halved. Will the bells ring when HS2 arrives, and will prices fall in the designer shops of The Mailbox? During the rest of the 18th century, Birmingham became a magnet for canal promoters and, in 1794, the

Birmingham Canal Navigations were formed, amounting to some 160 miles of waterway, of which 100 miles remain navigable in an area bounded by Wolverhampton, Walsall, Dudley and Tamworth.

Two and fourteen day visitor moorings are available either side of Brindley Place, a cornucopia of cafe bars and restaurants which lies at the heart of things now. For once the hackneyed analogy of Birmingham with Venice seems almost understated, and you cannot help but think that of all the British cities to see virtue in revitalizing their canals, Birmingham has made the best fist of it. From the piazzas of the Convention Centre the canal leads through Broad Street Tunnel (aka Black Sabbath Bridge in homage to the heavy metal rock band formed locally in 1968) to Gas Street Basin, the epitome - and for many the lost soul - of Birmingham's waterways. In fact Gas Street had come to exemplify the BCN to such an extent that it was often forgotten that the actual terminal wharf and offices of the Birmingham Canal

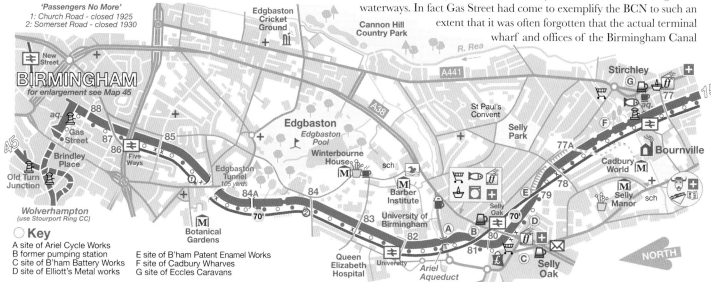

'Passengers No More'
1: Church Road - closed 1925
2: Somerset Road - closed 1930

○ Key
A site of Ariel Cycle Works
B former pumping station
C site of B'ham Battery Works
D site of Elliott's Metal works

E site of B'ham Patent Enamel Works
F site of Cadbury Wharves
G site of Eccles Caravans

44

lay to the east of here. Two arms terminated at the rear of the BCN company's handsomely symmetrical offices on Suffolk Street which, sadly, were demolished in 1928. Demolition controversially took its toll of the Gas Street canalscape in 1975 as well, by which time the planners should have known better, and British Waterways were never really forgiven for razing their rich heritage of 18th century waterside warehouses to the ground in a calculated move to sidestep a preservation order. For a time nothing was done to fill the void. Gas Street might have ceased to exist but for a community of residential boats

Gas Street 'Collage'

which lent a splash of colour and humanity to a decaying canalscape. A decade elapsed before the developer's proposals were realised in bricks and mortar, and the biggest irony of all is that the new pubs and offices emerged in a warehouse vernacular style of remarkable similarity to the bulldozed originals. The only post Seventies interlopers unsympathetic to the scale of the original Gas Street are the towering edifice of the Hyatt Hotel, and the imposing new Library to its rear.

Work began on the Worcester & Birmingham Canal from the Birmingham end in 1794, but it was not until 1815 that the route was completed throughout. Fearful of its water supply draining down into the Severn, the Birmingham Canal Company at first refused to be linked with the newcomer, and so laborious transhipment of cargoes took place across an infamous divide known as the 'Worcester Bar'. Eventually, however, a stop lock was provided between the two waterways, affording the BCN some measure of protection, yet enabling the passage of boats.

Quickly extricating itself from the wine bars and nightclubs of downtown Birmingham, the Worcester & Birmingham Canal turns right-angle past The Mailbox development - together with its lofty neighbour, The Cube - and makes for the sylvan suburbs of Edgbaston. It was this cloistered, arboreous entrance to and exit from the city that prompted Robert Aickman to express the aphorism: "Canals stretch green fingers into towns," a phrase coined aboard his first trip with the Rolt's aboard *Cressy* in April 1946. We can't help but share his enthusiasm, for this is a lovely stretch of canal - given its proximity to the city centre - and its towpath is enthusiastically embraced by walkers, runners and cyclists.

In cahoots with the Birmingham West Suburban Railway, opened in 1876, and now nose to tail with outer-suburban and inter-city trains, the canal negotiates Edgbaston Tunnel, whose towpath has been widened for the benefit of all those pedestrians and cyclists. The University of Birmingham is dominated by an Italianate tower affectionately known as 'Old Joe' after the university's main founder and first Chancellor, Joseph Chamberlain. In the absence of designated visitor moorings, boaters are pretty much honour-bound to keep going, but on foot there is every temptation to abandon the canal to its own devices and explore its seldom less than fascinating hinterland.

Erected in 2011, to carry the canal over Selly Oak's by-pass, Ariel Aqueduct derives its name from a former bicycle and motorcycle works once located nearby. Opened in 1896, the factory was built over 'Kerby's Pools', a Victorian venue for boating, shooting, athletics and cycling. Here too were Bournbrook Grounds where, in 1878, eight thousand spectators

'Old Joe'

Cadbury: from the canal

progenitors of the folding carton. Subsequently the premises were demolished to make way for student housing. Illustrative, on just one small patch of canalside land, of just how much change has accrued over a century and a half. Amongst many other notable local enterprises were the Birmingham Battery Works, 'batterers' of metal as opposed to makers of portable power sources; Elliott's Metal Works, which, amongst many other items, produced wire for telegraph lines and electric tramways - Neville Chamberlain worked in their offices before going into politics; and the Birmingham Patent Enamel Co., producers of countless advertising signs of the sort which used to adorn shops and railway stations.

The terracotta, chapel-like pumping house which overlooks the railway's crossing of the canal is a stoic survivor of Selly Oak's ongoing regeneration. It was built - the same year as the aforementioned cricket match - to pump water from a borehole, but became redundant with completion of the Elan Valley pipeline and was converted for use as an electricity sub-station. The substantial blue-brick framework of Bridge 78 conceals the fact that it carries that selfsame Elan Valley water main across the canal. Provision has been made at Battery Park retail development for restoration of the Lapal Canal, part of an ambitious scheme to reinstate the former Dudley No.2 Canal between Selly Oak and Halesowen.

Bournville railway station lies alongside the canal by Bridge 77. Bournville's garden village owes its existence to the altruism of Quakers Richard and George Cadbury who built a chocolate factory on a greenfield site in the vicinity in 1879. The name Bournville dates from that time: Bourn relating to a local watercourse, whilst the rather fanciful suffix of 'ville' was deemed to have desirable French overtones, more readily marketed than, say, Foundry Lane Chocolate. Cadbury made great use of the canal (see also Maps 20 and 33) and later the railway. In 1911 they became the first operator to use motorised boats on the canals, and their sizeable fleet was signwritten in Cadbury house style of chocolate and maroon. A large wharf known as Bournville Waterside stood along the offside of the canal, being linked to the works by the firm's private railway system which crossed the canal on Bridge 77A. All trace of the wharf has vanished under houses.

excitedly gathered to witness a representative side from Birmingham take on an Australian touring XI at cricket. In that era an over consisted of just four balls, and the local side were allowed to field twenty-two players. At one point play was halted for twenty minutes to retrieve the ball from one of the pools. In the end the match was drawn, being brought to what one might term a 'precipitate' end by a torrential downpour. One of the visiting antipodeans was none other than 'The Demon Bowler', Fred Spofforth, who went into the record books as the first man to take a Test Match hat-trick, at the Melbourne Cricket Ground the following year.

Ariel bicycles were made in Selly Oak up until 1932, and motorbikes until 1962. Thereafter the site was used by a company called Boxfoldia,

Edgbaston
Map 14

Developed residentially for the well-to-do by the Gough-Calthorpe family from the opening years of the 19th century, Edgbaston is a garden suburb any city in the world would be proud to cuddle up to. Architecturally eclectic, the houses are commonly set in extensive grounds. Some of the more grandiose examples, erected in an era of large families and servants, are no longer sustainable as family homes and have been turned into offices and institutions. Incidentally, the Gough-Calthorpes initially objected to the construction of the Worcester & Birmingham Canal, grudgingly acquiescing on the understanding that there would be no vulgar wharves or warehouses lining the waterway's passage through Edgbaston.

Things to Do
BARBER INSTITUTE - University of Birmingham. Tel: 0121 414 7333. Art gallery of international repute featuring works by Cezanne, Gainsborough, Magritte, Monet, Turner, Van Gogh etc. Open 10am - 5pm Mon-Fri and 11pm-5pm weekends. Admission free. B15 2TS
LAPWORTH MUSEUM OF GEOLOGY - University of Birmingham. Tel: 0121 414 7294. Open 10am-5pm Mon-Fri and 12-5pm weekends. B15 2TT
WINTERBOURNE HOUSE - Edgbaston. Tel: 0121 414 3003. Captivating Arts & Crafts house erected 1903 for the industrialist John Nettlefold of GKN fame. Gardens inspired by Gertrude Jekyll. Open from 10am daily. Shop and tea room. B15 2RT

Selly Oak
Map 14

Studenty enclave on the A38 with a wide choice of shops and food/drink outlets. Battery Retail Park features a canalside Sainsbury's supermarket. TouchBase Pears, overlooking Bridge 80, is a multi-purpose community centre with an emphasis on the needs of the deaf and blind.

Bournville
Map 14

Bournville exists in a chocolatey enclave all its own, and which of us wouldn't want to do just that! Perambulating its arboreally nomenclatured streets, one quickly succumbs to the Cadbury vision. Why can't all the world exist so well-adjustedly, so self-contentedly? Use of a CRT 'facilities' Yale key provides access from the secure (if not, ironically, salubrious) offside moorings opposite Bournville railway station.

Shopping
Useful row of shops on Sycamore Road opposite The Green: newsagent, butcher, pharmacy and bakery.

Things to Do
BOURNVILLE CARILLON - Linden Road. Tel: 0798 655 2770. 48 bells erected by George Cadbury in 1906 following an inspirational visit to Bruges. Performances on Saturdays at noon and 3pm throughout the year ex February. B30 1LB
CADBURY WORLD - Linden Road. Tel: 0121 393 6004. Self-guided tours 'choc-full of fun'. B30 2LU
SELLY MANOR - Maple Road. Tel: 0121 472 0199. A pair of medieval half-timbered buildings. Open from 10am daily Jun-Aug, Tue-Fri otherwise. B30 2AE

Stirchley
Map 15

Bournville Lane leads (past handsome three storey terraced villas with paired names) to Stirchley strung out along Pershore Road; a yang to Bournville's yin. Of note are the library and the public baths, the latter reconfigured as a community hub sans pool.

Eating & Drinking
ALICIA'S - Pershore Road. Tel: 0121 246 0947. Artisan pizzeria; eat in or take away. Open from 5pm Tue-Fri and from noon Sat. B30 2JR
WILDCAT - Pershore Road. Micropub open weekdays from 5pm, weekends from noon. B30 2JR

Shopping
Co-op, Farm Foods and convenience stores. Bakery (and cookery school) called Loaf open Tue-Sat. P. Browell is a traditional tobacconist established 1924.

Cotteridge
Map 15

Somewhat confusingly the location of King's Norton railway station. Shopping and fast food opportunities. Handsome 'Queen Anne' Fire Station. Cotteridge Wines on Pershore Road are open from noon and retail an exceptional choice of bottled beers. The legendary 11A/11C outer circle buses cross the canal on Bridge 75; two hour odysseys in their own right.

King's Norton
Map 15

It's only a short uphill walk to the centre, grouped about a pretty green and overlooked by the imposing spire of St Nicholas' Church. Queen Henrietta Maria stopped here overnight on her way to meet Charles I at Edge Hill. Half-timbered 17th century grammar school in churchyard. Lovely little Arts & Crafts library endowed by the Scottish philanthropist Andrew Carnegie in 1906. Extensive park and civic garden dating from the 1920s.

Eating & Drinking
MAHFIL - The Green. Tel: 0121 448 5820. Stylish Indian restaurant open from 5pm Mon-Sat and from noon Sun. B38 8RU
MOLLY'S - The Green. Tel: 0121 459 9500. Cheerful cafe for pre-canal exploring breakfasts. B38 8SD

Shopping
Facilities include: a pharmacy, Co-op convenience store, post office, newsagent and off licence. Farmers Market on The Green second Saturdays.

Things to Do
ST NICHOLAS PLACE - Tel: 0121 458 1223. Heritage Centre adjoining church. Tours Fri & Sat. B38 8RU

MOMENTARILY urban, though not overwhelmingly so, the canal weaves its way between industrial premises. Trade, after all, was why canals were built. Between bridges 75 and 73 the towpath swaps sides. Not on a whim, but because the Midland Railway once operated a transhipment basin on the west bank of the canal. The Birmingham & Gloucester Railway of 1840 crosses Bridge 74. Passenger trains, serving its seven local stations, were suspended during the Second World War, with closure being confirmed in 1946. But now there are firm plans to bring them back again. A small aqueduct carries the canal over the River Rea just north of Bridge 72.

Key
A site of Bournville MPD 21B
B former GKN screw works
C site of Lifford Wharf (MR)
D site of KN Metal Co.
E former Baldwins paper mill
F site of KN Brickworks
G former tug turning points

At King's Norton the Stratford Canal (Maps 8-13) joins the Worcester & Birmingham. Baldwins paper mill formerly overlooked the canal junction and large quantities of coal were brought here by narrowboat from Black Country mines to feed the mill's furnaces. The increasingly decrepit Junction House is backed by the soaring steeple of St Nicholas, the parish church of King's Norton, where the Rev W. Awdry of *Thomas the Tank Engine* fame was a curate during the Second World War.

At 2,726 yards, Wast Hill Tunnel is the Worcester & Birmingham's longest. It takes around half an hour to pass through and, whilst appearances can be deceptive, rest assured that there *is* room to pass oncoming craft inside its gloomy depths. Like all Worcester & Birmingham tunnels (except Edgbaston), it has no towpath. The lads who led their boat horses across the tunnel top in the past would be flummoxed now to find a housing estate built over much of their route, and a degree of diligence is required of latter-day towpath walkers if they are not to become disorientated. Follow our footprints, and you shouldn't go far wrong! On an historic note, look out for the semicircular brick-lined embrasures in the canal bank at either end of the tunnel - these are the remnants of the turning points for tugs which were once employed to haul unpowered craft through the tunnel.

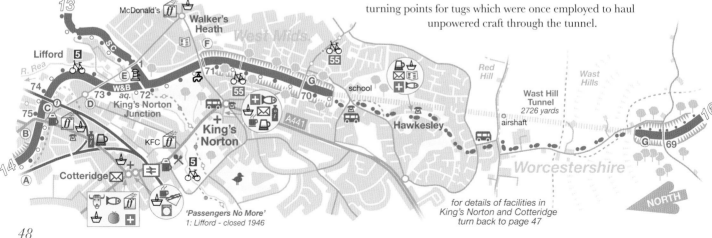

'Passengers No More'
1: Lifford - closed 1946

for details of facilities in
King's Norton and Cotteridge
turn back to page 47

16 WORCESTER & BIRMINGHAM CANAL Alvechurch 5mls/0lks/1½hrs

HOPWOOD was the temporary southern terminus of the canal for a decade from 1797. Consequently it became a busy spot, with wharf, weighbridge, stabling, limekilns, smithy and brickworks. There are panoramic views eastwards towards Weatheroak Hill crossed by the Roman's Ryknild Street. A feeder comes in from Upper Bittell Reservoir beside a now seemingly derelict canal employee's cottage near Bridge 66. The Lower Reservoir, rich in wildfowl, lies alongside the canal and is given a gorgeous wooded backdrop by the Lickey Hills. Only the Upper Reservoir feeds the canal, the Lower was provided to compensate millers whose water supplies from the Arrow had been detrimentally affected by construction of the canal.

South of Bridge 65, Lane House Aqueduct stood alongside a 'night soil' wharf, from whence Birmingham's sewage was distributed as fertilizer. A short section of the canal was re-routed in 1985 to accommodate the M42. Bridge 62 carries the electrified commuter line from Redditch through Birmingham to Lichfield. Wynn's Brickworks occupied the site now used for storage on the offside of the canal between bridges 61 and 60. Nowadays Scarfield Wharf is home to ABC's busy hire base, but in the early years of the canal a horse-drawn packet boat ran from here to Birmingham.

Delving delightfully into woodland, the canal reaches Shortwood Tunnel over which the old horse-path remains well-defined, and it is pleasant to wander across the top, fantasising that you've a horse to lead while your boat is hauled through the earth beneath your feet by one of the erstwhile tunnel tugs. Bridge 58 was known as Harris's Bridge after a local farmer. Milk churns and fresh produce were loaded here for consignment to Birmingham. It was once also known as a popular swimming site for the citizens of Redditch.

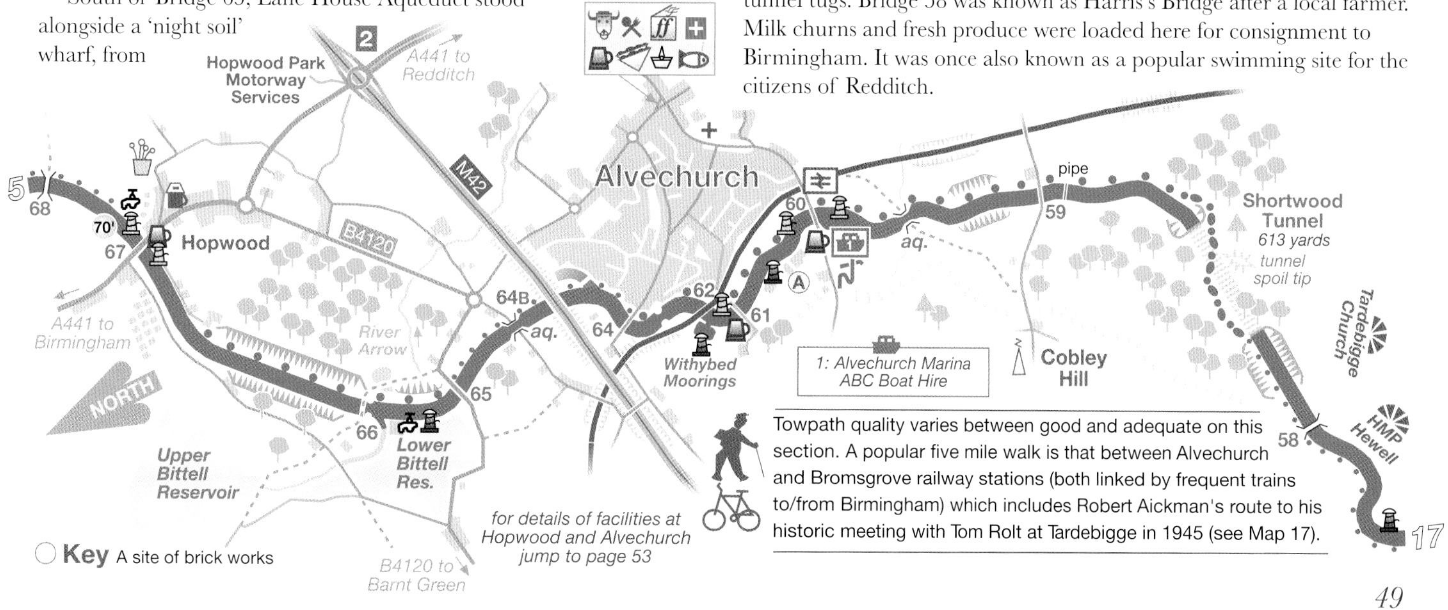

Hopwood Park Motorway Services
A441 to Redditch
2
M42
B4120
Alvechurch
Hopwood
A441 to Birmingham
NORTH
River Arrow
64B
aq.
64
62
61
60
59
58
65
66
67
68
70'
pipe
Shortwood Tunnel
613 yards
tunnel spoil tip
Tardebigge Church
HMP Hewell
Cobley Hill
1: Alvechurch Marina ABC Boat Hire
Withybed Moorings
Upper Bittell Reservoir
Lower Bittell Res.
B4120 to Barnt Green
Key A site of brick works
5
17

for details of facilities at Hopwood and Alvechurch jump to page 53

Towpath quality varies between good and adequate on this section. A popular five mile walk is that between Alvechurch and Bromsgrove railway stations (both linked by frequent trains to/from Birmingham) which includes Robert Aickman's route to his historic meeting with Tom Rolt at Tardebigge in 1945 (see Map 17).

TARDEBIGGE Tunnel separates the village's 'old' and 'new' wharves. The former, lying to the north, plays host to Anglo-Welsh's hire base now, but once it served a large pig farm to which food waste carried by boat from Birmingham was conveyed by aerial tramway to supplement the swines' voracious appetites. During the construction of Hewell Grange, between 1884 and 1891, the red sandstone, quarried near Runcorn in Cheshire, was brought in by boat and carried by horse-drawn tramway to the building site.

History is always rewriting itself, and canal history is no exception. When a plaque was erected to commemorate the first, auspicious meeting of L. T. C. Rolt and Robert Aickman at Tardebigge, it recorded the year as being 1946. Subsequently (with a self-effacing nudge from Pearsons who were in possession of contradictory evidence) it was altered to the year before. In similar fashion we had always been given to understand that the top lock was the deepest narrow chamber on the network, and that it had a rise/fall of 14 feet. In his admirably definitive book, *The Worcester & Birmingham Canal - Chronicles of the Cut*, the Revd. Alan White debunked this as a myth, affirming that the chamber's real height differential is a mere 12 feet. Enquiries to the Canal & River Trust resulted in the figure being put at 11 feet, which just goes to show, you should never believe anything you read in books!

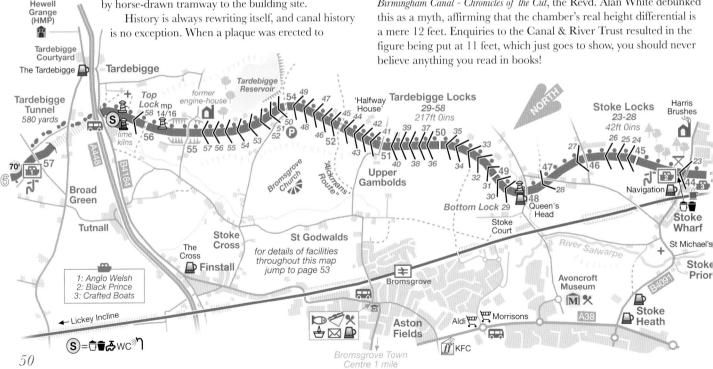

1: Anglo Welsh
2: Black Prince
3: Crafted Boats

for details of facilities throughout this map jump to page 53

S = 🚮 🚰 WC

Tardebigge New Wharf

the Second World War. One envies Rolt his rich roll call of characters: Mr Spiers the manager, 'with strange, frightened, restless eyes'; Mr Insull the 'portly and dignified' blacksmith; 'thickset, jovial' Tommy Hodges the boat-builder and repairer; Percy Hawkins the fitter and machinist, who kept his 19th century tools 'so beautifully clean and oiled', and George Bate the maker of lock-gates whose skill Rolt 'most admired'. Another acquaintanceship was struck with 'Jack' Warner, lock-keeper and unofficial 'master of ceremonies' at the Halfway House, a licensed farm by Lock 43. 'Jack' was more formally known to his daughter, Pat Warner, as John, and her book depicts day to day life around Tardebigge and its canal from an intriguingly different perspective to Rolt's. Indeed the unheralded arrival of *Cressy* at its mooring in 1941 provoked a degree of speculation amongst the tight-knit canal community that its occupants might be German spies.

The Reverend Alan White died - a month short of his 99th birthday - in 2017, and is commemorated by the milestone between bridges 56 and

A rite of passage, by any stretch of the imagination, Tardebigge Locks, coupled with the neighbouring flight at Stoke, amount to thirty-six locks in four miles. Other groups of locks, however fiendish, however formidable, pale into insignificance. The thirty chambers of the Tardebigge flight raise the canal over two hundred feet. When this section of the canal was first opened in 1808, a perpendicular lift designed by John Woodhouse was provided at the top, consisting of eight weights and pulleys operated by two men with fixed windlasses. Dysfunctionally prone to malfunction, and wasteful where water was concerned, it lasted just seven years before being replaced by a conventional lock, which is rather a pity, for canals thrive on eccentricity.

In addition to the Revd. White's learned tome, two other out-of-print books worth acquiring (try *www.abebooks.co.uk*) are L. T. C. Rolt's *Landscape with Canals* and Pat Warner's *Lock Keeper's Daughter*. All three, in their different ways and over-lapping time-lines, invoke intimate details of Tardebigge and the canal on its doorstep. Rolt's book paints a vivid picture of goings on around the New Wharf throughout his extended sojourn here during

Tardebigge Top Lock

Locking down Tardebigge

55: 14 miles from Birmingham and 16 from Worcester.

The gaunt engine house by Lock 57 ceased being employed for pumping around the time of the First World War. In the 1950s it was used as a jazz club; the scene, by all accounts, of some riotous nights. The cottage by Lock 53 was Pat Warner's childhood home. She devotes a chapter of her book to the neighbouring reservoir. Her father acted as a water baliff for Cadbury's angling club.

The picturesque lock-keeper's cottage between locks 31 and 32 is available for holiday lets from the Landmark Trust, the estimable body devoted to the rescue and refurbishment of worthwhile buildings in all shapes and sizes. It was the demolition of the junction house at Hurleston, on the Shropshire Union Canal, which 'maddened' the Trust's founder, John Smith, into creating the organisation in 1965. The cottage's last resident keeper, between 1953 and 1966, was Pat Warner's cousin, Dick Warner.

Only the briefest of pounds separates the Tardebigge and Stoke flights. Room enough, just, for half a dozen boats to moor for a breather and/or morale-boosting refreshments at the Queen's Head. Stoke Wharf plays host to a busy hire fleet. Nearby stands the factory of L. G. Harris & Co. manufacturers of paint brushes who can trace their origins back to 1928. They've been at Stoke Prior since 1937, but the present works dates from 1959.

Hopwood
Map 16

HOPWOOD HOUSE INN - canalside Bridge 67. Tel: 0121 445 1716. Comfortably furnished Marston's 'Rotisserie' pub/restaurant open from noon. B48 7AB. *Petrol station with convenience store to south of Bridge 67. Small garden centre nearby. Buses to/from Birmingham.*

Alvechurch
Map 16

Bloated Worcestershire village hugely expanded from its original core. Alan Smith, the ex Arsenal forward and Sky Sports pundit, played for the local football team. In the 1950s Dellow sports cars were made here. The church was much rebuilt by Butterfield.

Eating & Drinking
THE CROWN - canalside Bridge 61. Tel: 0121 445 2300. An unspoilt canalside pub. B48 7PN
NEW DILSHAD - Red Lion Street. Tel: 0121 445 5660. Village centre Indian restaurant open from 5pm daily (noon on Sundays). B48 7LF
THE WEIGHBRIDGE - canalside Bridge 60. Tel: 0121 445 5111. The 'weighbridge house' for a coal wharf in days gone by. Tillerman's Tipple is brewed for them by Weatheroak. Home cooked food lunchtimes and evenings ex Tue & Wed. *GBG entry. B48 7SQ Plus Chinese take-away and fish & chips in village centre.*

Shopping
Co-op (with ATM), pharmacy, *two* butchers, and a nice deli called Gin & Pickles (Tel: 0121 445 6769).

Connections
TRAINS - handy canalside station: West Midlands 20 minute frequency service (half-hourly Sun) to/from Redditch and Birmingham. Tel: 0345 748 4950.

Tardebigge
Map 17

'No village in the proper sense of the word', in Rolt's opinion eighty years ago, and nothing (as yet!) has occurred to alter that perception. To the south-east stands Hewell Grange, a late Victorian mansion, acquired by the government after the Second World War in lieu of death duties and subsequently used as a rather palatial prison.

Eating & Drinking
THE TARDEBIGGE - Hewell Lane. Tel: 01527 546724. Refurbished pub in what was long ago the village hall. Food from 11am daily (noon Mon). B97 6QZ

Connections
BUSES - Diamond services 42/3 operate hourly Mon-Sat (plus limited Sunday service) from stops above the southern tunnel mouth to/from Kidderminster (via Bromsgrove) and Redditch. Tel: 0871 200 2233.

Aston Fields
Map 17

A suburb of Bromsgrove surprisingly well endowed with facilities, notably Banners deli and hot food outlet established as long ago as 1906 (Tel: 01527 872581 - B60 2DZ) and they operate a cafe/restaurant as well (Tel: 01527 872889) open from 8am daily and providing evening meals Wed-Sat. Alternative eating-out opportunities include Fuso, an Italian restaurant (Tel: 01527 877789), Red & White, a Polish bistro (Tel: 01527 880068), Zinga, an Indian (Tel: 01527 871187) and 3A, a coffee & gin bar (Tel: 01527 874139). The Co-op convenience store contains a post office counter. Aston Fields is easily reached from Tardebigge by bus. Bromsgrove's recently enlarged and electrified railway station is here too, for taxis telephone Gold & Black on 01527 570707.

The Stokes
Map 17

A quintet - Heath, Pound, Prior, Wharf and Works - of scattered settlements in the vicinity of the canal.

Eating & Drinking
QUEEN'S HEAD - Sugarbrook Lane, Stoke Pound (Bridge 48). Tel: 01527 557007. Open daily from 11am. One of eight 'Lovely Pubs' in Warwickshire and Worcestershire. Full menu served 12-2.30pm and 5.30-9.30pm Mon-Sat, 12-7.30pm Sun. B60 3AU
NAVIGATION - Hanbury Road, Stoke Wharf (adjacent Bridge 44). Tel: 01527 837992. Comfortably refurbished pub. Food served from noon daily. B60 4LB

Things to Do
AVONCROFT - Stoke Heath (a mile west of Bridge 48). Tel: 01527 831363. Marvellous outdoor collection of reassembled buildings. Tea room & shop. B60 4JR

Stoke Works
Map 18

BOAT & RAILWAY - Shaw Lane, Stoke Works (Bridge 42). Tel: 01527 575597. Marston's/Banks's pub with a canalside terrace and skittle alley. Food from noon daily but not Sunday evenings. B60 4EQ
BOWLING GREEN - Shaw Lane (5 mins west of Bridge 41). Tel: 01527 861291. Lunch and dinner (from 6pm) Mon-Sat. B60 4BH

Hanbury Wharf
Map 18

EAGLE & SUN - Hanbury Road (Bridge 35). Tel: 01905 799266. Canalside pub serving food Mon-Sat 12-8.30pm and Sundays 12-7pm. WR9 7DX

Dunhampstead
Map 19

FORGE STUDIO - Bridge 30. Tel: 0751 796 1569. Andy Edwards hand paints canalware and sells gifts and guides as well as coffee and ice cream. WR9 7JX
FIR TREE INN - Trench Lane. Tel: 01905 774094. Comfortable country pub serving food Tue-Sat 12-2pm and 6-9pm and Sun 12-6pm. WR9 7JX

Tibberton
Map 19

BRIDGE INN - Plough Road (canalside Bridge 25). Tel: 01905 345144. Food served lunch and dinner (from 5.30pm) Tue-Sat and on Suns 12-4. WR9 7NQ
SPEED THE PLOUGH - Plough Road. Tel: 01905 345402. Under new management. WR9 7NQ.

NOWADAYS, Britain's salt industry is largely confined to Cheshire but, as the name Droitwich suggests, this part of Worcestershire was once a centre of salt making too. The salt obsessed Romans built a special road between Droitwich and Alcester to carry this valuable commodity. Similarly, the Worcester & Birmingham built the short Droitwich Junction Canal from Hanbury Wharf to carry the same cargo. Abandoned in 1939, it has become one of the success stories of the canal restoration movement, finally re-opening in 2011 and forming, along with the Droitwich Barge Canal what has become a hugely popular circular route - the Mid-Worcestershire Ring. If you're remaining loyal to the W& B's 'main line', it would be churlish not at least to stroll down the first three locks as far as Gateway Park, offering votive thanks as you go to those who steadfastly kept the faith with regard to the canal's second coming.

At the end of the 18th century, John Corbett, son of a local boatman, discovered large deposits of brine at Stoke Prior and developed one of the largest saltworks in the world on the site. It made his fortune. He met an Irish woman in Paris, married her and erected a replica French chateau for her on the outskirts of Droitwich, a town he transformed from one of industrial squalor into a fashionable spa. In its heyday the canalside works at Stoke was producing 200,000 tons of salt a year. The company had a fleet of fifty narrowboats and hundreds of railway wagons. Corbett died in 1901 and is buried at the pretty little church of St Michael's, Stoke Prior (Map 17). The 'John Corbett Way', a seven and a half mile waymarked trail, has been developed between Stoke Heath and Droitwich.

Attractive countryside returns at Astwood Locks, as canal and railway drift lazily through lush farmland overlooked by the wooded slopes of Summer Hill to the east. Westward views encompass Abberley and Woodbury hills beyond the River Severn. Closer at hand are the twin 700ft high masts of Wychbold radio transmitting station. Opened in 1934, its call sign "Droitwich Calling" became known throughout Britain and in many parts of Europe. During the Second World War Droitwich's long range transmitter broadcast the 'voice of freedom' throughout occupied Europe.

Hanbury Hall (NT)

NORTH

Hanbury Hall

AVON RING

MID-WORCS RING

B4090

mp 20/10 70'

Eagle & Sun

33

17

38

37

36

35

34

Hadzor

site of salt works 43

social club 42

Boat & Railway

Stoke Works

41

22 21 20 19 18 40

Bowling Green

Astwood Locks 17-22 42ft 0ins

Hanbury Wharf

Droitwich Junction Canal

1

2

3

Droitwich Spa Marina

Hadzor House

Roman Road

Gateway Park

22

Lots of public footpaths in this area, including one that leads beguilingly across pastures and parkland from Astwood Bottom Lock to Hanbury Hall, an imposing National Trust property dating from 1701 - Tel: 01527 821214. WR9 7EA

for details of facilities at Stoke Works see page 53

'Passengers No More' 1: Stoke Works - closed 1966

Wychbold

SKIRTING the mellow settlements of Shernal Green, Dunhampstead, Oddingley and Tibberton, the canal luxuriates in a sense of remoteness. High clumps of sedge border the canal, swaying with the passage of each boat emphasising the loneliness of the landscape. At Shernal Green the Wychavon Way - a 42-mile long distance footpath running from Holt Fleet on the River Severn (Map 24) to Winchcombe in Gloucestershire - makes its way over the canal.

Dunhampstead Tunnel is tiny compared to the 'big three' to the north, but like them it has no towpath, forcing walkers to take to the old horse-path through deciduous woodlands above. A hire base adds traffic to the canal at this point, whilst a canal shop and a country pub provide an excuse to break your journey. Four Scots pine strike a pose in a

neighbouring field like a boy band at a photo-shoot, or perhaps they are the transmogrified spirits of employees of a brick and tile works which stood on the site until around 1900.

Nowadays, Oddingley consists of little more than an ancient manor house, a tiny church, and a level-crossing. The pretty little Midland Railway signal cabin which stood here was removed in 2016, but has since found sanctuary at Shottle on the Ecclesbourne Valley Railway in Derbyshire.

Murder was done here in 1806. The vicar, George Parker, created considerable animosity in the neighbourhood by increasing the tithes due to him. On 24th June he was shot and killed, the assassin, witnessed fleeing towards neighbouring woodland, was never apprehended.

continued overleaf:

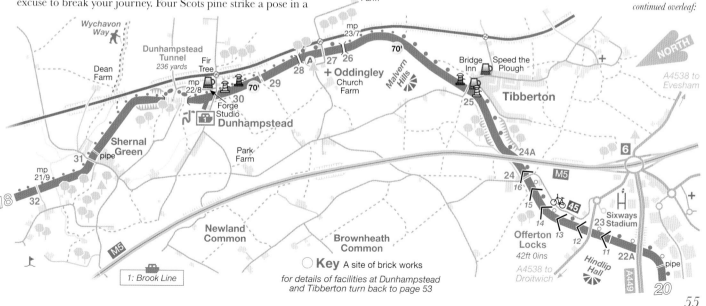

for details of facilities at Dunhampstead
and Tibberton turn back to page 53

continued from page 55:

Investigations, however, confirmed that it was a carpenter from Droitwich called Richard Hemming, the consensus being that he had been hired to murder the vicar by five parishoners led by one Samuel Evans, a retired army officer. With no murderer being apprehended, however, the law did not allow for any suspects to be charged. Twenty-four years later, a skeleton was discovered in a barn at Netherwood Farm, and it became apparent that Evans, since deceased himself, had murdered Hemming to hide all trace of the crime. In a subsequent show trial at Worcester Guildhall, three of the original conspirators were tried with aiding and abetting Hemming's murder but the case against them foundered on a number of legal niceties, and they went free, returning to Oddingley where the church bells were rung in celebration.

Southbound the Worcester & Birmingham recommences its descent to the Severn. Boating northwards you can take a breather. Worcester's industrial fringe makes its presence felt and muddy rugby players stomp across the footbridge at the tail of Lock 11. Worcester RUFC's Sixways Stadium stands to the south of the canal. In an era where belligerent sobriquets are *de rigueur*, the Warriors are amongst the leading clubs in the country, but we like to think of the club's more gentlemanly origins in the 1870s when they played in 'white shirts and blue knickerbockers'. Hindlip Hall (4934 to fans of the old GWR), headquarters of West Mercia Police and refuge, in its original Elizabethan guise, of two members of the Gunpowder Plot, dominates the hillside to the north-west.

Two aspects of this canal's working practice were remarkable. Boats kept *left* when passing each other and pairs of donkeys were widely used in place of horses to haul the boats. The animals worked well together as long as they 'knew' one another, but the introduction of a new donkey could cause considerable ructions. One of the last traders on the W&B was Charles Ballinger of Gloucester. He was still using horse-drawn boats as late as 1954, carrying coal from the Cannock area to Townsend's mill at Diglis. Occasionally he would have an 'uphill' cargo as well: matches from Gloucester to Birmingham, or flour from Worcester to Tipton; but by the beginning of the Sixties trade had deserted the canal.

Lock 11, Offerton

WORCESTER'S suburbs extend a warm welcome to incoming canallers - perfect hosts, they are not too intrusive - but there remains the little matter of ten locks to negotiate before you reach the running waters of the Severn. A large munitions factory was built at Blackpole during the First World War; specialising in bullets for both the British and *Russian* armies! After the war the works was purchased by Cadbury and concentrated on making cakes instead of cartridges. Cadbury employed water transport a good deal as we have already seen at Bournville (Map 14), and their wharf survives, albeit occupied by a cement plant now. A leisure centre and municipal golf course border the canal above Bilford Upper Lock. Worcester City FC sold their St George's Lane ground by Bridge 12 to property developers in 2013, and, after a period of playing their home games in Kidderminster have moved to Bromsgrove; their fan-base are entitled to feel disenfranchised. The properties erected are, however,

◯ Key
A former Munitions/Cadbury factory
B site of Railway Works
C site of Gas Works
D Shrub Hill Engineering Works
E sites of McKenzie & Holland Signal Works
F site of Vinegar Works
G site of Hardy & Padmore Foundry
H former Glove Works (Fownes Hotel)
I site of Porcelain Works
J former Flour Mill

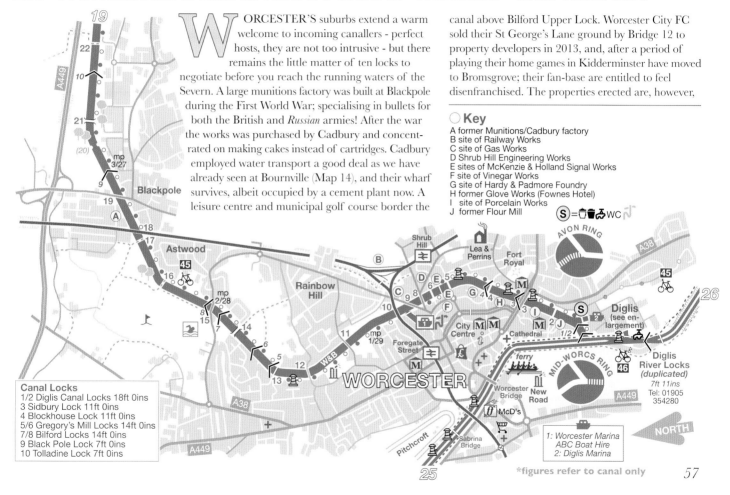

Canal Locks
1/2 Diglis Canal Locks 18ft 0ins
3 Sidbury Lock 11ft 0ins
4 Blockhouse Lock 11ft 0ins
5/6 Gregory's Mill Locks 14ft 0ins
7/8 Bilford Locks 14ft 0ins
9 Black Pole Lock 7ft 0ins
10 Tolladine Lock 7ft 0ins

Diglis River Locks (duplicated)
7ft 11ins
Tel: 01905 354280

1: Worcester Marina
ABC Boat Hire
2: Diglis Marina

*figures refer to canal only

not entirely unpleasing, and one admires the use of balconies and weatherboarding. A mural in a nearby bridge-hole recalls humble City's elimination of mighty Liverpool from the FA Cup on 15th January 1959.

By Bridge 11 the charmingly named Flagge Meadow playing fields of Worcester's ancient Royal Grammar School are overlooked by a handsome pavilion. Sir Edward Leader Williams, engineer of the Manchester Ship Canal, was a pupil, as indeed was his brother Benjamin Williams Leader (sic) the landscape artist. Another knighted Edward, Elgar, lived at Marl Bank on Rainbow Hill until his death in 1934. Controversially the property was demolished in 1969.

A shapely railway bridge (10) spans the canal by Lowesmoor Wharf. It has a hole cut out of it, presumably in order to lessen the weight of the structure as opposed to considerations of aesthetic virtue. Lowesmoor Wharf (aka Worcester Marina) is a good spot to moor securely close to the city centre - just slip beneath the roving bridge and make yourself known at the office.

For a cathedral city, Worcester attracted a surprisingly large amount of industry; spurred on, one imagines, by the connectivity provided by the river, canal and railway. The Italianate clock tower peeping over the canal by Bridge 8, belongs to the Shrub Hill Engineering Works of 1864. McKenzie & Holland's railway signalling works extended both sides of the canal. Hill, Evans & Co.'s Vinegar Works has been replaced by a shopping precinct, but was once served by a branch line railway which crossed the canal alongside Bridge 6. The lengthy saw-toothed building on the towpath side is a Firstbus garage; previously, and somewhat more illustriously, Midland Red.

On the offside, above Blockhouse Lock, on a site now occupied by Smiths News and Magnet, stood Hardy & Padmore's foundry, makers of all manner of cast iron items, such as the decorative dual lamp posts which still grace Worcester Bridge and the decorative cast iron railway bridge on Foregate Street. Interestingly, they also made barge stoves.

Locks at Blockhouse and Sidbury lower the canal towards the Severn. Between them, on the offside, Fownes Hotel was formerly a glove factory.

Virtually opposite stands the Commandery, which Charles II used as his headquarters during the Civil War Battle of Worcester in 1651, though it was originally a hospital and dates from as early as the 15th century. There is space here for half a dozen boats to moor overnight within euphonious earshot of the cathedral bells.

Sidbury Lock lies near the site of a gate in the city wall where a thousand Royalist troops are said to have been killed. Cromwell's men had captured the nearby fort and turned its canons on the escaping Cavaliers. The elevated fort is a pleasant park now, easily reached from the Commandery moorings. A panoramic plaque identifies major incidents of the Battle of Worcester and the gardens offer a marvellous view over the city and its multitudinous churches. Bridge 3 carries amusing sculptures of Civil War pikestaffs, shields and helmets.

Burgeoning apartment blocks usher the canal down to Diglis Basins. Old photographs of Royal Worcester's porcelain works depict a phalanx of four bottle kilns, so that the scene could easily be mistaken for North Staffordshire. Townsend's Flour Mill (by Bridge 2), was once an intensive user of water transport as well.

Diglis Basins opened in the 19th century to facilitate transhipment of cargoes between river and canal. One would have relished being here in their working heyday, marvelling at the constant comings and goings of boats of all shapes and sizes. When the river was in flood, river craft would ignore the locks and sail straight into the basins. On no account seek to emulate them!

⚠ A pair of broad locks separate the basins from the river. They are closed overnight, re-opening at eight in the morning. Entering or leaving the river can pose problems, especially if the current is flowing quickly, and getting your crew on or off for the locks needs careful consideration. The easiest access point is the pontoon immediately downstream of the lock entrance; if you're heading upstream the river's easily wide enough for you to turn once everyone's back on board. Coming downstream, turn after you've passed the entrance and you should find yourselves perfectly placed to drop your lock crew off on the pontoon. In any case, CRT often provide volunteer lock-keepers at Diglis now.

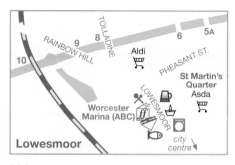

Lowesmoor

Worcester
Map 20

Descending from Birmingham to Worcester, the West Midlands are left intuitively behind, and you find yourself in streets where the patois has a distinct West Country burr. 'Royal' Worcester suffered more than most at the hands of the developers during the philistine Sixties (Ian Nairn, the late architectural writer and broadcaster, was incensed, and James Lees-Milne got into hot water for permitting his *Shell Guide to Worcestershire* to be too critical) but much making of amends has been done in recent years to enhance the city's fabric. The Cathedral, gazing devoutly over the Severn and containing the tomb of King John shares, with Gloucester and Hereford, Europe's oldest music festival, 'The Three Choirs'. From the deep well of Worcester's history you can draw inspiration from almost any era that captures your imagination. This was the 'faithful city' of the Civil War from which Charles II escaped following the final defeat of the Cavaliers. It was the home, for much of his life, of Sir Edward Elgar. Home too of that ensign of the empire, Lea & Perrins sauce - still produced on Midland Road. And here lies one of the loveliest cricketing venues, in England - Worcestershire's New Road ground.

Eating & Drinking
THE ANCHOR - Diglis. Tel: 01905 351094. Marston's local alongside Diglis Basins. Breakfasts from 9.30am. Skittle alley and canalside patio. WR5 3BW
BENEDICTO'S - Sidbury. Tel: 01905 21444. Italian on the Cathedral side of Sidbury Lock. WR1 2HZ
BROWNS AT THE QUAY - Quay Street. Tel: 01905 21800. Fine dining in former riverside mill. WR1 2JN
CENTENARY LOUNGE - The Cross. Tel: 01905 724242. Echoes of the old Great Western Railway and Jazz Age define this charming establishment. WR1 3PZ
DIGLIS HOUSE HOTEL - Severn Street. Tel: 01905 353518. Bar and restaurant food, open to non-residents throughout the day. Riverbank setting, former home of Benjamin Williams Leader. WR1 2NF
FIREFLY - Lowesmoor. Tel: 01905 616996. *Good Beer Guide* listed town pub. Opens noon daily. WR1 2SE
SAFFRONS - New Street. Tel: 01905 610505. *Good Food Guide* listed bistro. Closed Sundays. WR1 2DP

Shopping
The Shambles, Friar Street and New Street feature numerous fascinating little shops and small businesses. Crown Gate is the main shopping precinct with adjoining street markets on Tue-Sat. An Asda supermarket in the St Martin's Quarter on Lowesmoor is easily accessible from bridges 8/9 and/or Worcester Marina. Also handy on Lowesmoor are east European convenience stores, a bakery and a launderette. The Post Office is housed in W. H. Smith on High Street.

Things to Do
TOURIST INFORMATION CENTRE - The Guildhall, High Street. Tel: 01905 726311. Well stocked and welcomingly staffed! Closed Sundays. WR1 2EY
THE COMMANDERY - canalside by Sidbury Lock. Tel: 01905 361821. Civil War history. WR1 2HU
CITY MUSEUM & ART GALLERY - Foregate Street. Tel: 01902 25371. Admission free. One or two works by Benjamin Williams Leader (brother of the canal engineer Edward Leader Williams) best known for *February Fill Dyke* which hangs in Birmingham Art Gallery if you're going that way. WR1 1DT
GREYFRIARS - Friar Street. Tel: 01905 23571. National Trust 15th century timber framed house. WR1 2LZ
TUDOR HOUSE - Friar Street. Tel: 01905 612309. Local history displays in five hunded year old half-timbered house. Admission free. WR1 2NA
MUSEUM OF ROYAL WORCESTER - Severn Street. Tel: 01905 21247. Open daily from 10am. WR1 2ND

Connections
TRAINS - stations at Foregate Street and Shrub Hill. Services to/from the Malverns (and on through the hop-yards to Hereford) Droitwich, Kidderminster, Birmingham etc. Good service also to and from London Paddington. Tel: 0345 748 4950.
BUSES - links throughout the area, but of particular note are Stourport based independent Coniston services 294/6 connecting Worcester with Stourport half a dozen times per day (ex Sun) facilitating one-way walks along the Severn Way. Tel: 01299 823329.
TAXIS - Cathedral Cars. Tel: 01905 767400.

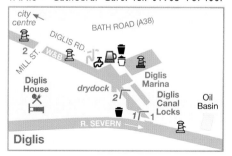

Diglis

21 DROITWICH CANALS Hawford & Salwarpe 4mls/8lks/4hrs*

'THERE are no wide prospects or startling beauties along this Salwarpe valley; it is for those who appreciate the smaller things - the noble trees on the slopes, the rich green of the meadows on the valley floor, still waters, and the quiet of deep country.' That was how Tom Rolt described the course of the Droitwich Barge Canal in 1949, by which time it had already been officially abandoned for a decade. Or should that be 'by *wych* time'? ... for *wych* was the name given to the smaller trows specially built to navigate from Droitwich down to the Severn with cargoes of salt, and Rolt, like us, was the sort of man who would have relished seeing such vessels going about the work for *wych* they had evolved.

Officially abandoned in 1939 - though disused as far as the Barge Canal was concerned by 1916, and 1929 in the case of the Junction - the seven and a bit miles of waterway between Hawford on the Severn and Hanbury on the Worcester & Birmingham Canal had decayed to such an extent that anyone with an ounce of common sense would have known that they were beyond redemption. Fortunately, canal enthusiasts are not noted for their common sense. When one sailed past the entrance lock at Hawford, buried in someone's front garden, and thought of how the A449's embanked dual-carriageway had been callously laid across the line of the canal, restoration seemed implausible. In the final analysis, the canals' shortness excited potential as opposed to consigning them to irrelevance. That and the fact that they were connected at either end with flourishing waterways which, taken as a whole, could be effectively trumpeted as a 'mini-ring' *par excellence*. In short, the scene was set for a revival: British Waterways' final flourish before being transformed from a nationalised industry into a charitable organisation.

The Barge Canal's towpath narrows in its central section but is generally good for walking and cycling alike. The Junction Canal is well-surfaced throughout.

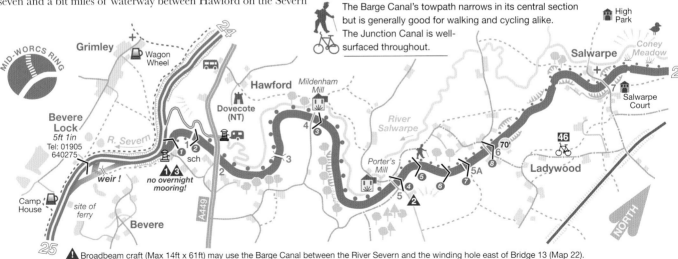

Broadbeam craft (Max 14ft x 61ft) may use the Barge Canal between the River Severn and the winding hole east of Bridge 13 (Map 22).

Eight, somewhat onerous, broad-beam locks carry the Barge Canal (surveyed by James Brindley but engineered by John Priddey and opened in 1771) up from the Severn at Hawford to its summit pound at Ladywood. Not to put too fine a point on it, the scenery is spell-binding. An audio trail (downloadable from CRT) has been recorded to interpret the canal's progress. Quite frankly, though, the soundtrack provided by nature is what you should really be listening to: cuckoos, chiff-chaffs, reed warblers; the murmur of insects, the munching of cattle; the inculcating breeze in the reed beds. At times the reeds are so high and thick that the canal and the towpath seem like separate entities, not yet introduced to each other.

Above Lock 2 the canal borders the grounds of a prep school before plunging into a newly-provided concrete tunnel beneath the A449. It doesn't take long, however, for the noise of traffic to be left behind, balm being provided by swaying poplars; some bearing mistletoe, should you need an excuse to kiss your companion: the person with you, that is, not this guide book! The bridges carry attractive blue number plates which have a sort of French feel about them. No.3 is also known as Linacre Bridge and it is one of the canal's original occupation bridges. Bridge 4, Mildenham Bridge, abuts Lock 3 and nearby is a retired example of several mills which were once a feature of the river valley. Looking at the River Salwarpe today, it's difficult to imagine there ever being enough flow in it to power machinery.

⚠ Advice for Boaters

1 Approaching the Droitwich Barge Canal from the Severn at Hawford you'll find two mooring pontoons. That on the left, nearest the lock itself, is for use when entering the lock. The one on the right is for waiting only and overnight mooring is prohibited.

2 To protect the privacy of the occupants of the cottage alongside Lock 4 access is restricted. Going uphill the person setting the lock will need to cross the road bridge to the offside. Going downhill a CRT Yale key will be required to reach the lockside.

3 River level gauges exist at Lock 1 on the Barge Canal, at Barge Lock in central Droitwich and at locks 6 and 7 on the Junction Canal.

4 Bridge 5 on the Junction Canal has restricted and variable headroom. Check for oncoming boats before proceeding.

A shallow cutting carries the canal away from the top lock and presently views open out across charmingly unspoilt countryside. The channel narrows at the site of a former swing-bridge. The cuttings at Salwarpe are much deeper and more bosky, whilst the canal bends sharply to pass beneath the high arch of Bridge 7. Cyclists are asked to dismount and boaters recommended to toot their horns to avoid an embarrassing meeting of bows on the bend. Sequestered at the end of a No Through Road, Salwarpe is notable for two fine buildings: St Michael's Church (with its giant Thuja trees, grown from seeds brought back from Tanganyika) and Salwarpe Court, a substantial 16th century house of half-timber and herring-bone brick. The entrance to Coney Meadow nature reserve lies alongside another abandoned swing-bridge.

Lock 1

ROITWICH wears its suburbs lightly, indeed the canal curtails them, and the towpath side of the Barge Canal's entrance from the south is bordered by playing fields and public open spaces.

As it reaches the centre of town - once a Dantesque scene of brine-extraction and evaporation - the canal passes beneath two railway bridges overlooked by a classic Great Western signal box and some fine examples of lower quadrant semaphore signals. Bridge 16 carries Kidderminster Road over the canal and ushers in Netherwich Basin where an inviting semi-circle of secure 'fish-bone' moorings are available, both for permanently moored craft and visitors.

Vines Park creates a delightful environment for the formal meeting of the Barge and Junction canals at Barge Lock. It derives its name from the Roman's vinicultural activities in the area.

Where at the height of the town's industrial past the canalside would have thronged in a steamy, smoky haze of salt works and brine pits, now it's a green sward, a public amenity enhanced by the return of boats and all the colourful activity they engender. Interestingly, the original line of the canal lies under the Saltway, but there is a cohesive quality about the new line which makes it appear entirely plausible. A recreation of the wych trow *Volunteer* reminds all and sundry of why the Barge Canal was built in the first place, and the statue of Saint Richard confirms that at least two miracles have occurred in the vicinity.

A trio of swing-bridges add charm to the canal's passage through Vines Park - a quartet if you count the one which spans the Barge Lock itself. They are padlocked to deter hooliganism, and you will need your trusty CRT Yale key to unlock them. Owing to subsidence brought about by brine extraction, Barge Lock is apparently fourteen feet higher than as originally built! The canal joins the river

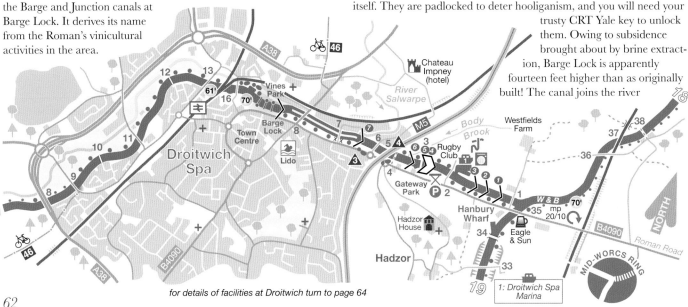

for details of facilities at Droitwich turn to page 64

at this point and, depending on fluctuations in water level, the lock may not require filling or emptying at all; though the gates should be closed after use. Under the watchful eye of St Augustine's church (its tower blackened by wafting smoke from the salt works), the navigation passes beneath another Bridge 8, the Junction Canal's bridges being numbered downwards to Hanbury Wharf. Handsomely decked out in gold paint, some credulity needs stretching to picture the era when the bridge featured a chapel. What a shame it was demolished in the 18th century, otherwise Droitwich could have joined the exclusive company of Rotherham, Bradford-on-Avon, Wakefield and the Cambridgeshire St Ives in retaining their bridge chapels.

In returning navigability to the Droitwich Junction Canal (opened by the Worcester & Birmingham Canal Company a little matter of seventy-three years after the Barge Canal) it has been necessary to detour from the original route to/from the town centre, resulting in a longer length of the River Salwarpe being adopted. Evidence of the former route of the canal can be seen in the form of an abandoned arch on the towpath side just east of Bridge 8. The Salwarpe is now utilised as far as Lock 7 - a different lock 7, you'll appreciate, from the Barge Canal's Lock 7 near Ladywood. This Lock 7, moreover, is completely new, and functionally built from concrete without the wing walls which traditionally nudge steerers into lock chambers; hence, perhaps, the requirement for two large blue and white, motorway-like arrows to be displayed indicating exactly where the 'hole' you should head for is!

It is fortunate that a culvert, provided to pass Body Brook beneath the M5 motorway, is of sufficient dimensions for narrowboats to squeeze through, otherwise the cost - let alone upheaval - of constructing a tunnel to carry the new line of the canal beneath the motorway might have rendered the whole project untenable. As things are, it's a tight enough squeeze, and even the gentle flow of Body Brook can make gaining headway a slow process travelling uphill. Lay-bys are provided at either end of what is known as Bridge 5 to hold back should an oncoming boat have already begun to pass beneath the motorway.

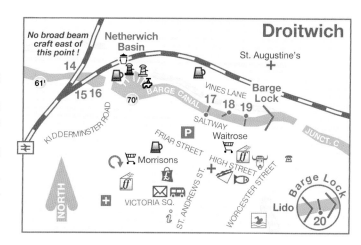

It will have already become apparent that the Junction Canal exudes an entirely different atmosphere to the Barge Canal, and not merely that it's narrower. Views along it are much more open and it attracts an altogether different class of flora and fauna. Three new locks - two of them merged into a 'staircase' pair with shared centre gates - lift the canal up past the Droitwich Rugby Club, again on a slightly different alignment to the original. A car park and picnic site encourage exploration of the new canal, whilst above Bridge 2 a two-hundred berth marina has been constructed, providing much needed facilities on this increasingly popular canal.

Regaining its original course, the canal ascends through three very deep (and original) locks to join the Worcester & Birmingham Canal at Hanbury Wharf. Small, but incredibly beautiful, the revitalised Droitwich Canals seem like £12m well spent, even if you simply go by the look of happiness on the faces of the people using them, whatever their means of propulsion.

Droitwich Spa

Map 22

A mild-mannered little town - pleased as punch to have a working waterway back on its doorstep - Droitwich revels in its salty past and you'll not go far without being reminded that the local brine is thirteen times saltier than the Med. Two local heroes vie for the town's affections: Saint Richard and John Corbett, the Salt King, the man responsible for the town's jaunty appellation

Eating & Drinking

BULLOCKS BISTRO - High Street. Tel: 01905 770897. Open Tue-Fri 10am-3pm and 6-10pm; Sat 9am-3pm and 6-10pm, and Sun 9am-4pm. WR9 8ES
GARDENERS ARMS - Vines Lane. Tel: 01905 772936. Congenial pub adjacent Vines Park moorings. Open from 11am daily, food served until 9pm. WR9 8LU
HOP POLE - Friar Street. Tel: 01905 770155. *Good Beer Guide* listed town pub easily reached from Netherwich Basin. Malvern Hills and Wye Valley ales.

PARK'S - Victoria Square. Tel: 01905 776633. Family run cafe open Mon-Sat 9am-4pm. WR9 8DS
PORTOFINO - Worcester Road. Tel: 01905 794799. Italian restaurant open Tue-Sat 12-2.30pm and 5.30-10pm; Sun 12-3pm and 6-9pm. WR9 8AB
RAILWAY INN - Kidderminster Road. Tel: 01905 771578. Banks's local with railway memorabilia adjoining the canal and overlooked by an authentic GWR 'lower quadrant'. Open daily from noon. WR9 9AY
SPICE FUSION - St Andrews Street. Tel: 01905 794188. Indian and Bangladeshi cuisine. Open from 5.30pm daily. WR9 8DY

Shopping

Waitrose's supermarket couldn't be handier, and Morrisons (with its recycling point) isn't far from the canal either. Independent shops (such as Lymers Butchers) along the subsidence-wrought High Street. All the ubiquitous chain stores in St Andrews Precinct, notable for its award-winning loos.

Things to Do

TOURIST INFORMATION & HERITAGE CENTRE - Victoria Square. Tel: 01905 774312. Housed on the former Brine Baths site, this fascinating little museum celebrates Droitwich's salty past; an audio-visual display bringing home the harsh working conditions. Another section is devoted to 'Droitwich Calling'. WR9 8DS
LIDO - Lido Park. Tel: 01905 799342. Outdoor saltwater heated swimming dating from 1935. Open late May through to early September: early swims from 6.30am (7.30am weekends) until 9am, thence 10am-7pm (6pm Weekends). WR9 8AA

Connections

BUSES - First Worcestershire 'Salt Road' service 144 operates between Worcester and Birmingham half hourly daily. Tel: 0871 200 2233.
TRAINS - West Midland services to/from Worcester, Birmingham, Kidderminster etc. Tel: 0345 748 4950
TAXIS - Vines. Tel: 01905 776100.

Vines Park

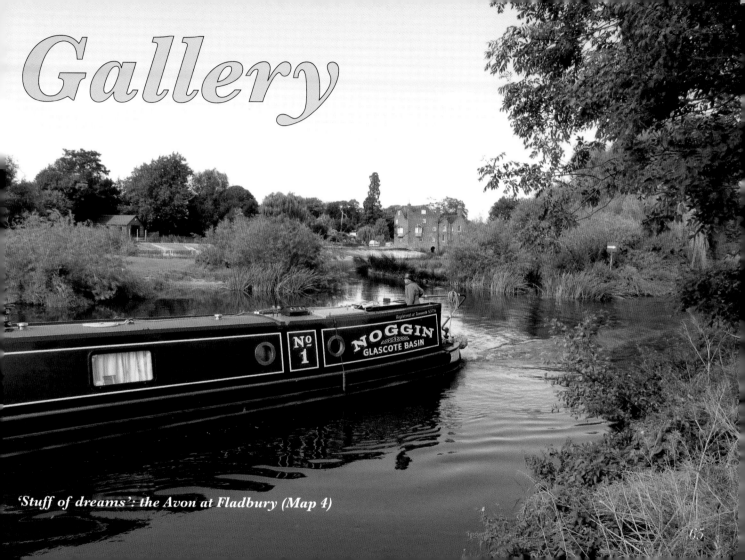

Gallery

'Stuff of dreams': the Avon at Fladbury (Map 4)

'Narrow and winding':
the Avon at Bidford (Map 6)

'Shakespeare's burial place':
Holy Trinity, Stratford (Map 7)

'The longest aqueduct in England': Edstone on the Stratford Canal (Map 9)

'What better memorial':
Bridge 39, Stratford Canal (Map 10)

'Seven chambers in close proximity': Lapworth Locks, Stratford Canal (Map 11)

'Reminiscent of the Oxford Canal':
Bridge 28, Stratford Canal (Map 11)

71

'Oak, alder, hazel': the Stratford Canal at Illshaw Heath (Map 12)

LITTLE OWL
ALVECHURCH MARINA

'Green fingers into towns': the Worcester & Birmingham Canal (Map 14)

73

'Countryside returns':
Astwood Bottom Lock,
Worcester & Birmingham
Canal (Map 18)

'Duplicated and automated':
Diglis River Locks, Worcester
(Maps 20 & 25)

'Blind bend': Sandy Point, River Severn (Map 28)

'Botticelli of bridge builders': Mythe Bridge, Tewkesbury (Map 29)

'*The high flank of Wainlode Hill*': Edward Elgar on the Severn (Map 30)

'*Gloucester Docks in all their glory*': Gloucester Lock, looking downstream (Map 31)

'A French chateau to shame': Ebley Mill on the Cotswold Canals (Map 37)

'Fifth and last of the roundhouses':
Inglesham Roundhouse (Map 44)

Wolverhampton (use Stourport Ring CC)

A4025

Stourport on Severn
site of power station

Town Centre

Stourport Marina

cider mill

Lincomb Lock
7ft 4ins
Tel: 01299 822887

Stourport Swifts FC

weir !

Redstone Rock

Areley Kings

site of WWII oil wharf

Winnall
site of Hampstall Ferry

Hampstall Inn

The Burf

Vine Yard

Severn Way

site of lock

site of lock

Dick Brook

Shrawley Wood

NORTH

Clacks Farm

Boreley

rather than engineering is the inhibiting factor, the fly in the ointment.

Those wishing to go and explore could do worse than emulate the architectural writer, Jonathan Meades, who availed himself of one of the little motor launches for hire by Stourport Bridge, to go spluttering upstream in search of the shanties which crowd the riverbank, in a 1990 television documentary. Far from being the butt of his famously verbose and withering scorn, he was smitten by their variously homespun and/or outlandish charm For all practical purposes, however, Stourport marks the head of navigation on the Severn, and it is here that the traveller by water exchanges the fluctuating currents of the river for the stolid waters of the Staffordshire & Worcestershire Canal, a route described in *Pearson's Stourport Ring Canal Companion.*

Stourport itself is one of the inland waterway system's great little treasures, a former transhipment port suffering from the delusion that it's a seaside resort. And whatever entrance the boater makes - locking up from the Severn under the benign gaze of the Tontine Hotel, or descending into the dripping depths of York Street Lock from the canal - there will be few steerers able to resist exploration of the basins, shunting back and forth like some busy tug; turning in wide

THE Severn has come down in the world, navigationally speaking. There was a time in the dim, and increasingly distant past, when it was boated commercially all the way upstream to the outskirts of Welshpool: Pool Quay - see Map 30 *Welsh Waters.* Boaters can only daydream of such voyages now: up through the Ironbridge Gorge, cradle of the industrial revolution; past the site of the Roman settlement of Uriconium; all but boxing the compass at Shrewsbury, islanded by a Housmanesque Severn stream. But such facilities, alas, were progressively abandoned during the second half of the 19th century, as the railways robbed the river of its trade. The railways in turn became viewed as obsolete. We have a propensity, like children rebelling against parental strictures, to undo great works. Up until 1963 you could catch a direct train from Stourport to Shrewsbury. Now the traveller between those two points has no recourse but to go by road. Progress is, perhaps, a dish that has been too long in the oven. From time to time there are campaigns to restore navigation - which theoretically remains a 'right' - at least as far as Shrewsbury. But, as with the majority of such well-meaning schemes, finance arcs or honing their reversing skills. The original and largest - known as the Upper Basin - opened in 1771, and connects through two wide-beam 'barge' locks with the river. These impressive (at least in narrowboater's eyes) chambers were built sturdily enough to withstand the Severn's perennial propensity for flooding, and capacious enough for the indigenous Severn Trows. Between the barge locks lies the smallest basin, thought to have been used as an assembly point and not as a wharf as such. A second link to the river, consisting of four narrow-beam locks in pairs of staircases, was opened in 1781. Again the locks are separated by a small basin from which a drydock extends. Manoeuvring a lengthy boat between the staircase pairs can be tricky, and it doesn't help one's sangfroid that there is often a sizeable crowd of onlookers who gain as much entertainment from your technique as from the adjacent fairground. At the top of the narrow locks, and contemporary with their construction, lies the Clock Basin, interconnected with the Upper Basin. On a peninsula between these upper, boat-filled expanses of water stands the glorious Clock Warehouse.

Once there were two basins which lay to the east of Mart Lane. Known expediently as the 'Further-most Basins', they dated from the early 19th century. The lower, reached through a wide lock, had a

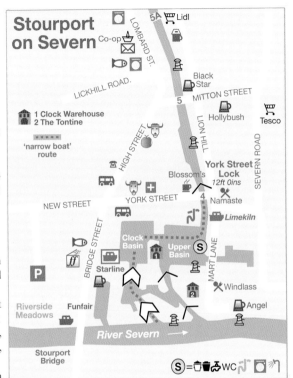

1 Clock Warehouse
2 The Tontine

'narrow boat' route

York Street Lock 12ft 0ins

> ⚠ The 'narrow boat' route through the basins at Stourport - from river to canal and vice versa - involves negotiating two staircase locks which are unusual in that there is no need to ensure that the lower chamber is empty when going down as overflow weirs automatically equate the levels. When joining the river and heading downstream, it's not a bad idea to telephone ahead to Lincomb Lock to let the keeper know you're coming.

brief existence, closing in 1866 when the town gas works took over the site. The other basin flourished in an Indian Summer of commercial activity between 1926 and 1949 when coal boats for the power station discharged in it; their dusty black cargoes of Cannock coalfield slack being unloaded by electric grab and carried in hoppers along an aerial ropeway to the power station's furnaces. Subsequently it was infilled and a timber yard occupied its site, but it has been re-excavated as the focal point of a re-generation scheme and is jostled now by modern apartments.

Another important element of the redevelopment of Stourport Basins concerns the return to life of the Tontine Hotel, refurbished for use as housing. It derived its unusual name from a system of speculative life insurance, the last surviving member of its original group of investors gaining full ownership of the building: fuel for skul-duggery one imagines and the possibility of a plot which would inspire most detective story writers. In its heyday it boasted a hundred bedrooms, a ballroom and formal gardens spilling down to the riverbank.

The River

The Severn's official head of navigation is just upstream of Stourport Bridge where the Gladder Brook enters from the west bank, though occasional convoys of shallow-

Redstone Rock

draughted diehards do journey upstream to Bewdley campaigning to restore navigation to the Upper Severn. One waterway project which did not materialise was for a canal from Stourport to Leominster. A token sod was dug opposite the basins in 1797, but the ludicrously ambitious through route never came to fruition. Stourport Bridge - the fourth on the site - was erected in 1870 to the designs of one Edward Wilson, an engineer involved in the construction of railways in the district at the time. It is notable for its unusual spiral staircase.

The River Stour's confluence with the Severn is muted, and no trace remains of Stourport's grandiose riverside power station, opened with a flourish by Stanley Baldwin in 1927. During the Second World War its

lofty chimneys were camouflaged in green and yellow to hide them from the Luftwaffe, a successful ruse as it turned out. Extended in 1950, it ceased generating in 1984 and has subsequently been replaced by housing. Alongside the entrance of the River Stour, from which the power station drew copious amounts of cooling water, stands a disused vinegar factory.

Stourport Boat Club held their first regatta in 1876 along a mile and a half course between Redstone Rock and a point upstream of Stourport Bridge. The event still takes place every August and attracts muscular competitors from far and wide. Caravans and camping accompany the river down to Redstone Rock, a refuge for outlaws in Cromwell's time. The wharves opposite, together with the industrial estate to the rear, were developed by the Severn & Canal Carrying Company in the nineteen-thirties; some of their initialled bollards are still extant. A considerable volume of oil traffic was dealt with here until the Sixties. Stourport Marina reflects the Severn's present day emphasis on leisure, but it would be nice if Harker's and Regent Oil's petrol barges still plied the river. B. A. Lane's books *Severn Tanking* and *Time & Tide* provide vivid 'first-hand' accounts of the lifestyle the tanker crews enjoyed. Or should that be endured? For they worked long hours for little financial reward; though as the author summarises: 'We enjoyed the life and there was not another job anywhere with comradeship like life on the Severn.' As for Stourport itself: 'It was nothing to find several craft waiting to discharge. We had to wait our turn, which could be any time during the day or night.' A whole way of life obliterated by lorries and pipelines.

Just below Stourport Marina stands a cider mill where, towards the end of summer, you'll see thirst-inducing lorry loads of apples being upended onto conveyor belts en route to the indoor presses.

Pending any progress with the Upper Severn scheme, Lincomb Lock is the highest on the Severn. It lies in a picturesque setting dominated by one of the sheer red sandstone cliffs which characterise the river in this part of the world. Downstream, on the port side, there is evidence of a petroleum jetty and camouflaged oil dumps dating back to the Second World War. Further on, the frivolities of 'Stourport-on-Sea' are rapidly forgotten as the Severn glides through some delightful Worcestershire countryside.

Pedestrians can enjoy the river by walking the Severn Way which keeps to the east bank between Stourport and Holt Fleet. Refreshment opportunities are, however, beyond reach since the ferries at Hampstall and Lenchford ceased to operate long ago. In 1919 the former was swamped in the wake of a passing steamer and sank, drowning nine unsuspecting unfortunates. Tragedy is never far from water.

It is difficult to grasp that Dick Brook, emerging imperceptibly from the woods on the west bank, was made navigable in the 17th century (by Andrew Yarranton, a Brindley before his time) to serve an iron forge located deep in the woods: woods which incidently are famous for their lime trees. L. T. C. Rolt moored here aboard *Cressy* and described the experience in topographical study *Worcestershire* published by Robert Hale in 1949. Gardening enthusiasts will recall that Clacks Farm played host to broadcasts of the BBC's *Gardeners World* for a number of years.

Stourport   Map 23

All the trappings of a seaside resort: funfairs and fish & chips, steamer trips, paddling pools and amusement arcades. Day trippers pour in from the land-locked West Midlands to let their hair down and make believe they are really in Barmouth or Weston-super-Mare. Marginally more in touch with reality, us boaters can swagger about the town pretending that we've just come up with a cargo of oil from Avonmouth.

Eating & Drinking

ANGEL INN - Severn Side. Tel: 01299 879480. Riverside Banks's pub offering B&B. Meals served at lunchtimes and evenings from 6pm Mon-Sat and between noon and 6pm Sun. DY13 9EW

BLACK STAR - Mitton Street (Bridge 5). Tel: 01299 488838. *Good Beer Guide* listed pub overlooking canal offering food and Wye Valley Ales. DY13 8YP

BLOSSOM'S - York Street. Tel: 01299 829442. Quaint canalside tea room. DY13 9EE

THE HOLLYBUSH - Mitton Street. Tel: 01299 827435. Black Country Ales and guests. DY13 9AA

NAMASTE - Lichfield Street. Tel: 01299 877448. Indian restaurant adjacent Bridge 4. DY13 9EU

RISING SUN - Lombard Street (canalside Bridge 5A). Tel: 01299 822530. Little Banks's backstreet local offering good value meals. DY13 8DU

THE WINDLASS - Stourport Basins. Tel: 01299 871742. Cafe/restaurant housed in former canal workshop and stable. Open 10am-4pm. DY13 9EW

Shopping

Co-op (with PO), Tesco Metro and Lidl supermarkets are most easily accessed from either side of Bridge 5A. Look out (on High Street) for Gough's, a butcher/greengrocer featuring gluten-free pies. Not just one, but *two* launderettes on Lombard Street.

Connections

BUSES - Diamond 3 links Stourport with Kidderminster every 20 mins Mon-Sat and approx. hourly Sun. Local independent Coniston services 294/6 run half a dozen times a day ex Sun to/from Worcester via Holt Heath. Tel: 0871 200 2233.

TAXIS - Terrys. Tel: 0771 235 1111.

24 RIVER SEVERN Holt Fleet & Bevere 5mls/2lks/1½hrs

'HOW is Worcestershire?' sang the Stourport-born singer /songwriter, Clifford T. Ward, and from these exceedingly pleasant reaches of the Severn you have little alternative other than to reply: still very lovely indeed. This is Britain's - rather than England's - lengthiest river: 221 miles in case you were wondering. It seems rather inadequate, that, at 42 miles, less than a fifth of it is currently navigable; a peculiarly British embarrassment. Neither is it legal to follow the whole of the Severn's course on foot - entrenched landowning interests have seen to that - and at Holt Fleet the Severn Way is forced into a lengthy, though not in itself uninteresting, detour; but care needs to be exercised as the path passes through the environs of a working quarry.

Holt Lock is picturesquely sited beneath high cliffs somewhat reminiscent of Stoke Bardolph on the Trent. Downstream the river passes beneath an

elegant iron bridge designed by Thomas Telford, dated 1828, fetchingly apparelled in green and cream, which sets it off rather nicely.

Happily, it is no longer necessary for canal enthusiasts to speak wistfully of the Droitwich Barge Canal in the past tense. The re-opening of this long abandoned waterway in 2011 was a remarkable achievement, as described in the text accompanying Maps 21 and 22. The last in the trio of automated locks which separate Stourport from Worcester is to be found at Bevere. Following restoration of the Droitwich canals, and the mini-ring thus formed, boat passages through the lock have increased significantly. Note Telford's charming little bridge which spans the weir stream.

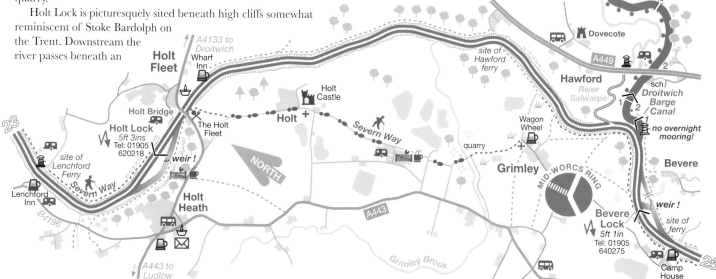

25 RIVER SEVERN Worcester 4mls/11k/1hr

WORCESTER'S affection for its riverside is clear, though perhaps not quite so commercially exploited as in its Edwardian heyday. We're all a bit too well-travelled now to be as excited at the thought of a steamer trip or a jaunt in a rowing boat as our forebears used to be. Old photographs expose a gallimaufry of vessels jostling for position: trows, tugs, lighters and narrowboats; paddle steamers, launches, rowing eights and skiffs. Once it must have seemed that the whole world and his wife wanted to be on the water. All but one of the city's ferry crossings have vanished too, though there are plans for a new footbridge in the vicinity of Gheluvelt Park, which gains its outlandish name from a Belgian village where the Worcestershire Regiment performed heroically in the First World War.

Enviable riverside properties - some of which would not look out of place on the Thames - look smugly down from the Henwick bank. A waterworks was opened on the Barbourne side in 1858, pumping water from the river prior to its being purified in filter beds. The Pump House survives and has been refurbished as an Environment Centre: though, regrettably no formal provision has been provided for boaters to moor up and visit.

Worcester's National Hunt race course can trace its riverside origins back as far as 1718. Then, as now, race meetings could be disrupted by the course finding itself under water. A recent revival has been the 'Land O'Plums' race which used to be run at Pershore up until around the time of the Second World War. Other sports were enjoyed on these meadows. In 1824 a bare fisted boxing match went eighty-four rounds.

Worcester Rowing Club was formed in 1874, though competitive rowing on the Severn was established even earlier than that. Fee payable visitor moorings are provided on the city side of the river either side of the ornate, cast iron railway bridge which carries the pretty Malvern and Hereford line across the river. The bridge is linked to Foregate Street station on a sinuous viaduct of 68 arches. A siding, known as The Butts, ran along the eastern bank of the river to serve industries along its bank, though the Dean and Chapter put their ecclesiastical feet firmly down

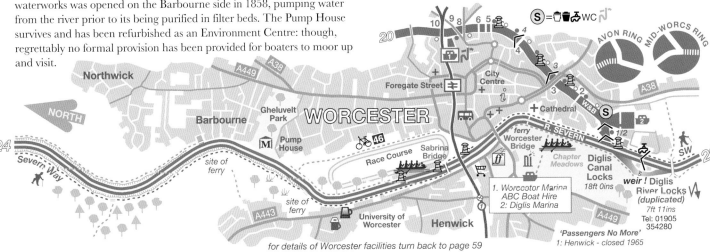

1. Worcester Marina ABC Boat Hire
2: Diglis Marina

'Passengers No More'
1: Henwick - closed 1965

for details of Worcester facilities turn back to page 59

when it was mooted that the line might continue below the Cathedral's west window and on down to Diglis.

Worcester Bridge was designed by John Gwynn and completed in 1781. Between 1882 and 1928 it carried trams, initially horsedrawn, latterly electric. When the bridge was widened in the 1930s, the old parapet found its way into Edward Elgar's garden, so enamoured was the composer of anything associated with his home town. Antiquated wharves and warehouses line the east bank of the river south of the bridge. A prominent landmark is the spire of St Andrew's (redundant and mostly demolished) church, nicknamed the 'Glovers' Needle' in homage to one of Worcester's old trades.

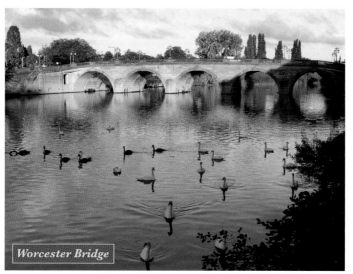

Worcester Bridge

The reach between Worcester Bridge and the Cathedral is designated a Swan Sanctuary in response to a period in the 1980s when swans were dying from lead poisoning, lead at that time being a component of angler's fishing weights. Fishing was subsequently banned and swans certainly now flourish on the river, as do herons, kingfishers and cormorants; even otters. Handy little bags of appropriate food for the swans and local duck population are available from riverside outlets.

On summer weekend afternoons and Bank Holidays a charming ferry operates in the vicinity of the Cathedral, rekindling scenes from days when such crossings were a common sight up and down the river. The ferrymen (and one lady!) are all volunteers and proceeds go to charity. Clinker built, the rowing boat, licensed to carry nine passengers, is called *Doris*, and the 'voyage', under the Cathedral's benign gaze, little less than heavenly.

Boating past the Cathedral is one of the inland waterways' most memorable experiences. Though one might justifiably call for the expertise of a tree surgeon so that the unimpaired views once enjoyed might be restored.

Worcestershire County Cricket Club's New Road ground can lay legitimate claim to being one of the most beautiful in the world. Seeking a suitable location to play, the club rented three 'sheep fields' from the Cathedral authorities. The first county match was against Yorkshire at the commencement of the 1899 season. The club's crest features a trio of black pears, several trees of which grow around the ground.

Downstream from the Cathedral, there is little suggestion of anticlimax. King's School's striking, prow-shaped boathouse catches the eye, as does the Diglis House Hotel, once home to the artist Benjamin Williams Leader. An incongruously mundane row of redbrick terraced villas ensues, bearing the names Florence, Gordon, Stanley and May. Perhaps they were built as accommodation for workers at the Royal Worcester porcelain works to the rear. A pair of broad-beam locks lift the Worcester & Birmingham Canal up into Diglis Basins ... more of which on Map 20.

Diglis, once home to a particularly noxious manure works, is now a honeycomb of apartment blocks. A boom prevents access to a former dock used by oil barges. Diglis River Locks are duplicated and automated, that on the east bank being the smaller, more regularly used, of the two. Downstream of the locks an impressive footbridge spans the river as it begins to make its way out into open countryside.

26 RIVER SEVERN Kempsey 4mls/0lks/1hr

LIKE a deferential waitress coming to clear the dishes, the River Teme makes little impact on the haughty Severn, but on its way down from the Welsh Marches, past Ludlow and through lush Herefordshire orchards and pastures, this lovely river hits heights of comeliness that the Severn seldom aspires to.

William Sandys (see Map 1), who was originally responsible for making the River Avon navigable, acquired the rights to make the Teme navigable up to Ludlow in the 17th century, but he never got around to doing anything about it. Perhaps the Civil War impeded his plans. Just a canon ball's trajectory from here the first skirmish of that conflict took place at Powick Bridge on September 23rd 1642. The Parliamentarians lost that battle but came from behind to win the war by defeating the Royalist forces on virtually the same battlefield nine years later. A long abandoned jetty again reminds us of the former trade in oil and petroleum along the river.

Carrington Bridge, which carries Worcester's Southern Link Road across the river, was in the process of being dual-carriagewayed while this edition was in preparation.

Severn Motor Yacht Club was founded in 1926. During the Second World War a number of the club's privately owned vessels were requisitioned by the Admiralty, some of which were lost on active service, as listed on a commemorative plaque in the club's picturesquely weatherboarded clubhouse.

South of Worcester the Severn pursues an undemonstrative course. There are brief glimpses for boaters of the Malvern Hills beyond the river's high, and largely uninspiring, banks. But if the scenery momentarily falters, the novelty of deep, wide water has yet to wear off. The walker - as so often on the Severn - has the better views, not least the architectural confection that is Stanbrook Abbey, a huge Gothic Revival assemblage designed by Edward Welby Pugin, son of Augustus Welby Northmore. The abbey's nuns upped sticks and moved to fresh fields in North Yorkshire in 2009, but the buildings have gained a new lease of life as a luxury hotel, conference centre and wedding venue. The Stanbrook Abbey Press gained an international reputation for its religious tracts. Hugh Whitemore's 1987 play *The Best of Friends* celebrated the three-way friendship which developed between Stanbrook's abbess Laurentia McLachlan, George Bernard Shaw and Sydney Cockerell.

Kempsey comes tentatively down to the riverbank, and its substantial, squat-towered church pokes its head above the boater's eyeline. Sources

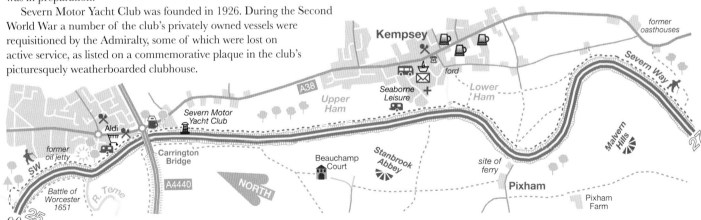

vary regarding the demise of Pixham Ferry, 1939 and 1947 being the most quoted parameters. It seems, though, that a larger vessel capable of carrying vehicles was destroyed in the floods of the former, and that a rowing boat carried bravely on until the latter. There was no formal road approach to the ferry stage on the Kempsey side, so cars had to be driven across the field avoiding potholes. The Croome Hunt used the ferry and archive photographs depict the horses and hounds packed aboard.

It is widely known that the Malvern Hills inspired much of Elgar's music, but the Severn was also his muse: 'I am still at heart the dreamy child who used to be found in the reeds by Severn side with a sheet of paper, trying to fix the sounds and longing for something great'. Between 1923-7 he lived in the neighbourhood, leasing nearby Napleton Grange.

One thrills to his 'falling sevenths' at every turn.

Kempsey

27 RIVER SEVERN Severn Stoke 5mls/0lks/1hr

UNBRIDGED, and ferry-less now, the Severn constitutes a natural obstacle all the way from Worcester's southern by-pass to Upton. Swaggering like a playground bully across its floodplain, it defies communities to get in its way, and they do their level best to not oblige; notwithstanding which, the villagers of Severn Stoke are regularly knee-deep in water. Webbed feet, though, seem a small price to pay for living in such glorious surroundings. High banks, it's true, preclude the best views from the perspective of a boat, but walkers on the Severn Way have beauty bestowed upon them in bucketfuls, the Malvern Hills being seldom out of sight, and never out of mind. The walker, furthermore, is at liberty to pause and take things in. His counterpart at the tiller or wheel is offered no formal moorings, and those with pets aboard, used to being able to offer 'walkies' on the towpath at the drop of a hat, should consider their pet's needs before blithely setting forth.

Clevelode was known for basket making, materials garnered from the riverbank osiers. The ferry was reputedly in use right up until the Second World War. Rhydd ferry probably ceased functioning at the time of the previous global conflict, though the ferryman's house remains. Submerged rocks at Rhydd caused problems before the locks were built, and indeed thereafter in times of drought. In 1847 a trow called *Prince* was holed here and sank. Cliffey Wood tumbles picturesquely down on the western bank. To the east are glimpses of the circular Panorama Tower at Croome D'Abitot in grounds landscaped by Capability Brown.

Stuccoed, crenellated, balconied and ever so slightly pompous, early 19th century Severn Bank juts above woodland on the east bank. In contrast, Severn End's origins can be followed back to the 15th Century, ancestral home of the Lechmere's, one of whom walked in Cromwell's funeral procession. Much of the property had to be rebuilt in the wake of a disastrous fire in 1896. Amusingly, it was the model for 'Brinkley Court', the country seat of Bertie Wooster's Aunt Dahlia in a number of P. G. Wodehouse's Jeeves stories. Wodehouse, it transpires, had a real aunt married to the vicar at Hanley Castle.

All the settlements which hang precariously around the river's neck would once have had wharves to which the Severn's indigenous trows would trade, bringing coal

The Severn Way is forced into a detour away from the riverbank in the neighbourhood of Severn Stoke, but is well signposted and the diversion has plenty of consolation prizes in the fine views offered.

A38

Rose & Crown

Panorama Tower (Croome)

Severn Stoke

Severn Bank

Sheepcote Farm

site of brickworks

site of ferry

Severn Way

26

Clevelode

site of ferry

Cliffey Wood

NORTH

Severn End

Hanley Castle

Malvern Hills

Rhydd

B4424

B4211 to Malvern

B4211

Three Kings

sch

Church End

B4209 to Malvern Wells

quarry

Fish Meadow

aggregates wharf

Severn Way

28

beware barges

Pool House

from the Forest of Dean and going back with the fruit and vegetable crops of this fertile plain. It is rewarding, then, to come upon one of the very last inland waterway traffics in the whole of Britain on a short stretch of the Severn between an aggregates quarry opposite Hanley Castle and a processing plant to the south of Upton upon Severn (Map 28). A fleet of widebeam barges - decked-out in blue and white and bearing piscatorial names - is operated by Thompson River Transport, an offshoot of Torbay Seaways & Stevedores, a company based in Torquay.

One feels privileged to encounter them: gliding downstream, gunwale deep with gravel, as illustrated above, or returning upstream 'in ballast', high out of the water like amphibious beasts of burden. Seeing them working is an experience every bit as spiritual as attending evensong in Worcester or Gloucester cathedrals. Notwithstanding the consequential loss of earnings, this guidebook's compiler would cheerfully corral all the ersatz narrowboats of the leisure age, together with their floating 'gin palace' cousins into Upton Marina and scuttle them like the German fleet in Scapa Flow, just for a glimpse of the Severn in its commercial pomp, heaving with barges, tugs and lighters, longboats and trows.

28 RIVER SEVERN Upton-upon-Severn 5mls/0lks/1hr

UPTON-UPON-SEVERN'S fleshpots come as welcome relief to the Severn's somewhat repetitive scenery, and, getting caught up in the excitement, the Severn Way swaps sides. Messrs Pevsner and Lees-Milne, men of impeccable architectural taste, fell over themselves to praise the present bridge, erected at the beginning of the Second World War: 'extremely fine' thought Nikolaus, 'impressive' considered James. Pearson, on the other hand, has never shared their enthusiasm, siding with L. T. C. Rolt in a preference for its predecessor, a swing bridge, the abutments of which can still be seen. In *Worcestershire*, Rolt painted a vivid picture of watermen lingering on the cutwater embrasures of this previous bridge: 'smoking, yarning, gazing down at the smoothly flowing water, or watching the activity on the wharves'. Each plod along the road of Progress apparently rids us of something worthwhile: fords give way to ferries, ferries to swing bridges, swing bridges to fixed structures devoid of any character. And now we can travel so quickly that the average journey makes no impression on us whatsoever, all of which succinctly explains the appeal of inland waterway travel.

Upton is a busy boating centre and visitor moorings are often at a premium, necessitating doubling or even tripling - up in a manner which behoves you to be considerate neighbours. The excursion vessel, *Conway Castle*, late of the Dart, sails from here, offering themed cruises and a weekly jaunt on summer Wednesdays down to Tewkesbury in an echo of the market boats of yore.

South of the town, the river arcs around the beautiful expanse of Upton Ham, 150 acres of flood plain and Lammas meadowland, so called because cattle are put out to graze on the Ham from 1st August, Lammas Day. Curlews and skylarks nest here, whilst knapweed and ladies smock thrive. The Malverns look lovely, ranged across the western horizon in all their poetic glory. Mind you, the Ham's inherent beauty, didn't prevent it from being used for military purposes down the years. A rifle range was constructed across it in the 19th century, and the Home Guard held manoeuvres on it during World War II.

The bridge which carried the Tewkesbury & Malvern Railway over the Severn was equipped with a sliding central section which could be

Map labels: A4104 to Pershore · Ryall · 'Passengers No More' 1: Upton - closed 1961 · aggregates wharf · beware barges · Upton Ham · Saxon's Lode · site of rly bridge · site of ferry · crse of Tewkesbury & Malvern rly · Malvern Hills · Bredon Hill · Sandy Point · Pepperpot · Town Centre · Upton upon Severn · P · WC · A4104 to Malvern · 1: Upton Marina · blind bend · Holdfast · M50 · aggregates wharf (dis) · Glos. · Worcs. · Severn Way · Queenhill · Bredon School · NORTH · site of ferry · 27 · 29

94

moved aside to permit tall-masted vessels to pass. The line - opened independently in 1864, but subsequently absorbed into the Midland Railway - never amounted to much more than a modest branchline, and its chief traffics appear to have been in fruit and vegetables, racing pigeons and anglers' specials. Upton became the line's western terminus when the section to Malvern was abandoned in 1952. Goods from Tewkesbury survived withdrawal of the passenger service in 1961 by three years.

There's a blind bend at Sandy Point demanding care from boaters in both directions. The hamlet of Holdfast was noted for its sweet peas, despatched by rail from Upton to Covent Garden in Edwardian times. To the north of the motorway lies the village of Queenhill, marked by the saddleback roof of its church, the work of Sir George Gilbert Scott. Across the roaring tarmac stands Bredon School, housed in a mock Jacobean mansion previously known as Pull Court.

Severn Stoke — Map 27

Black and white cottages necklaced along the A38. A poignant war memorial at the top of Ham Lane.

Eating & Drinking

ROSE & CROWN - Church Lane. Tel: 01905 371249. Half-timbered, flood-prone Marston's pub accessible from the Severn Way. Bar and restaurant food. Open from 11.30am daily (noon Sun). WR8 9JQ

Connections

BUSES - First services 332 & 333 operate infrequently to/from Worcester and Upton. Tel: 0871 200 2233.

Hanley Castle — Map 27

Whilst inaccessible to boaters and walkers on the Severn Way, this charming village merits inclusion on the grounds of its historic pub, well worth taking the trouble to visit via Upton by taxi or bike. Reversing the common trend, pupils from all over the district are bused into the rural High School which can trace its orgins back to the 14th century.

Eating & Drinking

THREE KINGS - Church End. Tel: 01684 592686. One of the great unspoilt pubs of England justifiably listed on CAMRA's National Inventory. Dates from the 15th century and in the same family since 1911. WR8 0BL

Upton-upon-Severn — Map 28

They barely bother to take the bunting down in this jaunty little riverine town. What with its jazz, folk, blues, steam and water festivals there's hardly any point. Indeed, the spirit of the Severn pervades the place to such an extent that it exudes the atmosphere of a small coastal port - Upton upon Sea, perhaps, rather than upon Severn. The illusion is enhanced by the resemblance of the cupola-topped old church - known locally as The Pepperpot - to a lighthouse. Its high-spired Victorian replacement looks its best when viewed across The Ham against a backdrop of the Malvern Hills. Limited visitor pontoon moorings are provided upstream of the bridge within sight of the splendid Regal Garage with its 1930s styling, manned pumps and array of veteran recovery vehicles.

Eating & Drinking

Pubs jostle for pole position on the waterfront and it would be invidious of us to list one above another. Here, though, is a brief selection of establishments further into town:
HENRY'S - High Street. Tel: 01684 438300. Charming cafe surrounded by books and antiques. WR8 0HB
PUNDITS - Old Street. Tel: 01684 591022. Cosy Bangladeshi restaurant and takeaway. WR8 0HN
THE SECRET MESS - Church Street. Tel: 01684 594892. Stylish little restaurant. WR8 0HT
THRISHNA - Old Street. Tel: 01684 594900. A viable alternative if Pundits is full. WR8 0HW
UPTON CHIPPY - New Street. Tel: 01684 592230. Eat in or take away fish & chips. WR8 0HR
THE WHEELHOUSE - Upton Marina. Tel: 01684 594224. Boater-friendly bar/restaurant open from 10am daily. WR8 0PB
WHITE LION HOTEL - High Street. Tel: 01684 592551. Comfortable hotel (mentioned in *Tom Jones* by Henry Fielding) with popular Brasserie. WR8 0HJ

Shopping

Inveterate travellers will make a bee-line for The Map Shop (Tel: 01684 593146) on the High Street whose wide range of maps and guide books encompasses the whole world, the *Canal Companions* included. More practically, there are Spar and Co-op convenience stores, a post office, wine merchants and a launderette.

Things to Do

TOURIST INFORMATION & HERITAGE CENTRE - Church Street. Tel: 01684 594200. Housed within 'The Pepperpot'. Open 10-5 Mon-Sat (ex Thur) Apr-Sep; 10-4 Mon, Fri & Sat Oct-Mar. WR8 0HB
TUDOR HOUSE MUSEUM - Church Street. Local history & memorabilia. Tel: 01684 592447.
SEVERN LEISURE CRUISES - Waterside. Tel: 01684 593112. River cruises aboard *Conway Castle*. WR8 0HG

Connections

BUSES - services 332 and 333 operate to/from Worcester; ditto 363 which continues to Tewkesbury, and is thus useful for Severn Way walkers. Service 365 runs to/from Malvern. Tel: 0871 200 2233.
TAXIS - Upton Dial-a-Cab. Tel: 01684 593939.

29 RIVER SEVERN Tewkesbury 5mls/11k/1hr

note overlap and 180°
spin with Map 1

1: Tewkesbury Marina

Tewkesbury
(see enlargement P.9)

Aldi

Tewkesbury
Park

Deerhurst

Odda's
Chapel

St Mary's

Abbey

Leisure
Centre

Cheltenham College
Boat House
ferry

Severn Way

site of
ferry

Chaceley
Stock

Yew
Tree

Avon
Sailing
Club

Avon
Lock
water
works

Severn Ham

Lower
Lode

semi-tidal

Chaceley

weir !

The
Mythe

Mythe
Bridge

Upper
Lode
Lock
Tel: 01684
293138

AVON RING

Bushley

Glos.

NORTH

Worcs.

SEPARATING Gloucestershire (east bank) and Worcestershire (west bank) the Severn flows down to Mythe Bridge. You only have to see it to guess that it is the work of that Botticelli of bridge builders, Thomas Telford. Completed in 1826, and thus predating its near twin at Holt Fleet (Map 24) by a couple of years, this is one of half a dozen bridges that Telford threw across the Severn. Its setting, below the wooded heights of The Mythe - featuring the earthworks of a motte & bailey castle - is sublime, though a more imaginative paint scheme might enhance it further. Walkers on the Severn Way get to cross the bridge, and pay homage to its toll house and kiosk as it leaves the river briefly, to visit Tewkesbury. The

Tewkesbury & Malvern Railway had to dig a 420 yards long tunnel to burrow under the high ground.

A large water treatment works overlooks the Severn's confluence with the navigable channel of the Avon. But boaters bound for Gloucester or Sharpness proceed to Upper Lode Lock, which was built in 1858 to alleviate the problem of shallows upstream. The river skirts its

⚠ Advice for Boaters

1. Leaving or entering the Severn, for or from the Avon, it is important to avoid the sandbar. Give this a wide berth by keeping over towards the southern bank as you turn into the Avon, or by making sure that Mythe Bridge is in view before turning upstream into the Severn.

for details of facilities at Tewkesbury turn to page 9; for Lower Lode, Chaceley Stock and Deerhurst turn to page 99

The Mythe

eponymous ham, 177 acres of meadowland, it being a rare winter when it's not submerged. Sir Arthur Quiller-Couch's *Ode Upon Eckington Bridge* claims that 'Man shall outlast his battles, they have swept from Naseby Field to Severn Ham'. History has proved him right. So far!

Traditionally, the keeper at Upper Lode Lock would lower newcoming downstreamers to the Severn a bucket - not, disappointingly, full of freshly caught elvers - but containing a useful sheet of instructions pertaining to the passage downstream. Researching this edition we were told that it had been a long time since head office sent any out, though, to be fair to them, the Canal & River Trust do publish a comprehensively useful *User's Guide to the River Severn Navigation* which we can thoroughly recommend. It can

be downloaded on the internet, or obtained in person from CRT's regional office on Dock Road, Gloucester.

Though nominally a freshwater river above Gloucester, the Severn can be tidal on 'high springs' as far as Upper Lode, and even occasionally beyond. At such times the keeper may advise you to proceed no further until the tide ebbs. A second channel of the Avon enters the Severn at Lower Lode, from where the view of Tewkesbury Abbey, with Bredon Hill as a backdrop, is quite breathtaking. How sad it is that access to Deerhurst and its Saxon church and chapel is denied the boater; it is hard to imagine the cost of a mooring pontoon would prove prohibitive. Time and time again boaters are denied legitimate access to interesting places.

30 RIVER SEVERN Apperley & Ashleworth 6mls/0lks/1hr

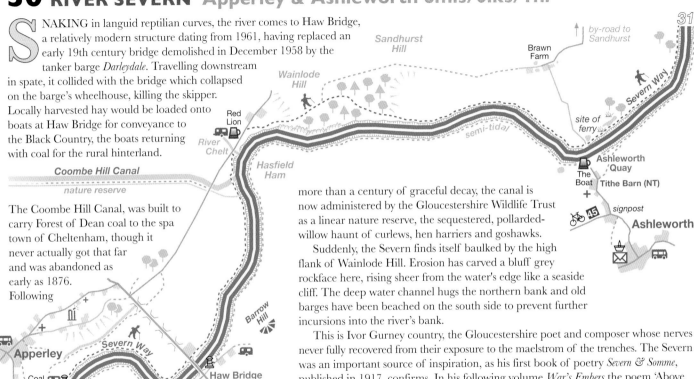

SNAKING in languid reptilian curves, the river comes to Haw Bridge, a relatively modern structure dating from 1961, having replaced an early 19th century bridge demolished in December 1958 by the tanker barge *Darleydale*. Travelling downstream in spate, it collided with the bridge which collapsed on the barge's wheelhouse, killing the skipper. Locally harvested hay would be loaded onto boats at Haw Bridge for conveyance to the Black Country, the boats returning with coal for the rural hinterland.

The Coombe Hill Canal, was built to carry Forest of Dean coal to the spa town of Cheltenham, though it never actually got that far and was abandoned as early as 1876. Following

more than a century of graceful decay, the canal is now administered by the Gloucestershire Wildlife Trust as a linear nature reserve, the sequestered, pollarded-willow haunt of curlews, hen harriers and goshawks.

Suddenly, the Severn finds itself baulked by the high flank of Wainlode Hill. Erosion has carved a bluff grey rockface here, rising sheer from the water's edge like a seaside cliff. The deep water channel hugs the northern bank and old barges have been beached on the south side to prevent further incursions into the river's bank.

This is Ivor Gurney country, the Gloucestershire poet and composer whose nerves never fully recovered from their exposure to the maelstrom of the trenches. The Severn was an important source of inspiration, as his first book of poetry *Severn & Somme*, published in 1917, confirms. In his following volume *War's Embers* the poem 'Above Ashleworth' was inspired by the view from Barrow Hill. Gurney, together with his champion, Gerald Finzi, are commemorated in Gloucester Cathedral by colourful windows created by Tom Denny. And while we're on the subject of composers, spare a thought for Herbert Howells, another 'Gloucestershire Lad', often inspired by local landscapes. Try the Benedictus from his *Missa Sabrinensis* or Severn Mass.

Lower Lode
Map 29

Eating & Drinking

LOWER LODE INN - Forthampton. Tel: 01684 293224. A customers' mooring pontoon provides access to this rambling riverside inn which operates an outboard-engined ferry (Tel: 0743 209 8184) across to the Tewkesbury bank during the summer months. Open from noon daily. Bar and restaurant food, B&B and a good choice of locally sourced real ales. GL19 4RE

Chaceley Stock
Map 29

Riverside hamlet a mile east of Chaceley itself. Elver and bacon omelette is apparently a local delicacy. *Chaceley* was the name of a Healing's of Tewkesbury grain barge, built by Harkers of Knottingley in 1964 and originally known as *Nora Easting*. Now shortened, and converted for leisure use, it has reverted to its original name, but is still to be seen in the vicinity.

Eating & Drinking

YEW TREE INN - Tel: 01452 780333. Isolated riverside inn at site of Deerhurst ferry. Open Tue-Sat 12-2pm and 6-11pm. Open Sun 12-5pm. Generously portioned, home made food. Doom Bar and guest ales. Apartment for let. Pontoon moorings exclusively for customers. GL19 4EQ

Deerhurst
Map 29

Floodgates defy the Severn to do its worst, and it often obliges. St Mary's church is Anglo-Saxon, dating from the 8th century. Pride of place goes to a sculpture of the Virgin and Child, an astonishing relic. The font is far more modern, 9th century at least! And as if this was not enough for one back of beyond village to boast, nearby stands another Saxon survival known as Odda's Chapel. *Deerhurst* was also a Healing's grain barge. Other members of the small fleet bore the names of Severnside villages: *Tirley*, *Bushley* and *Apperley*.

Apperley
Map 30

Once a village known for apple growing and salmon fishing, Apperley now exists chiefly as a commuter base for folk who work in Gloucester and Cheltenham and there is no longer enough daytime activity to support a shop. The local cricket club can trace their origins back to the middle of the 19th century. One of their stalwarts, who rejoiced in the name of Alf Dipper, played for England. The likes of Bob Willis, John Emburey, Herschelle Gibbs (SA), Gordon Greenidge and Courtney Walsh (WI) have graced the ground at one time or another.

Eating & Drinking

THE COAL HOUSE - Gabb Lane. Tel: 01452 780211. Riverside inn with pontoon moorings exclusively for patrons. Restricted opening hours: Fri & Sat evenings from 6.30pm and Sun lunch 12-3pm. Steak on the Stone signature dish. Apartment for let. GL17 4DN

Connections

BUSES - Stagecoach service 351 links Apperley four or five times daily (ex Sun) with Gloucester and Tewkesbury, a highly enjoyable ride in its own right, never mind its usefulness to Severn Way walkers. Tel: 0871 200 2233.

Haw Bridge
Map 30

Macabre scene, in 1938, of the as yet unsolved 'Cheltenham Torso Murder Mystery' concerning a retired army captain, whose headless and limbless body was found in the river by fishermen; his lover, a male dancer who subsequently committed suicide; and the latter's mother, an illegal abortionist.

Connections

BUSES - Stagecoach service 351 connects Haw Bridge four or five times daily (ex Sun) with Gloucester, and/or Tewkesbury. Tel: 0871 200 2233.

Wainlode Hill
Map 30

Eating & Drinking

RED LION - Wainlode Hill. Tel: 01452 730935. Riverside but *no* easy mooring. What Severn Way walkers lose over Ashleworth, they gain with this charming brick-built inn. Food served from noon daily. Camping to rear. GL2 9LW

Ashleworth
Map 30

Follow the lane inland from the pub and you'll quickly come upon Ashleworth's magnificent Tithe Barn cared for by the National Trust. Past that stands Ashleworth Court, built of blue lias and dating from 1460. Frustratingly it's in private hands, but tucked away between it and the Tithe Barn is the village's splendid church of St Andrew & Bartholomew. The interior is utterly charming, though we're not sure, given the temptations of The Boat - that we would readily subscribe to the wall-painted advice in the South Aisle to be 'there fore sober and watch unto prayer'.

Eating & Drinking

THE BOAT - Ashleworth Quay. Tel: 01452 700272 Mooring pontoon for customers. Has shed some of its innocent charm since it passed out of the Jelf family, but catering, formerly limited to lunchtime rolls, has been upgraded to basket meals and burgers, ideal accompaniment for the most part locally brewed ales. No unnecessary noise, just the soft congenial burr of Gloucestershire voices. Humbly yet beautifully appointed, photographs of elvering and the long gone ferry on the walls. Closed Mondays. GL19 4HZ

Shopping

PO stores in village centre an idyllic ten minutes walk west of Quay. Note the quaint (but in need of new paint) signpost at the first junction you come to.

Connections

BUSES - service 351 as Haw Bridge.

31 RIVER SEVERN Gloucester 4mls/11k/1hr

LONG Reach leads to Upper Parting. These old river names have an evocative resonance. And there were deeper subtleties: the navigable channel downstream of the Parting was known to working boatmen as 'Skipper's Length', whilst that above was known as 'Mates'. The tradition was that barge skippers would be at the wheel for the tortuous, narrow exit channel from Gloucester, being relieved by the mate once Upper Parting had been reached .

The now unnavigable western channel of the Severn, which loops past the village of Maisemore, was used to gain access to the Herefordshire & Gloucestershire Canal, a 34 mile rural waterway which took fifty years to build. Within forty years of completion in 1845 it had largely been converted into a railway. Twenty years ago no one would have considered that the H & G could ever be made navigable again, but other 'impossible' restoration projects have been achieved, and 'never' is no longer a word in any self-respecting canal activist's vocabulary. The junction basin at Over has been

cosmetically restored, though being on a tidal reach of the Severn it cannot be accessed by inland waterway craft. As a taste of things hopefully to come, boat trips are operated along a short length of the canal.

The navigable, eastern channel of the Severn must have demanded all the barge skipper's fund of experience. If you have been used to the motorway breadth of the river down from Tewkesbury, this B-road backwater comes as something of a shock. It forms a surreptitious approach to the city, for the overhanging willows hide any view which might otherwise be had of the cathedral, but in its favour lies

◯ Key
A site of Tar Works
B former Moreland's Match Manufactory
C site of Carriage & Wagon Works
D site of Castle Meads Power Station

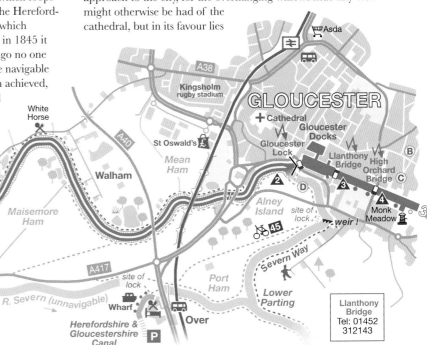

Llanthony
Bridge
Tel: 01452
312143

100

⚠ Advice for Boaters

1. On reaching Upper Parting, boaters are encouraged to telephone ahead to the lock-keeper at Gloucester - Tel: 01452 310832 - so that the lock up into Gloucester Docks can be made ready for them.

2. Approaching Gloucester Lock beware the current drawing you towards the unnavigable channel to Lower Parting. The quay wall to your left has chains through which a line should be looped until the green light signals that you can enter the lock. Attach your stern line first.

3. Llanthony Bridge requires raising for craft proceeding to/from the Gloucester & Sharpness Canal.

4. Headroom at High Orchard Bridge is 13 feet / 4 metres.

the fact that it ushers you into the very centre of the city without experiencing any of the drab outskirts which form a welcoming committee to most centres of population these days.

A series of bridges span the river as roads and railways converge

Gloucester Lock

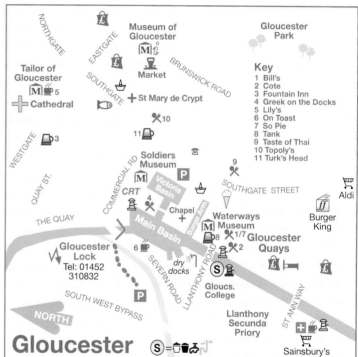

Key

1 Bill's
2 Cote
3 Fountain Inn
4 Greek on the Docks
5 Lily's
6 On Toast
7 So Pie
8 Tank
9 Taste of Thai
10 Topoly's
11 Turk's Head

Gloucester

on the city centre, before you reach the long wall of the old River Quay, where vessels which had navigated the tidal Severn used to berth prior to the development of the docks and the ship canal from Sharpness. An unlikely line of plum trees defines the quay now, though it is not a place for boats to linger, other than whilst waiting for access to the lock (see Note 2).

Downstream of The Quay the river branches again, the right hand unnavigable channel leading round to Lower Parting. Between 1943 and 1969

Castle Meads Power Station stood alongside this reach. Three coastal vessels were built to bring South Wales coal to the plant, but it proved impractical to reach the unloading point because of silting caused by the discharge from Gloucester Lock, so coal was delivered by rail.

Gloucester Lock dates from 1812 and was originally in the form of a staircase pair. Now it is one deep chamber, mechanised and spanned by a liftbridge carrying a busy road around the docks. Though it feels odd to be going *up* a lock on a journey *down*stream, Gloucester Docks are gradually revealed in all their grandeur, and it is with a sense of exhilaration that you proceed into the Main Basin to seek out a mooring amidst these splendid surroundings. The two main visitor mooring points suitable for canal craft are in the north-east corner of the Main Basin and immediately south of Llanthony Bridge. Both are marked on the enlargement on page 99; both can be noisy when the bars shut!

Cargo-handling may be history, but the docks retain considerable appeal. And if the handsome warehouses host offices now in place of wheat and maize and barley, and if there are more shoppers than stevedores, there is still much to exercise the imagination. In certain lights the setting can be seen as Atkinson Grimshaw - the Yorkshire bred Victorian artist, much given to atmospheric dockland scenes - must have been inspired by. His finished canvas hangs in the Museum of Gloucester. The Mariners' Chapel was erected in 1849 to care for the spiritual needs of the docks' itinerant and international population of seamen. The interior is usually open to visitors and a service is held each Sunday at 3pm. Ivor Gurney was the chapel's organist before the Great War. In the south-western corner of the Main Basin, overlooked by the Alexandra Warehouse, a pair of drydocks are used by T. Nielsen & Co, one of the world's leading specialists in the repair, restoration and construction of traditional ships and rigging.

Dragging oneself away from Gloucester isn't easy, but the allure of the Gloucester & Sharpness Canal is equally hard to resist. Its egress from the city would hardly be recognisable to the old salts of its working past. We don't work 'til we drop now, we shop, as manifested by the Gloucester Quays complex of designer outlets. And when we're not shopping, we're eating and drinking, as evinced by a concomitant rash of restaurants and bars. The remnants of Llanthony Secunda Priory, a 12th century offshoot of its mid-Wales namesake, provide a pious sense of proportion in the midst of all this debauchery. Little remains of the Gloucester Railway Carriage & Wagon Company's 28 acre site, once the city's largest employer, and manufacturers of many a London tube train, British Railway's diesel multiple unit, or foreign potentate's luxury train. Ditto Moreland's factory on Bristol Road, makers of England's Glory matches. Matchmakers (of the non matrimonial variety) need timber, and a feature of the canal at this point were extensive ponds where logs could be soaked to prevent drying out and cracking prior to use. Moreland's Riga Wharf owed its name to the fact that much of the timber was imported from Latvia. Used for private moorings now, the dock at Monk Meadow was once dominated by a giant grain silo.

Main Basin

Gloucester
Map 31

Seagulls reinforce the maritime ambience of this charming 'West Country' city. Charles Dickens was amazed to find merchant seamen wandering conspicuously along the streets of what he imagined would be a quiet cathedral city. He followed one and discovered 'endless intricacies of dock and huge three-masted ships'. Naturally, there are no sailors to be followed today, and, in any case, one has one's reputation to consider. Henry Vollam Morton - the Bill Bryson of the inter war years - was more drawn to the city's match girls, who were in the habit, he discovered when researching *In Search of England*, of perambulating Southgate and Northgate dressed, like Botticelli maidens, in flowered voile.

Most users of this guidebook, however, will be wondering what Gloucester *itself* is like, having already become acquainted with the docks. In truth it's a bit of a curate's egg, a bit of a Mahler symphony, consisting of serene passages and alleyways interspersed with strident concrete shopping precincts which could be anywhere. Here and there, though, you encounter evidence of the Roman 'Glevum', stressing Gloucester's longevity. The city has, however, in its cathedral, a masterpiece of medieval architecture, an act of faith which transcends the perceived shortcomings of modern life. Here is the largest stained glass window in England; the intricate fan vaulting of the cloisters; and the tomb of King Edward II, murdered at nearby Berkeley Castle in 1327; and, in a corner of the Lady Chapel, those aforementioned stained glass windows by Tom Denny, celebrating the English composers Ivor Gurney and Gerald Finzi. Gurney, together with his friend Herbert Howells, attended the premier of Ralph Vaughan Williams's *Tallis Fantasia* in the cathedral in 1910, and they walked the city's streets all night, too overwhelmed to sleep!

Eating & Drinking

BILL'S - Llanthony Road. Tel: 01452 309151. Open from 8am daily (9am Sun). Rapidly out-growing its Sussex origins, Bill's can now be found in many towns. Especially good for vegetarian/vegan cusine. GL1 5SH

COTE - Gloucester Quays. Tel: 01452 228268. Open daily from 8am (9am weekends). Reliable French chain. We ate here *twice* on our research trips. GL1 5SH

FOUNTAIN INN - Westgate Street. Tel: 01452 522562. *Good Beer Guide* recommended 17th century inn within a stone's throw of the docks. GL1 2NW

GREEK ON THE DOCKS - Merchant's Quay. Tel:01452 524574. Couldn't be handier for the visitor moorings. Open daily from 11.30am. GL1 2ES

LILY'S - College Court. Tel: 01452 307060. Quaint tea room and daytime restaurant. GL1 2NJ

ON TOAST - The Docks. Tel: 01452 505440. Modern cafe and take-away beside the main basin. GL1 2LE

SO PIE - Llanthony Road. Tel: 01452 557648. Open Tue-Fri 12-3pm and 5-9pm and weekends from noon. Atmospheric restaurant for pie aficionados. GL1 5QU

TANK - Llanthony Road. Tel: 01452 690541. Gloucester Brewery 'tap' adjacent to the National Waterways Museum. Food served Mon-Thur 12-3pm and 5-9pm and Fri-Sun from noon. GL1 2EH

TASTE OF THAI - Southgate Street. Tel: 01452 520894. Thai restaurant adjacent dockland. GL1 1UT

THE LOCK KEEPERS - Over. Tel: 01452 332900. Restaurant/rooms alongside H&G Canal. GL2 8DB

TOPOLY'S - Southgate Street. Tel: 01452 331062. Old fashioned Italian within easy reach of the docks. Open 12-2pm and 6.30-10.30pm daily. GL1 1TX

TURK'S HEAD - Southgate. Tel: 0777 198 2356. Quirky micro pub. *Not* child friendly. GL1 2LX

WHITE HORSE - Sandhurst Road. Tel: 01452 414651. Out of town riverside pub transformed into a Chinese restaurant. No formal moorings alas. GL2 9NG

Shopping

To some extent the Gloucester Quays development of designer outlets on the south side of the docks seems to have sucked some of the life out of the city's traditional centre, for the main thoroughfares are startlingly bereft of quality shops, an honourable exception being Farmhouse Deli on Northgate. Sainsbury's are well placed for boaters by High Orchard Bridge. Quayside Books & Prints on Commercial Road often has a good choice of inland waterway related titles. Gloucester Antiques Centre on Westgate is well worth a rummage.

Things to Do

TOURIST INFORMATION - Brunswick Street. Tel: 01452 396572. (Museum of Glos.). GL1 1HP

NATIONAL WATERWAYS MUSEUM - Llanthony Warehouse. Tel: 01452 318200. Inland waterway history displays housed in former grain warehouse. Floating exhibits include a Severn dumb barge and a fully restored steam dredger. 45 minute trips aboard Dunkirk veteran *Queen Boadicea II*. Admission fee runs annually facilitating repeat visits. GL12EH

MUSEUM OF GLOUCESTER - Brunswick Road. Tel: 01452 396131. Desultory local displays. GL1 1HP

TAILOR OF GLOUCESTER - College Green. Tel: 01452 422856. Beatrix Potter museum/shop. GL1 2NJ

SOLDIERS OF GLOUCESTERSHIRE MUSEUM - The Docks. Tel: 01452 522682. Local heroism in the former Custom House. Key displays concerning 'The Glosters' defiance during the Korean War. GL1 2HE

Connections

BUSES - useful links with Tewkesbury (71/35) and Stroud (64/66). Sharpness can be reached by changing at Dursley (60/62). Tel: 0871 200 2233.

TRAINS - services to/from Birmingham, London and Bristol and the Golden Valley. Tel: 0345 748 4950.

TAXIS - A2B Taxis. Tel: 01452 222222.

STRIDING boldy out of the county town, the Gloucester & Sharpness Canal certainly exudes the air of a commercial waterway, one on which you might confidently - not to say nervously - anticipate a close encounter with an ocean-going vessel at any given moment. Alas, such apprehensions are unfounded, there has been no coastal trade, to speak of, up to Gloucester for forty years. Housing estates have burgeoned beside the canal and the industries which once relied upon water transport have forgotten its existence. Solely the occasional convolvulus-strangled bollard, or the fact that railway lines remain embedded in the towpath suggest that serious commerce was once enacted here.

What was originally known as the Gloucester & Berkeley Ship Canal (for it was to be two miles longer than as finished, and destined to rejoin the Severn estuary at Berkeley Pill) was promoted in the *fin de siecle* years of the 18th century to by-pass the treacherous shallows and mercurial tides of the lower Severn. In common with the majority of engineering projects - right up to the present day - it took much more money and much more time to complete than was initially envisaged ... thirty years in fact. Its original engineer, Robert Mylne was sacked, and it fell to the ubiquitous Master Telford to finish it. For a century and a half the canal more than adequately fulfilled its function. Not until we perversely concentrated the carriage of goods on the most environmentally unsound means at mankind's disposal was it rendered obsolete.

Hempsted is the first of many keeper-operated swing bridges which span the canal at regular intervals. Sims, Rea and Sellars apart, G&S bridges lack sufficient headroom for even low-slung pleasure craft, but the rumour mill usually works well and they appear to open for your passage as if by magic.

Rea Bridge is graced by an ornately classical keeper's house, notable for its Doric-columned portico. These charming structures are to become increasingly familiar as the canal journeys south. North of Sellars Bridge the canal widens at the site of an oil terminal which received supplies by Bowker & King's 1000 ton coastal vessels trading from Llandarcy refinery near Neath in South Wales until the early 1980s. The former quay remains intact, and, in a fitting gesture to the maritime past, roads in the housing estate which took the terminal's place are named, not after Yorkshire dales, but Harker tanker barges which plied the canal.

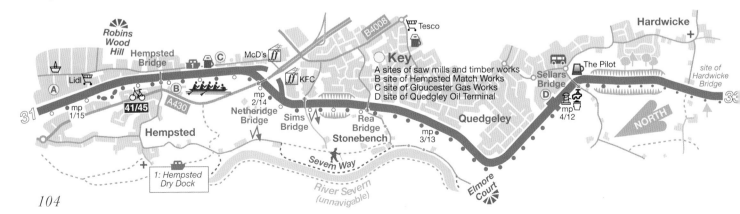

TRAVERSING a low-slung landscape, seemingly lost in a topographical void between the Cotswolds and the Forest of Dean, the Gloucester & Sharpness Canal has an alien feel about it. Islanded between the canal and the river are farms of Holstein Friesian milking herds which could be convincingly used to film a drama set in Denmark. A derelict dumb barge lies moored listlessly against the bank with a mock cargo of reeds and water. Hardwicke Court is the work of Sir Robert Smirke and features in Simon Jenkins's *England's Thousand Best Houses*. Its occupants' view to the south-east has become somewhat compromised by a futuristic 'energy from waste' facility.

Saul Junction will once again be able to live up to its name when the ambitious Cotswold Canals restoration project is realised - see Map 36. The Stroudwater Canal predated the G&S by almost fifty years and was formally abandoned in 1954, though trade had ceased a dozen years earlier.

Pending restoration, the junction is still a fascinating location, lent added prominence by the presence of a sizeable marina and working boatyard. The Cotswold Canals Trust have a heritage centre and trip boat at Saul and the Willow Trust also operate a pair of trip boats for the disabled. Car parks bring landborne visitors and Wycliffe College come here to row. So, all in all, there's rarely a dull moment. We would recommend a ramble along the reedy towpath of the Stroudwater Canal to Framilode.

By Fretherne Bridge stands an industrial estate which, in a previous existence, belonged to Cadbury's. George Cadbury, son of one of the chocolate manufacturer's founders, was a keen advocate of water transport and made sure that the works made the most of its canalside setting. Sugar, transhipped at Bristol Docks, came in by barge, as did milk collected in churns from bridges along the canal. During the various stages of the

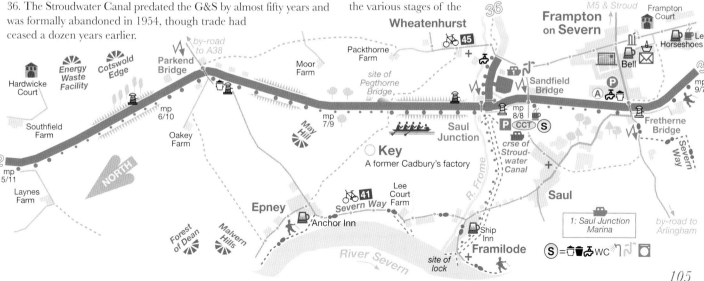

Key
A former Cadbury's factory

1: Saul Junction Marina

(S) = WC

manufacturing process, chocolate in its constituent parts was conveyed backwards and forwards between the Cadbury factories at Frampton, Blackpole (Map 20) and Bournville (Map 14) by boat. Cadbury invested in the Severn & Canal Carrying fleet, introducing motorised narrowboats, known colloquially as 'longboats' on the Severn. The last cargo of chocolate 'crumb' was carried from Frampton to Bournville circa 1961.

Hardwicke — Map 32
Eating & Drinking
THE PILOT - Sellars Road. Tel: 01452 690807. Open daily from noon. Food served Mon-Thur 12-3pm and 5-10pm, throughout from noon Fri-Sun. GL2 4QD

Epney — Map 33
Eating & Drinking
THE ANCHOR - Epney. Tel: 01452 740433. Open lunchtimes and evenings (from 6pm) Mon-Thur and from 11.30am onwards Fri-Sun. GL2 7LN

Frampton-on-Severn — Map 33
Frampton reminds you of another village grouped haphazardly about an extensive green on another extremity of the inland waterways - Nun Monkton on the Yorkshire Ouse. Fair Rosamund - Henry II's mistress - is reputed to have been born here. Rosamund's Green incorporates a cricket pitch, a trio of duckponds, and an array of horse chestnuts overlooked by a heterogeneous collection of houses from the large to the small, from the merely heavenly to the inherently sublime. Peacocks call from the 18th century purlieus of Frampton Court and many of the trees on the green have circular seats mandatorily made for watching the world go by. An avenue of chestnuts known locally as 'The Narles' leads to the church of St Mary the Virgin. Frampton United play in the Gloucestershire County League and their badge reflects their watery location.

Eating & Drinking
THE BELL INN - The Green. Tel: 01452 740346. Bar and restaurant food and accommodation. GL2 7EP

LEY BISTRO - The Green. Tel: 01452 740077. Cafe open daily for breakfasts, lunches and teas. GL2 7DY
THREE HORSESHOES - The Green. Tel: 01452 742100. Convivial *Good Beer Guide* listed local famous for its 3-Shu pie and boule pitch to the rear. Home made food, Uley bitter brewed nearby. GL2 7DY

Shopping
Excellent new-build timber shop called, appropriately enough 'The Green Shop' offering a range of provisions plus hot snacks for hungry walkers; PO counter too. Open daily 8am-6pm (4pm Sun).

Connections
BUSES - minimalist weekday Stagecoach commuter service 60F to/from Gloucester. Tel: 0871 200 2233.
TAXIS - Saul Taxis. Tel: 01453 826763

Framilode — Map 33
A 'blowy, Severn-tided place' in the words of Ivor Gurney who kept his sailing boat *Dorothy* here. His poem *The Lock Keeper* concerns the lifestyle of the contemporary incumbent, James Harris. A good location to see the Severn Bore: www.severn-bore.co.uk

Eating & Drinking
THE SHIP INN - Tel: 01452 764050. Charming pub beside a reedy length of the former Stroudwater Canal. Good food, local ales and accommodation. Closed Mondays. Food served 12-2.30pm and 5.30-9pm weekdays and from noon throughout at weekends. Bath Ales and St Austell. GL2 7LH

Saul — Map 33
Shopless, publess, but far from devoid of interest, particularly in that a number of its houses feature unusual friezes above their front doors. The name isn't biblical, but derived, rather, from the French for willow - *saule*. The Cotswold Canals Trust have one of their admirable visitor centres alongside CRT's services block at Saul Junction - Tel: 0785 402 6504. Also, nice little cafe called The Stables (Tel: 01452 741965 - GL2 7LA) by Sandfield Swing Bridge.

Slimbridge — Map 34
The village straggles down from the A38 past Slimbridge's high spired church to Shepherd's Patch, beyond which the road crosses the canal swing-bridge and makes a bee-line for the Wetlands Trust.

Eating & Drinking
BLACK SHED - Shepherd's Patch. Tel: 01453 890609. Canalside cafe-bar open daily from 9am. Closes 6pm Sun-Tue and 11pm Wed-Sat. GL2 7BP
TUDOR ARMS - adjacent Patch Bridge. Tel: 01453 890306. Family owned country inn with a good choice of bar and restaurant meals. Breakfast served from 7.30am (8am weekends) until 11am. Main menu thereafter from noon. Beers from Uleys, Wadworth and Wye Valley. Accommodation. GL2 7BP

Things to Do
ADVENTURE BIKE HIRE - from the Black Shed. Tel: 0737 832 1048. GL2 7BP
SLIMBRIDGE WETLAND CENTRE - Bowditch (half a mile north-west of Patch Bridge). Tel: 01453 891900. Open daily from 9.30am to 5pm all year round. Brilliant views across the Severn from its observation tower. Guided tours around its founder, Sir Peter Scott's, house/museum. Special Severn Bore linked events. Cafe and shop. GL2 7BT

JOINED by the 'Severn Way', the canal continues its delightfully bucolic progress, making its way past willow-fringed dykes draining fields extending down to the flood bank of the Severn; a seething, boiling mass of cafeteria tea-coloured water at high tide. Frampton's isolated parish church overlooks Splatt Bridge, one of several still hand operated by their keepers, as illustrated overleaf. Interestingly, the swing bridges were originally constructed with two leaves, it being the keeper's responsibility to work one side, and a 'passman' who'd cycle along the towpath, accompanying vessels as required. A mineral railway once ran from a quay by Splatt Bridge to extensive gravel pits east of the canal.

The River Cam feeds the canal just above Cambridge Arms Bridge. At one time there was a lock at the entrance to the river, facilitating the passage of boats upstream to a wharf at the village of Cambridge a mile to the south-east. The house overlooking the feeder has been extensively rebuilt, but it was originally a shanty, once a common feature along the Gloucester & Sharpness from the 1930s onwards.

Built initially as holiday homes, many were gradually upgraded for domestic use throughout the year. Often self-built by their owners on land owned by the Sharpness Dock Company, some were actually constructed from materials brought along the canal by barge. Once there were almost a hundred of them, now less than half a dozen remain inhabited; we can't be without our 'mod cons' now.

A curious corrugated iron building, aptly named the 'black shed', stands alongside Patch Bridge. It dates from 1910, being used to store incoming grain prior to transport to a mill in the neighbouring town of Cam. It was requisitioned by the war department during the First World War. Now it houses a cafe and boat and bicycle hire facilities.

So prostrate is the landscape, that the eye is drawn to far horizons. Eastwards stands the Cotswold Edge, a lengthy escarpment punctuated by individual summits such as Stinchcombe Hill above Dursley, Cam Long Down, and Uley Long Barrow, known locally as Hetty Pegler's Tump after Hester, wife of a 17th century landowner called Henry Pegler. To the north-west, far beyond the Severn, lies the much cherished Gloucestershire landmark of May Hill (971ft), topped by a prominent clump of pine trees, planted to commemorate Victoria's Golden Jubilee.

continued overleaf:

Map labels

by-road to Cambridge & A38

feeder

The Marshes

Hetty Pegler's Tump

Cambridge Arms Bridge 6

by-road to Slimbridge & A38

41

Cam Long Down

Shepherd's Patch

Tudor Arms

Ryall's Farm

mp 11/5

May Hill

5 Patch Bridge

mp 12/4

Church End

41

P

mp 10/6

7 Splatt Bridge

Severn Way

Awre Church

New Grounds

River Severn

Slimbridge Wetland Centre

M

The Warth

Severn Way

Stinchcombe Hill

NORTH

1: Gloucester Narrowboats

mp 13/3

33

35

Saul Junction

continued from page 107:

May Day is traditionally welcomed in on its summit by Morris dancers; Edward Thomas is said to have written his poem *Words* on it: 'Let me sometimes dance with you, or climb or stand perhaps in ecstasy'; and the composer Gerald Finzi's ashes were scattered on its summit in 1973 - some seventeen years after his untimely demise at the age of 55.

Slimbridge is derived from 'slyme bridge', a reference to the once marshy nature of the surrounding landscape. The New Grounds are exactly that, land reclaimed from the river's tidal grasp during the 16th and 17th centuries. They provide rich pastures for cattle and once featured a number of decoys for the catching of duck. Nowadays, of course, it is with the preservation of duck and wildfowl that the area is concerned, since Peter Scott's establishment here of the Slimbridge Wildfowl and Wetland Trust in 1946. Son of the ill fated Antarctic explorer, Sir Peter Scott was the original Vice-President of the Inland Waterways Association, a close friend of Robert Aickman and one time husband of the novelist and early IWA secretary Elizabeth Jane Howard. In the early days of the Wildfowl Trust Peter Scott brought a converted narrowboat called *Beatrice* to Shepherd's Patch to provide accommodation for visiting ornithologists.

Splatt Bridge

Purton Upper

ONE senses, even without glancing at the map, that the Gloucester & Sharpness Canal's dreamlike progress across the Vale of Berkeley is drawing to a close. Yet, like all enjoyable dreams, you're anxious to cling on to it for as long as possible.

Though the eye is naturally drawn to the Severn's mesmerisingly wide expanse, it's worth looking momentarily in the opposite direction where a plantation masks the existence of an old duck decoy pool, a system of trapping wildfowl for the larder employing hooped nets, tapering edges and keepers dogs. At the beginning of January 1908 the keeper caught two hundred wild duck in one day. Salmon fishing with lave nets was another local activity. Purton folk were, reputedly, of above average girth. Diminishing stocks and stricter controls have brought lave netting to an end on this side of the Severn, though it can still be witnessed at Portskewett on the Monmouthshire bank of the estuary.

Presently the canal curves past a treatment plant which extracts water on behalf of the population of Bristol - lucky Bristolians! A pair of swing bridges (operated by a single keeper at the lower bridge who uses CCTV) span the waterway as it winds around to the very edge of the Severn with the seemingly close yet tantalisingly inaccessible hills of Dean forming the horizon.

'Friends of Purton' are a group devoted to the preservation and interpretation of upwards of eighty abandoned vessels - trows, schooners, barges, lighters - beached on Purton's shoreline to combat erosion. Painstakingly, each historic vessel has been identified and had its key dates itemised, the result being an open air 'museum' of no little poignancy and resonance. The canal widens at the site of former timber ponds.

Savouring panoramic views of the Severn estuary, you reach the remains of a swing bridge, which once carried a railway; not only over the canal, but over to the far side of the Severn as well! Opened in 1879, primarily to carry Forest of Dean coal across to Sharpness Docks, it consisted of twenty-one fixed arches spanning the estuary and a moveable arch, propelled by steam, over the canal. The cylindrical base of the moveable arch, together with a couple of masonry

continued overleaf:

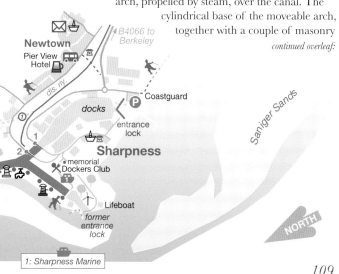

arches on the opposite bank, are this astonishing structure's sole remnants, though an interpretive panel and adjacent model help to envisage how impressive it must have looked. During the Second World War practising RAF pilots were in the dare-devil habit of flying *beneath* the bridge.

On a fog-bound October evening in 1960, *Arkendale* and *Wastdale*, two Harker petrol barges heading for Gloucester, missed the entrance to Sharpness Docks and collided with the bridge, demolishing one of the piers and bringing two of its girder spans down on themselves. Their unstable cargoes ingnited, and the blaze was worsened by the severing of a gas main on the bridge itself. Eyewitnesses described how the whole river was set alight. There were five fatalities from the barges, but things could have been worse, a group of contractors working on the bridge had clocked off early to listen to a Henry Cooper boxing bout on the radio. The remains of the two barges still lie off Purton. As for the railway, tragically it never re-opened, though Sharpness retained a shuttle service to the main Bristol-Birmingham line at Berkeley Road until 1964. A group calling themselves the Vale of Berkeley Railway, are attempting to preserve what's left.

So it would have been nice to know Sharpness when Tom and Angela Rolt moored *Cressy* here for 'a memorable month of summer' in 1948, and to have shared with them their train rides over the bridge to Lydney and the Forest of Dean. At that time there was considerable petroleum tanker barge traffic between Avonmouth and Worcester and Stourport, together with the occasional passage of a coastal vessel bound for Gloucester. Over the intervening half century cargoes ebbed and flowed almost as furiously as the Severn itself, but the last regular through traffic was in the shape of Healing's barges which plied between Avonmouth and Tewkesbury until 1998. Lock-wheeler fondly remembers journeying up the estuary from Avonmouth aboard *Chaceley* with 250 tonnes of Canadian wheat in his salad days as a cub reporter with *Waterways World*. Fondly, that is, in retrospect, for in rereading his article forty years later he is reminded that the sea-lock at Avonmouth opened to reveal 'a maelstrom of foaming waters, surging and seething out across the wind-whipped estuary', and that he and the crew 'huddled in the wheelhouse, as wave succeeded wave: over the bows, over the gunnel, and in through the wheelhouse window'; boy that boy could overwrite!

Yet the docks live on, operated now by the Victoria Group, whose portfolio also includes Boston (Lincs), Bromborough (Wirral), Plymouth, and Seaham (Co. Durham). Annual tonnage is in the region of a healthy half a million - fertilizer from France, Germany and North Africa; cement from northern Spain; timber, paper, coal, wheat and grain - though perhaps it neatly illustrates shortcomings in our balance of trade and manufacturing prowess that exports are restricted to scrap metal. Ships of up to 6000 tonnes are able to pass through the entrance lock - which has dimensions of 320 feet long by 57 feet wide - and if you want to see them you should position yourself at the picnic site on the south side of the jetty about half an hour before high water. Gloucester Harbour Trustees list comings and goings on their website: *www.gloucesterharbourtrustees.org.uk*

The original course of the canal veers to the right, making its approach to the former entrance lock along an arm now used for moorings. Here, lay berthed the mercantile training ship *Vindicatrix*, celebrated by a memorial near the Dockers Club. *Vindicatrix* had a fascinating history. She was launched on the Clyde in 1893 bearing the name *Arranmore*. In 1910 she came under German ownership, becoming a U-Boat crew's rest ship in Heligoland. At the end of the First World War she was repatriated, renamed and berthed in Gravesend as part of a sea training school, subsequently evacuated to Sharpness at the onset of the Second World War. The school went back to Gravesend in 1966 and *Vindicatrix*, in a scene which must have been reminiscent of Turner's *Fighting Temeraire*, was towed across the Severn estuary to Newport for breaking up.

The original lock - overlooked by the Harbour Master's classically styled house - is abandoned, but it enjoyed a brief new lease of life during the Second World War as an alternative point of entry in case of bomb damage. The lock apparatus from this period remains in place, the work of Cowans Sheldon, the Carlisle engineering firm perhaps better known for their railway cranes and turntables. A small detail, for sure, but emblematic of this resilient little port's intrinsic and abiding appeal.

Purton
Map 35

There was a flour mill here once, and on Derby Day they used to run their own horse race along the foreshore known as the Royal Drift. Now the chief attraction lies in the ships' graveyard. The village lies in the territory of the Berkeley Hunt, notable in that the Master and his staff wear yellow coats with green collars as opposed to the traditional hunting pink. Teas are served in the tiny church of St John the Evangelist on Sunday afternoons.

Eating & Drinking

BERKELEY ARMS - Tel: 01453 811262. Timeless throwback deservedly listed on CAMRA'S National Inventory of Historic Pub Interiors. Open weekend lunchtimes and evenings daily from 7pm. There aren't many pubs left like this now, so make a pilgrimage while you can. Wickwar Bob on tap. Panoramic views across the Severn from the garden. GL13 9HU

Sharpness
Map 35

A humbler counterpart to Goole on the Yorkshire Ouse, where life revolves around the enduring relationship between tides and docks. Scintillating views down the estuary to the Severn bridges and nuclear power plants. You are reminded of the centre forward's prerequisite: Sharpness in front of Goole.

Eating & Drinking

SHARPNESS DOCKERS CLUB - The Docks. Tel: 01453 811477. You don't have to be a docker (let alone a member) to enjoy the considerable hospitality of this social club housed in what was once the Sharpness Hotel; one of three in the village. Archive scenes of the docks and railways adorn the walls, the food is tasty and filling, and the beer comes from Wickwar just down the road. Oh yes, and skittles too. Perfect! Open Mon-Thur 7-11pm and Fri-Sat lunchtimes and evenings from 7pm. GL13 9UN

PIER VIEW HOTEL - Oldminster Road. Tel: 01453 811255. Open lunchtimes and evenings (from 7pm) daily. GL13 9NA

Shopping

Dock Shop (open mornings from 6am (ex Sun) until lunchtime) in dock precincts. Mace convenience store and PO in Newtown.

Connections

BUSES - Stagecoach service 62 links Sharpness with Dursley (where 60 connects with Gloucester) and Bristol (via Berkeley) approximately bi-hourly Mon-Sat. Tel: 0871 200 2233. TAXIS - A2B Dursley. Tel: 01453 548483.

Sharpness

EMBOLDENED by the award of £4 million from Highways England, to cover the cost of reinstating the canal at the A38/A419 interchange, and optimistic of Heritage Fund finance from the National Lottery, the Cotswold Canals Trust can forsee a time, in the not too distant future, when Stroud is once again linked to the navigable inland waterways system. Canal restorers have learned the art of patience the hard way. In good faith, the 5th edition of this guide book, published in 2003, predicted that the former Stroudwater and Thames & Severn canals - branded collectively nowadays as the Cotswold Canals - would be fully restored by 2010. If ambition and finance were in equal supply this might well have been achieved. But civil engineering projects are prone to 'optimism bias' - all the more so where inland waterways are involved - whilst public purse-string holders are genetically myopic to the all round benefits of working waterways, wilfully ignoring the wider benefits which accrue.

Opened in 1779, and measuring eight miles in length with thirteen widebeam locks, the Stroud-

water Navigation enjoyed considerable prosperity before the Railway Age. And even thereafter, up until the Second World War, a moderate amount of local trade, predominantly in the guise of Forest of Dean mined coal, continued to use the route. As we have seen, navigable status was abandoned in 1954, though remarkably the company still exists.

Don't start off too quickly walking eastwards: contemplate the Severn; gaze across its broad expanse to the hilly outline of the Forest of Dean; pay a visit perhaps to St Peter's Romanesque little church; then set your face towards the Cotswold escarpment - Sapperton Tunnel is almost twenty miles away and three hundred and sixty feet higher. Framilode Lock was tidal and was well known to the poet and composer Ivor Gurney (see Map 30) who kept his sailing boat *Dorothy* with the keeper. The lock lies buried in a private garden now. A reedy length of canal, more or less 'in water', runs past the Ship Inn, is culverted beneath the by-road to Saul, then promptly peters out as the path to Saul Junction follows

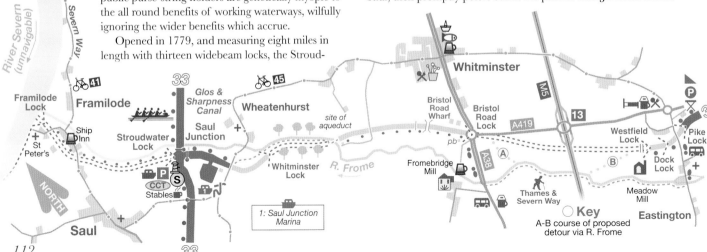

Framilode

Fromebridge Mill has been converted into a popular pub and restaurant. Walking beside the Frome would be an idyllic exercise but for the racket emanating from the M5, an immense and unceasing barrier of noise of El Alamein artillery barrage intensity. At least, in passing through the dark confines of the tunnel beneath the motorway - as boats will eventually do - you can pretend to be a rock star emerging from your dressing room to a stadium filled with delirious fans.

Passing Meadow Mill you reach the northern outskirts of the village of Eastington and rediscover the original course of the navigation at Pike Bridge, rebuilt to navigational height in 2005. Dock Lock derived its utilitarian name from the presence of the Stroudwater company's boatyard and maintenance depot at this point. There was once a cider house on site. Pike Lock is overlooked by a cottage which latterly provided accommodation for a lock-keeper, but which originally - and hence its name - was a toll house on the local turnpike road.

the southern bank of the River Frome, channelled beside pollarded willows, to reach the Gloucester & Sharpness Canal at Saul Junction.

The first few hundred yards of the Stroudwater east of Saul have remained in use as linear moorings after the navigation was officially abandoned. These end abruptly at the site of a swing-bridge by which means the Frampton to Whitminster by-road (NCR 45) crossed the canal. In order to re-open the canal to boats, it will need to be reinstated.

East of here sections of the canal have been obliterated, not least an aqueduct over the River Frome. Where the substantial obstacle of the M5 motorway is concerned, the strategy is to detour into the River Frome. Oddly, this has historic precedence, for in the mid 18th century, a certain Mr Kemmett adapted the river to carry coal to the cloth mills of the Stroud Valley. Clearly a man ahead of his time, he didn't use locks (which would have interfered with the flow of water to mills) but a sequence of lifting points, where containers of coal would be transferred by double-jibbed cranes from vessels on the lower level to counterparts on the upper.

Whitminster

37 STROUDWATER NAVIGATION Stonehouse 4mls/6lks

BLUNDER Lock gained its pejorative name from a miscalculation of water levels when the canal was being built. The mistake may have been deliberate on the part of an engineer who'd been given notice to quit; revenge being, as they say, a dish best served cold. Newtown Lock commemorates David Boakes, an early stalwart of restoration. It was re-opened (in heavy rain) by the Prince of Wales in 1992. The towpath changes sides at Roving Bridge and proceeds to Bond's Mill Bridge, the world's first plastic lift bridge - sturdier than it sounds. The circular gatehouse alongside the lift bridge was originally built as a pill box with a machine gun emplacement on its roof. Bond's Mill can trace its history back to early in the 18th century, but during the Second World War it was used as a 'shadow factory' by the Sperry Gyroscope Company of Brentford. Queen Mary visited the works to boost morale in 1941. After the war, aerial photographs of the site were unearthed at the Luftwaffe headquarters in Lubeck, revealing that an attack was planned in 1943, though fortunately it never took place. On summer Sunday afternoons the gatehouse is open as a visitor centre for the Cotswold Canals Trust. As the canal proceeds eastwards, panoramic hill views are revealed to the south-east, down as far as Hetty Pegler's Tump - see Map 34.

On its high embankment, the main line railway between Birmingham and Bristol presents an expensive challenge to the restorationists, though Network Rail are said to be sympathetically predisposed. A culvert of navigable dimensions will have to be inserted. The Gloucester-based transport artist, Rob Rowland, has painted a pretty scene of a horse-drawn boat passing beneath the bridge as a steam train, hauled by one of the GWR's original County class 4-4-0s, puffs elegantly by overhead.

Beyond the railway the canal broadens into a wide lily-filled pool known as 'The Ocean'. In all likelihood it predated construction of the canal, and may once have been a fishpond for Stonehouse Court, an extensive Elizabethan building renovated by Lutyens and now an hotel. Ocean swing-bridge was reinstalled in 2012. Nearby stands the charming church of St Cyr's which apparently relinquished part of its churchyard to the canal builders. Two attractive houses abut Nutshell Bridge and are curiously linked by a passage beneath it. The route of the old Midland Railway line to Nailsworth (adopted as a cycle path) crosses the canal on a cast iron bridge and there was once a transhipment wharf here. A private swing-bridge spans the canal at Ryeford as

'Passengers No More'
1: Stonehouse Bristol Road - csd 1965
2: Ryeford - csd 1949
3: Ebley Crossing Halt - csd 1964
4: Cashes Green Halt - csd 1964
5: Downfield Crossing Halt - csd 1964

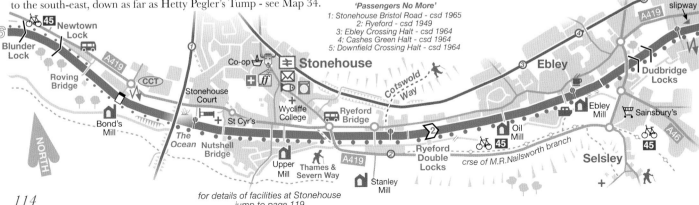

for details of facilities at Stonehouse jump to page 119

Stonehouse

the Cotswold Way swoops briefly down to join the canal on its hundred mile way from Chipping Campden to Bath.

Ryeford Locks are one of only two staircase pairs on the Cotswold Canals, the other, as yet unrestored, is at Dudgrove (Map 44) on the Thames & Severn Canal near Inglesham. To the rear of the isolated lock cottage you can see the unusual French Gothic church tower of G. F. Bodley's hillside church at Selsley. Bodley was fortuitously in the employ of Samuel Stephens Marling, the owner of Ebley Mill, when much of its fabric was destroyed by fire in 1859. "Run me off a fulling mill, when you've got a moment, would you, Bodley?" must have been Marling's approach, and the result is a handsome mid-Victorian factory that would put many a French chateau to shame. Available locally, Ian Mackintosh's book *Cathedral of Cloth* paints a vivid picture of the mill's history. Textile production ceased in 1981, but, appropriately enough, it is now the headquarters of Stroud District Council, enthusiastic proponents of the canal's rebirth. *Perseverance*, the Cotswold Canals Trust's trip-boat, plies this length of the canal on Saturday afternoons and Bank Holiday Mondays from April to September, as pictured on page 81. Keep your eyes peeled for the workboats *Warp* and *Weft* as well, their names inspired by the weaving process. The restoration of Dudbridge Locks have resulted in an ingenious hydro-electric scheme which employs excess water going down the by-washes to generate green electricity.

HOW invigorating it must feel to live alongside this Lazarus-like canal, and how satisfying to be involved in its resurrection. The Stroudwater and Thames & Severn canals met historically at Wallbridge Basin on the western outskirts of Stroud (one 'l' on the mileposts!). A contemporary letter, dated 20th November 1789, records the 'marriage' of Father Thames and Madam Sabrina, or, in other words, the opening of the canal throughout. Within a month Staffordshire coal was being delivered to Lechlade, and 'plenty of punch, wine and other liquors' were being provided in celebration at the New Inn at the expense of the wharfinger Mr Wells. One can only hope to witness similar largesse when the Cotswold Canals re-open in their entirety, at some hopefully not too distant point in the future.

To all intents and purposes, the canal appears fully restored as far as Hope Mill Lock, though a certain amount of residual dredging was still being undertaken on the occasion of our most recent research. The old transhipment port of Brimscombe is the target for Phase 1a of the restoration scheme. Redeveloped as an industrial estate, the wheel will turn full circle when it becomes a 'port' once more. Significant challenges remain to the east where the course of the canal has been built upon, but momentum is clearly with the scheme, and there is no reason to suppose Brimscombe won't be reached ere long.

Meanwhile, we may still relish the Thames & Severn Canal's lovely journey up the Golden Valley on foot. Wherever your gaze falls, there are contrasting images

'Passengers No More'
1: Stroud Cheapside - csd 1949
2: Bowbridge Crossing Halt - csd 1964
3: Ham Mill Halt - csd 1964
4: Brimscombe Bridge Halt - csd 1964
5: Brimscombe - csd 1964
6 - St Mary's Crossing Halt - csd 1964
7 - Chalford - csd 1964

= mills

for details of facilities at Stroud, Brimscombe and Chalford jump to page 119

Fully restored, Bowbridge Lock

of the lawnmower in 1830. Present day boaters appear to have inherited the prodigious thirst of their bargee forebears and should revel in this local brew when navigation returns. Hope Mill was also the site of Abdela & Mitchell's (formerly Edwin Clarke's) boatyard, builders of river boats and pleasure steamers which saw service in some amazingly far-flung corners of the world. On the approach to Brimscombe the canal rubs shoulders with the neat little ground where Brimscombe & Thrupp FC play their home games in the Hellenic League.

No avid canal enthusiast would have been immune to the fascination of Brimscombe in its heyday. The need for an inland port was brought about by the necessity of transferring goods between vessels of a different gauge: Severn 'trows' and Thames barges of the 'western' kind as well as a requirement to store items pending final delivery or further transport. Locks on the Stroudwater and Thames & Severn, though widebeam, were of differing dimensions. To save water, the Thames & Severn locks were reduced in length around 1841 and in the final years of trade

to enjoy, as the valley's industrial floor plays off against its rural horizons. Comparisons with the Rochdale and Huddersfield Narrow canals' Trans-Pennine routes are easily evoked, though here in Gloucestershire the theme takes on a mellower appearance.

Replica milestones measure the miles, and indeed half miles too. Most of the over-bridges are traditionally hump-backed, but Jubilee Bridge is an attractive structure of cast iron latticework, built to enable workers to reach the mills from their houses up on the hillside beyond the railway. So dense was industry in this constricted valley that the Great Western Railway opened a necklace of wayside halts served by push & pull trains.

Whilst the original Stroud Brewery (having been acquired by Whitbread) was closed in 1967, a micro-brewery bearing the same name was established in 2006. New premises in the vicinity of Hope Mill Lock were erected in 2019, together with a canalside 'tap'. One of their avowedly organic beers is known as Budding in homage to Edward Beard Budding, local inventor

Paddington-bound at Ham Mill Lock

carriers found the ubiquitous narrowboat a more suitable craft for working on the Thames & Severn than the wide-beam barges of old.

Brimscombe basin offered a hundred and seventy five thousand square feet of capacity and was said to have been able to accommodate up to a hundred vessels simultaneously. Notable features included the company's head offices, a transit shed, warehousing and a boat weighing machine used for establishing tolls. A central island was incorporated for the secure storage of goods which might, unprotected, have caught the attention of the thieving classes. The main warehouse found unusual use as a school following the demise of the canal and was unfortunately demolished in 1964. Port Mill, an attractive survivor, is home to Renewables First, a hydro and wind power company, whilst neighbouring Bourne Mill is home to Ark Cycles. It's heartening to see these old mills finding new sustainable uses.

Walkers face brief detours at both Brimscombe and Chalford, though nothing too machiavellian. Brimscombe railway station boasted a small

Chalford Roundhouse

Clayfield Mill

engine shed for stabling bankers for the climb to Sapperton summit. On to St Mary's Lock, canal and railway - accompanied by the Frome chuckling transparently over it's clear gravel bed - create a mutually exclusive environment away from the traffic on the A419. An access lane to St Mary's Mill swoops down to cross the railway by way of a traditionally-gated level crossing guarded by a tiny signal box. Piped beneath the railway, the canal briefly loses confidence before reappearing at Ile's Mill Lock overlooked by a mellow and now domesticised Clayfield Mill.

It grows increasingly difficult not to be overawed by the beauty of the canal's surroundings, as indeed was Temple Thurston on his famous voyage along the canal with the *Flower of Gloster* in 1910. He likened the surrounding scenery to Switzerland, something hacks are over-inclined to do when faced with precipitously hilly districts of England. Nevertheless his heart was in the right place and you too will be entranced by these 'blue slate roofs' viewed against a 'golden distance'. At Chalford you come upon the first of the Thames & Severn's keynote roundhouses.

Stonehouse Map 37

Stonehouse will come into its own when boaters begin to use the Stroudwater Navigation once again. In the meantime, walkers will probably want to press on to Stroud where the facilities are closer to hand.

Eating & Drinking
STONEHOUSE COURT HOTEL - Bristol Road. Tel: 01453 794950. A nice place to stay while exploring the Cotswold Canals, or punctuate your walk with afternoon tea on the terrace. GL10 3RA

Shopping
Good range of shops on High Street less than 10 minutes walk north of the canal.

Connections
TRAINS - see Stroud.
BUSES - Stagecoach 61 runs hourly Mon-Sat to/from Dursley and Stroud offering useful pick up/set down points along the canal. Tel 0871 200 2233.

Stroud Map 38

A codicil to the Cotswolds, with a spirited tradition of independent outlook, the textile town of Stroud tumbles down the valley side with the profile of a dry ski slope. Gradients notwithstanding, Stroud is a likeable place to wander around, several fine buildings vying for attention, none finer than the splendidly classical Subscription Rooms of 1833. In its heyday as a wool town Stroud was famous for its military tunics, now those mills left in production - out of the hundred and fifty which once functioned in the Frome Valley - are renowned for the production of snooker table cloth and Wimbledon tennis ball felt.

Eating & Drinking
WOODRUFFS ORGANIC CAFE - High Street. Tel: 01453 759195. Exemplifies Stroud in both outlook and atmosphere; heavenly cakes. GL5 1AJ

Shopping
Stroud's precipitous High Street is refreshingly bereft of chain stores and congenially populated by individual retailers of more enterprising outlook. Stroud Bookshop is an increasingly rare example of an independently owned new bookdealer. Made in Stroud on Kendrick Street reflects the area's status as a haven for craftsmen and artists, and has links with the Farmers Market held every Saturday.

Things to Do
THE MUSEUM IN THE PARK - Stratford Park. Tel: 01453 763394. Local heritage. GL5 4AF

Connections
TRAINS - Great Western Railway services along the Golden Valley to/from Gloucester (via Stonehouse) hourly through trains to/from London Paddington via Swindon. Tel: 0345 700 0125.
BUSES - Stagecoach service 52 threads its way through the Golden Valley via Brimscombe and Chalford to Cirencester Mon-Sat and is consequently of good use to towpath walkers. Ditto Cotswold Green 54/A which calls also at Sapperton. Tel: 0871 200 2233.
TAXIS - Stroud Taxis. Tel: 01453 750211.

Brimscombe Map 38

Eating & Drinking
STROUD BREWERY BAR - London Road. Tel: 01453 887122. Canalside brewery tap open 11am-11pm daily (closes 5pm Sun & Mon) Wood-fired pizzas. GL5 2BY

Shopping
Useful facilities for passing walkers include a fish & chip shop, and post office stores.

Chalford Map 38

Cuddled in the lap of the Golden Valley, Chalford deserves to be savoured in its own right rather than just an adjunct to the canal. Indeed, there is something to be said for the walker detouring along the gorgeous by-road between Bell Lock and Golden Valley Lock to get a more intimate view of the higgledy-piggledy houses which define its character.

Eating & Drinking
LAVENDER BAKEHOUSE - London Road. Tel: 01453 889239. Splendid cafe serving breakfasts (from 9am) lunches and teas. Upstairs gallery. GL6 8NW

Connections
BUSES - Cotswold Green service 54/A runs Mon-Sat between Stroud and Cirencester calling also at Sapperton. Tel: 0871 200 2233.

Frampton Mansell Map 39

Eating & Drinking
CROWN INN - Tel: 01285 760601. Charming *Good Beer Guide* listed 17th century inn offering annex accommodation. GL6 8JG

Shopping
JOLLY NICE - Tel: 01285 760868. Farm Shop and cafe on A419. GL6 8HZ

Sapperton Map 39

Idyllic settlement perched above its famous tunnel offering easy access to view the western portal. Historic links with proponents of the Arts & Crafts movement.

Eating & Drinking
THE BELL - Tel: 01285 760298. Well-appointed country inn and restaurant. Lunches and dinners (from 6pm) Mon-Sat. Food served Sun 12-4.30pm. GL7 6LE
THE DANEWAY - Dane Lane. Tel: 01285 760297. 'Canalside' inn known as the Bricklayers Arms when the Thames & Severn was open. Food served from noon daily. Camping available. GL7 6AN

Connections
BUSES - Cotswold Green 54/A. Tel: 0871 200 2233.

TO descend from a train at Kemble (Map 40), walk across the top of Sapperton Tunnel, and continue down past the embowered lock chambers of the Golden Valley, is to experience one of the most compellingly enjoyable walks in England. Lock-wheeler is not unique in this opinion. Doyen canoeist, William Bliss, described camping close to Sapperton's western portal one honey-scented evening in his 1933 masterpiece *The Heart of England By Waterway*. Accompanied by the soundtrack of a nightingale's song, he explored the tunnel-mouth's environs and came to the inescapable conclusion that 'nowhere else in the world but on an English river or canal could such beauty of night and scent and sound have been mine'.

East of Chalford, one begins to feel the climb. The accompanying railway, engineered by the redoubtable Brunel, makes its parallel ascent upon a sequence of blue brick viaducts, originally of timber construction. Paddington-bound, the sleek green IETs go growling up the 1 in 60, but it would have been nice to hear the Brimscombe bankers of yore in cacophonous syncopation with the locomotive at the head of the train.

Beyond Valley Lock, civilisation is left largely astern, and woodland creates a very real sense of remoteness. In these very woods, Eynsham Harry prepared a mid-day meal of wild hops, whilst Temple Thurston counted seventeen varieties of wild flower. Footpaths splay off into the trees, agitating to be explored, and the Golden Valley lives up to the implications of its name as the canal shares its upward trajectory with the

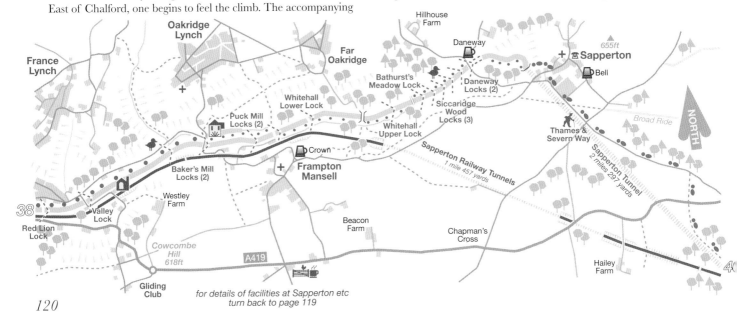

Oakridge Lynch
Hillhouse Farm
Daneway
655ft
France Lynch
Far Oakridge
Sapperton
Bell
Bathurst's Meadow Lock
Daneway Locks (2)
Whitehall Lower Lock
Puck Mill Locks (2)
Siccaridge Wood Locks (3)
Whitehall Upper Lock
Broad Ride
Crown
Thames & Severn Way
Baker's Mill Locks (2)
Frampton Mansell
Sapperton Railway Tunnels
1 mile 457 yards
Sapperton Tunnel
2 miles 297 yards
Westley Farm
38
Valley Lock
Beacon Farm
Red Lion Lock
Chapman's Cross
Cowcombe Hill 618ft
A419
Hailey Farm
Gliding Club

for details of facilities at Sapperton etc turn back to page 119

River Frome, bounding down its bed in the opposite direction. 'WD 1784' engraved on the arch of Whitehall Bridge refers to William Dennis, the mason responsible for this section of Josiah Clowes' canal.

Sacrilege in some circles, but ambivalent thoughts arise: these long abandoned lock chambers are like tumuli; should we really disturb them? Even in the canal's heyday, working up or down the final flight of seven locks to and from the summit at Daneway was often problematical given the paucity of water supply. Consumption was reduced by about 20% following shortening of the lock chambers. A series of side-ponds had already been added in 1823, but every drop of water continued to count. By 1893 matters had grown so bad that the canal east of Chalford was closed. It re-opened six years later, but was still wracked by water problems. Encountering just one other boat (captained by an elderly lady humming quietly to herself at the tiller) Temple Thurston remarked that in places they barely floated at all, much to the chagrin of Fanny the boat horse. A quarter of a century later the author Geoffrey Boumphrey and a companion were unable to progress this far even by canoe as described in his book *Down River*, an account of a tour on the Severn and the Thames and, where possible, the Cotswold Canals, published in 1936. In the event Boumphrey and his pal 'George' had to portage their canoes by car between Chalford and Cricklade.

The canal widened into a wharf and basin between the two Daneway locks, the upper of which is overlooked by an inn, once the Bricklayer's Arms now simply The Daneway. The higher lock has been infilled to provide the pub with a car park; future patrons of the beer garden will

Sapperton Tunnel (Daneway Portal)

have the ring-side view of an excavated lock chamber. The summit lies 362 feet above sea level, but it rapidly becomes apparent as you twist in an easterly, becoming south-easterly direction away from Daneway, that the canal can go no further save by subterranean methods. And indeed, within less than half a mile, the neighbouring ridge rears suddenly up in defiance and the western portal of Sapperton is revealed, battlemented as if it means business.

3,817 yards long (impressive enough, but roundly beaten by the Huddersfield Narrow Canal's Standedge tunnel which is 5,698 yards long) and up to 200 feet below the surface of the Cotswold landscape it burrows through, Sapperton Tunnel was five years in the making. George III came to inspect it on Saturday 19th July 1788 as an antidote to taking the waters in nearby Cheltenham. Contemporary accounts suggest that His Majesty expressed astonishment. So, more practically, did Temple Thurston, who lay on his back with Eynsham Harry for four damp and sepulchral hours to propel the *Flower of Gloster* through the tunnel. Curiously, he refers to a barge in a lock and the dazzling light of the setting sun when he emerges from the tunnel's eastern portal. Disorientation, or poetic licence? In its working days a four-hourly cycle of entry times was the order of the day. A realistic account of a boat being legged through the tunnel enlivens the opening pages of C. S. Forester's adventure *Hornblower and the Atropos*. Pending restoration, we have to walk across the top in the footsteps of the old boat horses and mules. For a heady moment one imagines that the dung on the road through Sapperton village is still steaming from those animals, until it becomes apparent that horse-riding is a popular activity amongst the rides of Oakley Wood.

SMALL BLUE butterflies flutter over the grassland between the A419 and the cool, dark interior of Hailey Woods, where your attention is drawn to fungi, and whether they are edible or not. Short of having a mycologist at hand, discretion is undoubtedly the best part of valour.

Walking over the top of Sapperton Tunnel gives you plenty of time to marvel at its existence ... and, indeed, yours as well. From time to time you catch sight of spoil heaps planted with beech trees which bring to mind all the activity of those human moles who dug the tunnel over two centuries ago. If you were enamoured of the Gothic portal at the western end of the canal tunnel, you will be surprised to discover, not a mirror image at the eastern end, but a design of quite different Classical style: a sort of double A-side in pop single terms. An interpretive panel explains how the tunnel was constructed, whilst noting that the last recorded passage of a boat bearing cargo was a vessel named *Gem* on 11th May 1911. Humphrey Household, in his seminal history of the canal published by David & Charles in 1969, records that it was carrying 20 tons of stone. Above, and to the left of the portal, stands the Tunnel House Inn, erected during construction of the canal to provide accommodation

and refreshment. It still fulfils the latter purpose admirably, though the original third storey was destroyed by fire in 1952. The inn was once visited by John Betjeman and his father: shame he wasn't moved to write a poem about it.

Coates Roundhouse differs from Chalford in that its conical roof is inverted as a means of gathering water for domestic use. Originally the ground floor would have been used as stabling. Forcibly closed on health grounds in the 1950s, it now resembles an abandoned lighthouse. A competent historic transport artist should be encouraged to capture it on canvas in juxtaposition with a train crossing the canal on the neighbouring skew bridge.

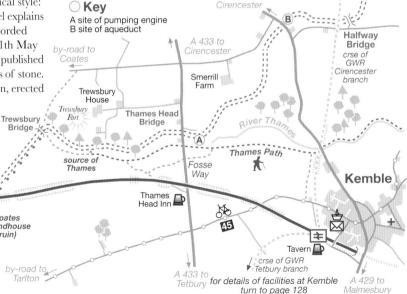

○ **Key**
A site of pumping engine
B site of aqueduct

The summit section of the Thames & Severn is 8 miles and 13 chains in length. Sadly the canal east of Sapperton is not so well-defined as in the Golden Valley, and at Trewsbury Bridge it ceases to be a right of way. Long distance walkers are not, however, abandoned entirely to their own devices for the Thames & Severn Way merges, a couple of fields away, with the Thames Path, at the beginning of its trek to London, a mere 184 miles away.

Dense tree growth masks the line of the canal, hiding Trewsbury House, a substantial Victorian mansion, together with its neighbouring ancient hillfort, from view. A stone marks the source of the River Thames, an iconic little piece of English soil. At one time a reclining sculpture of Old Father Thames stood at the site, but it was prone to vandalism and moved to the safer environment of St John's Lock near Lechlade (Map 44).

The course of the canal encounters an even older transport link, the Roman's Fosse Way, and comes upon the site of a pumping house which supplied three million gallons of much-needed water a day to the summit from a well sunk 64 feet below the surface. The first edition of Humphrey Household's aforementioned history of the canal featured an engaging coloured plate of this significant structure, with a sail-powered barge passing. The pump fell out of use in 1912 after navigation was abandoned across the summit, and subsequently became a victim of the drive for scrap metal during the Second World War. A private dwelling now occupies the site.

Smerrill Aqueduct carried the canal across the road between Cirencester and Kemble. Its stone arch was removed soon after navigation ceased. There is a photograph of it in Household's book. Prone - as was much of the canal - to leakage, stop-gates were installed either side. A small

Sapperton Tunnel (Coates Portal)

Coates Roundhouse

red sandstone viaduct remains intact carrying the trackbed of the Kemble to Cirencester branch line across both a by-road and the course of the canal. Strange how moving such remnants can be, even when disfigured by modern height limit road signage. The railway was opened in 1841 to Brunel's broad gauge. It closed in 1964, though part of the terminus remains extant at Cirencester, forlornly overlooking a car park.

Halfway Bridge, ruinous, yet intact, reflects the fact that the canal at this point is approximately halfway on its twenty-eight and three-quarters of a mile journey between Wallbridge (Map 38) and Inglesham (Map 44).

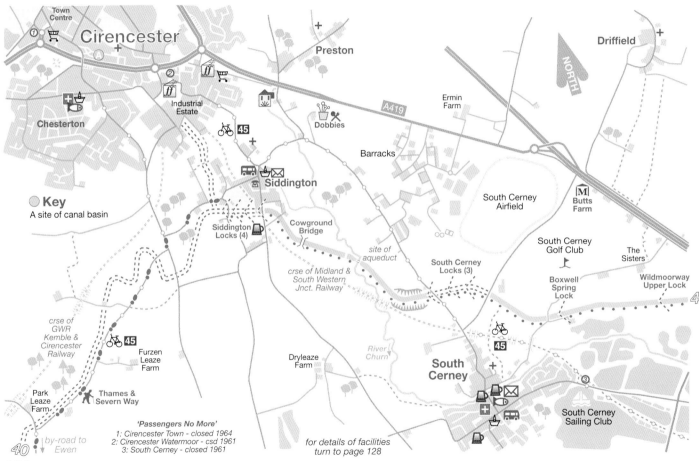

Town Centre

Cirencester

Chesterton

Industrial Estate

45

Preston

Driffield

NORTH

A419

Ermin Farm

Dobbies

Barracks

Siddington

Key

A site of canal basin

Siddington Locks (4)

Cowground Bridge

site of aqueduct

crse of Midland & South Western Jnct. Railway

South Cerney Airfield

Butts Farm

South Cerney Golf Club

The Sisters

South Cerney Locks (3)

Boxwell Spring Lock

Wildmoorway Upper Lock

42

crse of GWR Kemble & Cirencester Railway

Furzen Leaze Farm

Dryleaze Farm

River Churn

45

South Cerney

Park Leaze Farm

Thames & Severn Way

South Cerney Sailing Club

'Passengers No More'
1: Cirencester Town - closed 1964
2: Cirencester Watermoor - csd 1961
3: South Cerney - closed 1961

by-road to Ewen

40

for details of facilities turn to page 128

WITH a detour via the village of Ewen, the Thames & Severn Way proceeds along fairly quiet by-roads, shadowing the course of the canal as closely as is feasible to Siddington. Cirencester has expanded considerably in recent years, gobbling up the course of the arm which once led to a terminal wharf on Querns Road off Sheep Street near the centre of town. Scant evidence that it ever existed remains to be found, more's the pity, and the wharf house itself was demolished in 1975, at a time when authorities cared even less about such things than they seem to do now. 'Another Whitchurch, another Leek', as we pithily put it in an earlier edition.

At Siddington, a quartet of locks commenced the canal's descent eastwards to the Thames at Inglesham. Their combined fall totalled 39 feet, and the substantial remains of the central pair are easily explored. Frustratingly, a house has been erected upon the site of the bottom chamber, something of a challenge to the restorationists; though not insurmountable, given a hefty wrecking-ball. Between the third and fourth locks, another transport casualty of what passes for progress - and far less likely to ever be revived - was the Midland & South Western Junction Railway. It was one of those obscure yet delightful cross country lines, of no apparent use to anyone apart from railway enthusiasts. Linking Cheltenham with Southampton, it did, however, flourish briefly, as a means for northerners, bent on emigrating to the Antipodes, to reach their port of embarkation.

South of Siddington the towpath is well-defined. Traditionally hump-backed in appearance, Cowground Bridge has been restored recently, and presents an encouraging sight. The same cannot be said, though, of the following swing-bridge, which has suffered the indignity of having a fairly ramshackle farm track laid across it. Ditto the Churn Aqueduct, replaced by a footbridge. The Churn rises up on the Cotswold plateau to the south of Cheltenham and has its confluence with the Thames at Cricklade. It was one of a 'baker's dozen' of tributaries lyrically described by the poet and topographer Brian Waters in his *Thirteen Rivers to the Thames* published by Dent in 1964. In it he noted that water-mills are as frequently encountered on the Thames and its tributaries as public houses along an English road,

a comparison which time has not dealt kindly with. There is still, for eyes attuned to such things, evidence of an irrigation system, which Waters drew his readers attention to, whereby the meadowlands beside the Churn were deliberately flooded in winter, in order to protect the grass from freezing, and also to allow rich nutrients in the river water to enhance the grazing properties of the meadows the following spring.

A bosky cutting leads to South Cerney Locks. The top chamber has been levelled as part of the much remodelled former wharf house's garden. Across the neighbouring by-road, all sense that there was ever a canal suddenly vanishes, though a right of way remains across the fields. On the adjoining hillside the control tower and hangars of RAF South Cerney draw the eye, though the site is now predominantly used as an army barracks. Paralleling the canal, the old railway has been upgraded as a footpath and cycleway (NCR 45).

The course of the canal regains its integrity where another by-road crosses it adjacent to South Cerney Golf Club's substantial club house. A worthwhile detour from the towpath just before Boxwell Spring Lock will take you to a multi-arched bridge over the old railway line. Steps lead down to the cycleway, and in doing so provide a fascinating view of the structure's segmented arches which find a curious counterpoint in the viaduct which carries the (not remotely connected) Great Western Railway over the canal on the eastern outskirts of Stroud (Map 38).

Bowxell Spring Lock is a mere 3ft 6ins deep. A plaque commemorates David Miles Marshall 1951-2012 'Musician, Thespian and Engineer' - an intriguing mix - whose 'rich baritone echoed from the depths of the chamber as he laid bricks: a visionary anticipating reopening of the canal'; amen to that.

South Cerney was the home, for a number of years, of the venerated canal historian, IWA founder, and David & Charles co-publisher, Charles Hadfield. No mere sentimentalist where canals were concerned, he doubted if future generations would find them quite so unequivocally fascinating, worrying that our legacy might be judged by what we had preserved as opposed to what we had created. Food for thought!

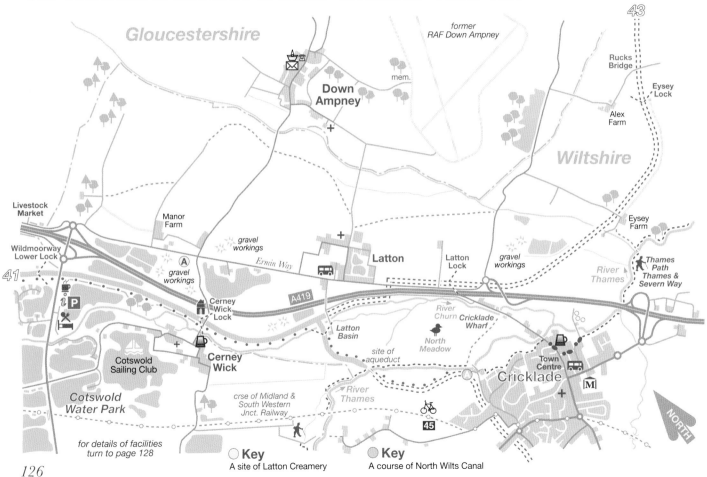

Gloucestershire

43

former RAF Down Ampney

Rucks Bridge

Eysey Lock

Down Ampney

mem.

Alex Farm

Wiltshire

Livestock Market

Manor Farm

Eysey Farm

gravel workings

Wildmoorway Lower Lock

Ermin Way

Latton

Latton Lock

gravel workings

River Thames

41

A

gravel workings

Thames Path Thames & Severn Way

A419

Cerney Wick Lock

Latton Basin

River Churn

Cricklade Wharf

Cotswold Sailing Club

Cerney Wick

site of aqueduct

North Meadow

Town Centre

Cricklade

M

Cotswold Water Park

crse of Midland & South Western Jnct. Railway

River Thames

45

NORTH

for details of facilities turn to page 128

126

○ **Key**
A site of Latton Creamery

● **Key**
A course of North Wilts Canal

Cerney Wick Lock & Roundhouse

NOTWITHSTANDING the hubbub emanating 'off stage' from the A419 - a road which, as originally designated, stretched from Hungerford on the Kennet & Avon Canal to Quedgeley on the Gloucester & Sharpness Canal - the canal's tree-lined progress is decidedly ethereal. The mileposts have been reinstated, enabling walkers to calculate their pace.

Below Wildmoorway Lower Lock, the canal skirts Cotswold Water Park, forty square miles featuring over a hundred and fifty lakes. One can't fail to be impressed by the way these former gravel workings have been transformed from eyesores into environmental success stories, but why on earth didn't they restore the canal as an integral part of the same project?

Cerney Wick Lock is overlooked by the third of the Thames & Severn Canal's five surviving roundhouses. This one is privately occupied. The lock chamber boasts top gates, but the road bridge spanning its tail has been lowered and the canal culverted beneath. Latton Basin marked the junction with the North Wilts Canal which linked the Thames & Severn

with the Wilts & Berks Canal at Swindon; one can only marvel at the routes lost to present day boaters by official neglect and indifference in the early years of the 20th century. Ironically, nowadays the North Wilts provides walkers with the best option for progress, because the Thames & Severn between Latton and Inglesham is for the most part infilled and no longer a right of way. A solid path follows the course of the North Wilts to the outskirts of Cricklade, where the Thames & Severn Way and Thames Path merge. The basin at Cricklade Wharf was infilled long ago, though the impressive wharf building remains intact. The canal lobby gained a minor victory in 1997 when the A419 was dual carriagewayed and provided with sufficient headroom for a canal fully restored to navigable standards. It awaits only the boats!

Kemble
Map 40

The best thing about Kemble is its Tudoresque railway station, formerly the junction for branches to Cirencester and Tetbury, short-sightedly truncated in the 1960s. Furthermore, as a railhead, Kemble forms an ideal jumping-off point for exploring the eastern end of Sapperton Tunnel and the source of the Thames.

Eating & Drinking
TAVERN INN - Station Road. Tel: 01285 770216. Cosy Arkells pub. Food and skittle alley. GL7 6AX
THAMES HEAD INN - Tetbury Road (A433). Tel: 01285 770259. Country pub with camping site. Food served from 11am (noon suns) throughout. GL7 6NZ
TUNNEL HOUSE INN - Tel: 01285 770702. Characterful pub adjacent eastern portal of Sapperton Tunnel open from 11am: food served lunch and evening (from 6pm) Mon-Sat and 12-4pm Sun. Beer choice includes Bristol Beer Factory, Ramsbury and Ulley, plus guests. GL7 6PW

Shopping
Small post office store.

Connections
TRAINS - hourly Great Western Railway service to/from Gloucester via Stroud and Paddington via Swindon. Tel: 0345 700 0125. *Nice cafe on station!*

Siddington
Map 41

Suburbanised outlier of Cirencester.

Eating & Drinking
THE GREYHOUND - Ashton Road. Tel: 01285 653573. Comfortable stone-flagged Wadworth pub adjacent course of the Thames & Severn Canal. Lunch daily and dinner Mon-Sat from 6pm. GL7 6HR

Shopping
Convenience store with post office.

Cirencester
Map 41

A fundamentally gorgeous town of Roman origin straddling the Fosse Way, Cirencester/Corinium was riven from the rail network by those chumps Beeching & Marples in 1964. A fully restored inland waterway on its doorstep would go someway to redressing the isolation thus incurred.

Eating & Drinking
JACKS - Black Jack Street. Tel: 01285 640888. Fabulous cafe & kitchen open from 9am (10am Sun). GL7 2AA

Shopping
Flourishing shopping centre for a well-heeled Cotswold hinterland. Waitrose supermarket.

Things to Do
CORINIUM MUSEUM - Park Street. Tel: 01285 655611. Devoted principally to Roman Cirencester (hence the name), but additional displays bring the area's history up to date. Open daily. GL7 2BX

Connections
BUSES - Stagecoach 51 runs hourly (bi-hourly Sun) via Cricklade to/from Swindon. Tel: 0871 200 2233.

South Cerney
Map 41

Eating & Drinking
GATEWAY CAFE - Spine Road. Tel: 01285 862627. Water Park/information centre cafe open 9am-5pm daily. Handy for morale-boosting coffee/cakes when walking the Thames & Severn towpath. GL7 5TL

Shopping
Co-op, post office and pharmacy.

Things to Do
COTSWOLD WATER PARK - 40 square miles of former gravel pits transformed into an outstanding leisure resource. Tel: 01285 868096. GL7 5TL

Connections
BUSES - Stagecoach 51 as Cirencester.

Down Ampney
Map 42

Ralph Vaughan Williams was born here in 1872 and is justifiably commemorated within the parish church of All Saints. Indeed he named his famous hymn tune *Come Down O Love Divine* after his birthplace. Another stained glass window recalls those who took part in Operation Market Garden in 1944, having flown from the nearby wartime airfield.

Shopping
Community shop with post office facility and cafe.

Cricklade
Map 42

Ancient Wiltshire town (can this really be in the same county as Salisbury!) dominated by the substantial 16th century tower of the parish church of St Sampson of Dol. High Street slopes agreeably down from the Jubilee Clock of 1897 to the Town Bridge spanning the infant Thames.

Eating & Drinking
RED LION - High Street. Tel: 01793 750776. *Good Beer Guide* listed pub offering useful accommodation if you're exploring the T&S/Thames Path. Home-brewed 'Hop & Kettle' ales. Food served Wed-Sat lunch and evenings from 6.30pm; Sundays 12-5pm. SN6 6DD *Plus other pubs, an Indian restaurant, and fast food outlets.*

Shopping
Tesco Express (with post office), pharmacy, two butchers and a bakery.

Things to Do
CRICKLADE MUSEUM - Calcutt Street. Tel: 0745 376 6744. Local history displays, including the fascinating story of Cricklade Pottery. Open Saturday mornings ex December and Wednesday afternoons April to September. SN6 6BD

Connections
BUSES - Stagecoach 51 as Cirencester.

43 THAMES & SEVERN CANAL Kempsford 4mls/0lks

SHYNESS overcomes the Thames & Severn between Cricklade and Inglesham, for, pending restoration, it is not feasible for members of the general public to pursue the line of the canal in a satisfactory, let alone enjoyable, manner. There are, nonetheless, one or two highlights the diligent explorer will find of interest. A public footpath affords access to the site of Marston Meysey Wharf, private property now, but retaining an overbridge and a roundhouse, the latter tastefully assimilated into a modern dwelling. Enjoy the view, by all means, but respect the owner's privacy, as with all such mementoes of the canal in its prime. Old maps illuminate the canal's eastward progress. We can recommend the National Library of Scotland's online archive. The next convincing proof that it existed hereabouts is Oatlands Bridge, a high and dry remnant in a field close to the road on the outskirts of Kempsford. According to Handford & Viner's indispensible Stroudwater and Thames & Severn Canals Towpath Guide of 1988, at least one of its bricks is embossed with the name of the Stonehouse Brick & Tile Co.,

evidence, surely, of materials being conveyed along the line of the canal by boat, if not for construction, then at least for maintenance in later years. A clue to the canal's former existence can be found in Kempsford village, where a side-road, exiting the High Street near The George inn, is named Wharf Lane. Here, though once again on private land, is to be seen a wharf house clearly related to the one at Cricklade.

Kempsford lies on the Thames, and the two watercourses lay closely parallel for some distance, though nowadays, owing to access constraints, the Thames Path is divorced from the riverbank in this locality. When Robert Whitworth was first surveying the Thames & Severn Canal, consideration was given to making its junction with the Thames at Kempsford as opposed to Inglesham. Long ago the river formed the boundary between Mercia and Wessex. Now it contents itself with dividing Gloucestershire from Wiltshire. East of Kempsford the canal continues infilled and all but invisible on the last lap of its journey to join the Thames.

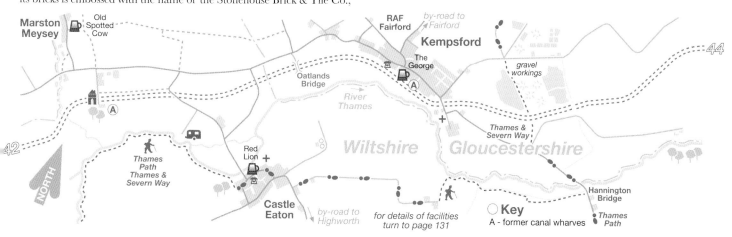

for details of facilities turn to page 131

Key
A - former canal wharves

EVEN the humble appendices in Humphrey Household's history of the Thames & Severn make illuminating reading. From them one can glean the costs of building a barge at Brimscombe in 1791 were £160 16s 10d, or at least what the estimate was; the number of staff employed at sundry points along the line; and the the rise/fall measurements of the locks. But perhaps the most telling statistics, mirroring the waterway's rise and fall, were Appendix 6 and 7 respectively which show gross receipts and dividends paid to shareholders. The former, arranged in tabular from 1797 to 1881, peaked in the early 1840s at a time when, rather ironically, the canal was busy conveying building materials for the Swindon to Cheltenham railway. As for dividends, they were hardly ever substantial, and in many years none were paid at all, 1853 being the last occasion when a cheque plopped through the letterboxes of those who had so optimistically invested in the canal.

Dudgrove Double Lock was peculiar in having chambers of unequal depth: the upper having a fall of 9 feet, the lower just 2ft 6ins. Inglesham marks the canal's last throw of the dice, so to speak. The restorationists have set up camp here - literally and emotionally - determined to make the lock usable again as a statement of intent, a prelude to all the soothsaying toil to come if Lechlade is ever to be reconnected to Stroud. The lock stands cheek by jowl by the fifth and last of the canal's remaining roundhouses. It would be hard to imagine a more iconic necklace of structures; other than Martello towers perhaps.

From Inglesham, the most obvious return to civilisation and the present tense lies via Lechlade and the navigable Thames. Pearsons, however, prefer to repair to the sequestered church of St John the Baptist, cared for by those visionaries, the Churches Conservation Trust, and sing a psalm or two for a better world to come.

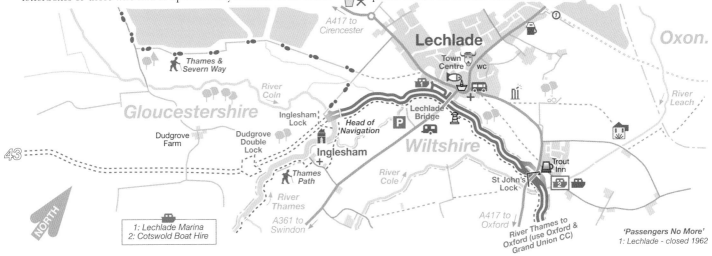

1: Lechlade Marina
2: Cotswold Boat Hire

'Passengers No More'
1: Lechlade - closed 1962

Marston Meysey
Map 43

Isolated Wiltshire village. The church of St James was erected in 1876 to the design of the English Gothic Revivalist architect, James Brooks, and features glass by Kempe and Clayton & Bell.

Eating & Drinking
OLD SPOTTED COW - The Street. Tel: 01285 810264. Cosy country pub dating from 1820. Food served lunch and evening (from 7pm) Mon-Sat and 12-2.30pm Sun. SN6 6LQ

Castle Eaton
Map 43

Village on the south bank of the Thames; once of Wiltshire but now in something called 'Swindon'! St Mary the Virgin, abutting the river, boasts Norman doorways and an Early English chancel. It was restored by Butterfield circa 1860 and is notable for its unusual 14th century bell turret.

Eating & Drinking
RED LION - The Street. Tel: 01285 706533. Comfortably refurbished Donnington Brewery (Stow in the Wold) pub. Food is served lunch and evening (from 6pm) Tue-Thur, and throughout from 12.30pm Fri-Sun. SN6 6JZ

Kempsford
Map 43

Village on the north, Gloucestershire bank of the Thames. There was a battle here in 800 between opposing forces from Mercia and Wessex. RAF Fairford has been largely mothballed since used by USAF B52s during the Iraq War, though it still hosts the annual Royal International Air Tattoo over the third weekend of July.

Eating & Drinking
THE GEORGE - High Street. Tel: 01285 810236. An Arkells county pub, notable in that the brewery's founder was born in the village in 1802. GL7 4EQ

Inglesham
Map 44

Sequestered hamlet at the north-eastern tip of Wiltshire. The 13th century church of St John the Baptist was saved by William Morris in the 19th century, and is notable for its wall paintings, and a stone carving of the Madonna and Child. John Betjeman arrived here by punt whilst filming a documentary for the BBC in the early 1960s.

Lechlade
Map 44

Lechlade - a little town with a lot going for it - has been looking a bit frowzy of late, though perhaps that might be said of the whole of Britain. Not that we don't still have a lot of time for Lechlade, though, with its graceful thoroughfares of mellow Cotswold stone dominated by St Lawrence's church which Shelley (having rowed all the way from Windsor) immortalised in his poem *Summer Evening Meditation* in 1815. Gracing the south-east corner of Gloucestershire, it once lay cheek by jowl with Oxfordshire, Wiltshire and Berkshire too; though the latter shrank southwards following the abhorrent boundary changes foisted on us by the Heath government in 1974.

Eating & Drinking
KHUSHI - Burford Street. Tel: 01367 252956. Indian restaurant open from 5.30pm daily (12pm throughout on Sundays). GL7 3AP
LYNWOOD & CO - Market Square. Tel: 01367 253707. Well-appointed cafe open from 8am until 4pm (2pm on Sundays). GL7 3AB
NEW INN - Market Square. Tel: 01367 252296. Hotel with garden running down to the riverbank. GL7 3AB
RIVERSIDE INN - Park End Wharf. Tel: 01367 252534. Arkells (of Swindon) pub offering breakfasts daily 8 10am and main menu Mon-Sat 12-3pm and 6-8.30pm, and on Sundays between noon and 5pm. Accommodation also available. GL7 3AQ

TEA CHEST - Park End Wharf. Tel: 01367 253015. riverside tea room. GL7 3AQ
TROUT INN - Faringdon Road (adjacent St John's Lock). Tel: 01367 252313. Comfortable country inn overlooking weir pool. Customer moorings. Food served lunch and evenings (from 7pm) daily. GL7 3HA
VERA'S KITCHEN - Burford Street. Tel: 01367 252677. Quaint tea room open from 8am daily; also offers B&B accommodation. GL7 3AP

Shopping
A well-stocked Londis convenience store located on the corner of the Market Square (6.30am-10pm daily) caters for most day to day requirements, but on Oak Street you'll also find the excellent butcher/greengrocer/deli shop of Bayliss & Cutler. Also worthy of mention is the artisan bakery Sourdough Revolution on High Street. Other outlets include a post office, pharmacy, pet shop, antiques arcade and, somewhat surreally, a shop devoted to the all year round sale of Christmas presents. Hillier Garden Centre lies about a mile west of the town on the Fairford Road and features the Mulberry & Thyme cafe/restaurant (Tel: 01367 252372).

Things to Do
COTSWOLD CANALS TRUST - chartered river trips aboard Thames launch *Inglesham*. Tel: 01453 752568.
COTSWOLD CANOE HIRE/SWINDON WATERSPORTS - Park End Wharf. Tel: 01367 252303. Canoe and rowing boat hire. GL7 3AQ

Connections
BUSES - Stagecoach services 76/77 provide Lechlade with a fairly sparsely timetabled link to Fairford and Cirencester from Monday to Saturday. In the opposite direction they run to Highworth which has connections to Swindon. Tel: 0871 200 2233.
TAXIS - CT'S. Tel: 01367 252575.

BIRMINGHAM

Scale: 4 inches to a mile

To Wolverhampton (use Stourport Ring CC)

Round House

Lego Land

Arena B'ham

Oozells Loop

Sea Life

Brindley Place

ICC

Theatre

Library

Centenary Square

Paradise Forum

BROAD STREET

Gas Street Basin

1: Sherborne Wharf

The Mailbox

Pen Museum

Jewellery Quarter

Saturday Bridge

St Paul's

Old Turn Jnct.

Cambrian Wharf

Tindal CRT

Coffin Works

Farmer's Bridge Locks 1-13
80ft 0ins

Ludgate Hill

Livery Street

Snow Hill

Barker Bridge

535

B & F

Lancaster Street

Aston Road

Tesco express

Aston Jnct.

Aston Locks

Love Lane

Science Park

Lister St.

Heneage St.

St Chad's Cathedral (RC)

Snow Hill Station

Art Gallery

COLMORE ROW

St Philip's Cathedral (CoE)

Colmore Circus

Lancaster Circus

Aston University

Old Square

NEW STREET

CORPORATION ST.

Metro Eastside extension

New St. Station

Rotunda

Holloway Circus

China Town

Bull Ring

Markets

St Martin's

Back to Backs (NT)

HIGH ST.

Moor St. Station

HS2 station development site

Thinktank

City University

Curzon Street Tunnel

Fazeley St.

Typhoo (Digbeth) Basin(s)

96 — 95C

Warwick Bar

River Rea

The Bond

Coach Station

Custard Factory

Ashted Tunnel

Ashted Locks
36ft 0ins

Belmont Row

Curzon Street

Boaters may require 'water conservation' handcuff keys to access paddle gear on some of the locks on this map

1 Bistrot Pierre
2 Itihaas
3 Marco Pierre White
4 Maribel
5 Noel's
6 Warehouse Cafe
7 The Wellington
8 The Woodman

Key
A former FMC warehouses
B BCN Cottage 65
C former Typhoo tea factory
D Gun Barrel Proof House
E Curzon Street L&B terminus
F Belmont Works
G site of General Hospital
H site of Tower Cycle Works
I site of Perryian Pen Works

B & F = Birmingham & Fazeley Canal
BCN = Birmingham Canal Navigations
DB = Digbeth Branch (B&F)
GU = Grand Union Canal
W & B = Worcester & Birmingham Canal

S1 = CG

S2 = WC

for details of facilities in central Birmingham turn to page 137

46

*figures relate to Old Turn-Warwick Bar

(use South Mids/Stourport Ring CCs)

BIRMINGHAM reinvented its canals in the mid 1980s, transforming them from an increasingly embarrassing eyesore into a cynosure of much admired urban renewal. History sadly didn't record the Damascene moment. Perhaps some bored conference delegate allowed their gaze to rest upon the tea trolley and saw the magic words 'Just Add Water'. Whatever the source of inspiration, it has manifestly paid dividends. Though, were one inclined to quibble, it would be even more rewarding to see the benefits extend beyond the city centre's high footfall focal points. By the time the inquisitive visitor has descended into the saturnine bowels of Snow Hill, apprehension has a tendency to set in, and with it, every inclination to turn back. Not that canal die-hards don't occasionally savour a tasty slice of dissolution. Truth be told, it accompanies them everywhere.

City Centre Canals

The pivotal point of Birmingham's dense 'More than Venice' canal network is Old Turn (aka Deep Cutting/Farmer's Bridge) Junction. Overlooked by Arena Birmingham and the National Sea Life Centre, there is an unexpected sense of harmony between the 18th century canal and its ultra-modern environment. Water buses and trip boats offer visitors a taste of the enjoyment to be had from navigating these waters. Bicycles can be hired from a butty boat permanently moored at the junction. Moor here (2 and 14 day visitor moorings are available) and savour, however fleetingly, the sense of being a proud inhabitant of Britain's 'Second City'. Incidentally, the circular island in the middle of the junction pool dates from World War II, and was put there to make it easier to block-off the canal in the event of breaches brought about by bomb damage.

Birmingham & Fazeley Canal

Farmer's Bridge Locks pass dramatically beneath the northern periphery of the city centre, affording boaters and towpath users alike an off-beat perspective of the neighbourhood. At Cambrian Wharf there are boaters' facilities and a Canal & River Trust Information Centre, where even the most inane enquiry is met with courtesy, if not necessarily insight. The canal broadens into a basin which once lead to the Newhall and Gibsons branches serving wharves nearer the city centre. Cambrian Wharf was redeveloped in 1969, a template for revitalizing the city's canals. But one senses that time has passed it by, and nowadays it feels subservient to the likes of Brindleyplace and The Mailbox. In the 18th century work began on an impressive crescent of town houses: Brum in homage to Bath. Then, as a bit of a nuisance, the Napoleonic Wars intervened, and only about a third of the houses were erected, and even those were demolished in the 1960s and replaced by an ungainly quartet of tower blocks.

The dramatic descent to Aston Junction commences at Lock 1. Replica gas lamps are a reminder that the flight was once so busy with working boats it was used day and night. Saturday Bridge carries Summer Row across the canal, and is said to have derived its name from the custom of boatmen being paid their wages here each Saturday. Lock 6 provides an opportunity to visit the fascinating Coffin Works visitor centre.

Below Lock 7 the towpath rises to cross a former arm. Here stood Birmingham's Museum of Science & Industry before most of its exhibits were moved to Thinktank. Earlier it had been the site of Elkington's vast electro-plating works. Locks 10 and 11 lie in a cavern beneath the BT Tower of 1967. Just shy of five hundred feet high, it is Birmingham's tallest building, though only half the height of London's Shard.

Assuming you're agile enough to straddle a low wall, there is access alongside Lock 11 to Ludgate Hill and the calm oasis of St Paul's Square, a pocket of the city redolent of an older, and, who's not to say, wiser Birmingham. In *Towns in Britain* (Five Leaves 2014) those perceptive arbiters of good town planning, Adrian Jones and Chris Matthews, felt it had the potential to be Birmingham's 'Clerkenwell'. Quite! St Paul's itself was erected in 1779 to the designs of Roger Eyken, the tower and spire being added by Francis Goodwin (see also Map 46) in 1823. The 18th century industrialist and partner of James Watt, Matthew Boulton,

Barker Bridge

by a Dr John Ash, who called upon 'the Nobility and Gentry' to contribute financially. Investors, however, were reputedly slow to come forward. The Birmingham Canal was being subscribed to at the same time and naturally offered greater returns!

Lancaster Street Bridge is jostled by student accommodation blocks where once stood a bicycle factory. Indeed, all manner of industry clustered along the canal. Nearby lay the Perryian Pen Works. Birmingham was once the pre-eminent centre of pen and nib manufacture. The towpath see-saws over a trio of side-bridges which once spanned arms.

Digbeth Branch

Aston Junction marks the egress of the Digbeth Branch opened in 1799. It descends through the six locks of the Ashted flight to a junction with the Warwick & Birmingham Canal, later part of the Grand Union. Forty years ago Aston Science Park seemed futuristic. Rebranded, it feels rather out on a limb now; more of a habitat for Canada geese than scientists. There are 2 day visitor moorings and a winding hole between Lister Street

Near Aston Junction

worshipped here so regularly he was allocated his own pew (No.23).

Between Locks 12 and 13 the canal negotiates a stygian vault under Snow Hill railway station; closed and subsequently demolished at some cost in 1972, but re-opened and rebuilt at more cost (though markedly less flamboyance) just fifteen years later. Lock 13 marks the foot of the flight. Nearby stands St Chad's, Pugin's Roman Catholic Cathedral of 1841, indiscriminatingly juxtaposed with a skyscraper.

From Snow Hill to Aston Junction the canal, clear of locks for a welcome respite, widens and is less claustrophobically engulfed by the high canyons of commerce. Encapsulating mankind's propensity for inequality, St Chad's Sanctuary for asylum seekers and refugees stands cheek by jowl with Snow Hill Wharf's luxury apartment block. Near Barker Bridge - an elegant cast iron span supported by brick piers and abutments dating from 1842 - stood the city's original General Hospital opened in 1779. It had been promoted and Heneage Street bridges, but little in the way of nearby amenities to prolong a stay.

Below the top lock the canal plunges immediately into the confines of Ashted Tunnel before emerging into the 'work-in-progess' world of Eastside and the burgeoning campus of Birmingham City University. Overlooking Belmont Row Bridge, an old lock-keeper's cottage has so far escaped demolition, though no one seems to know what to do with it yet.

Beyond the bottom lock, the canal enters a curving tunnel beneath a series of railway lines to which HS2, on the approach to its new Curzon Street terminus, is in the process of being added. As early excavation work progressed in this respect, the foundations of an 1837, Robert Stephenson designed roundhouse were unearthed, including a turntable with sixteen radiating 'roads' for the stabling of locomotives.

Once your eyes have reaccustomed to daylight - or what passes for it

Warwick Bar

on the Birmingham Canal Navigations - the canal has reached Warwick Bar and its T-shaped junction with the Warwick & Birmingham Canal. Self-effacingly hidden behind a brick wall on the opposite bank to the towpath is one of the city's least known but most remarkable buildings, the Gun Barrel Proof House, dating from 1813, and still fulfilling its original purpose more than two centuries on.

To the west the branch proceeds beneath Fazeley Street into a pair of truncated arms once lucratively busy with trade to and from Digbeth's many food factories, notably Typhoo Tea. It remains to be seen if the rejuvenation of Eastside will impact beneficially on Warwick Bar. From time to time sundry initiatives have attempted to smarten it up, but it always seems to revert back to a rather shabby default setting ... shabby, that is, without the chic. It is tedious to moralize, but improvements are futile if not succeeded by regular maintenance.

Ashted Locks

Warwick & Birmingham Canal

The stop lock (whose cosmetically reinstated gates are left permanently open) was constructed to separate the waters of the Birmingham & Fazeley (later BCN) and Warwick & Birmingham (later Grand Union) canal companies. Alongside the remains of the stop lock stands a warehouse with an awning supported by cast-iron pillars over an arm lying parallel to the narrows. At one time it was leased by Geest the fruit importers and earned the sobriquet 'Banana Warehouse'. Earlier still it belonged to Pickfords, canal carriers of some importance before they made their name with heavy road transport. Beyond lies New Warwick Wharf, marked by the tall curved wall of Fellows, Morton & Clayton's warehouse built in 1935 in belated response to modernisation of the canal from London. This confident 'Art Deco' style of architecture - emblazoned with the company's name along Fazeley Street to this day - was not rewarded by a significant increase in trade, and, having been for a number of years used by HP Sauce, it now houses a conglomeration of small businesses.

Crossing the River Rea - an unsung (and, in central Birmingham, much culverted) tributary of the Tame - the canal encounters more FMC warehousing built of alternate courses of red and blue brick, and equipped with weather-boarded elevators and an attractive saw-tooth valanced canopy over a side arm. Known now as 'The Bond', it has become a centre for graphic art based enterprises. Directly opposite the towpath rises and falls over a side bridge spanning an arm which once led into one of the City of Birmingham's Salvage Department basins. Horsedrawn rubbish boats operated between here and the Small Heath destructor (Map 46) until 1965. All that detritus suggests they could still play a role.

Quarter of a mile to the west - though just off the map - stands the celebrated Custard Factory, a redevelopment of a works where Bird's famous custard powder was made until 1963. Nowadays it's a hub for start-ups, artisan shops, and eating places. An exemplar of what can be done with otherwise unwanted industrial buildings, if a little bit of imagination from developers and investors is brought to the party.

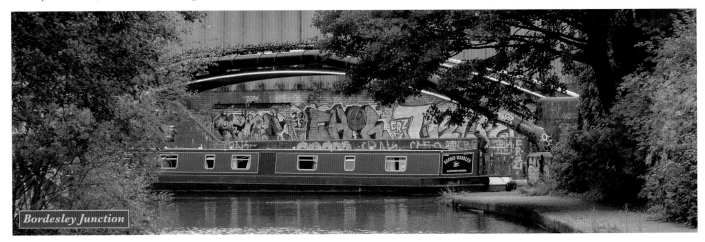

Bordesley Junction

Birmingham

Somewhat belatedly, 'Brum' has woken up to the error of its ways, reaching the inevitable, and long-overdue conclusion, that there is more to life than the motor car. Not that there isn't a good deal of reparation to be made - 'going forward'. The concrete and petrol fuelled debaucheries of the Nineteen Sixties and Seventies all but annihilated the self-styled 'Second City's' cohesive Georgian, Victorian and Edwardian core. Pedestrianised survivors found themselves herded into subfusc corridors of gloom beneath grid-locked roads from which occasional glimpses were afforded of a canal network which - specious comparisons with Venice apart - had slipped from the city's tribal memory. Much of this discredited legacy can be laid at the door of two knights of the realm: Herbert Manzoni, the City Engineer, and Frank Price, Council Leader and Mayor, who went on to become a not entirely unappreciated Chairman of the British Waterways Board for some sixteen years. Notable casualties of their remorseless redevelopment schemes included the Market Hall, Central Library, Liberal Club and Technical College. Chillingly, Manzoni openly averred to have 'never been certain as to the value of tangible links with the past', a point of view unlikely to resonate with seasoned *Canal Companion* aficionados. Manifestly in safer hands now, Birmingham is an increasingly rewarding city to explore, and the humble pedestrian is no longer considered a second class citizen; well, not entirely!

Eating & Drinking
BISTROT PIERRE - Gas Street. Tel: 0121 616 0730. Canalside French restaurant from noon daily. B1 2JT
ITIHAAS - Fleet/Newhall Streets. Tel: 0121 212 3383. Well thought of Indian restaurant overlooking Farmers Bridge Locks. B3 1JL

MARCO PIERRE WHITE - The Cube. Tel: 0121 634 3433. Steakhouse, bar and grill 25 floors up. Panoramic city views. Food served from noon daily. B1 1PR
MARIBEL - Brindley Place. Tel: 0121 633 4944. Fine dining. Lunch Tue-Fri and dinner Tue-Sat. B1 2JB
NOEL'S - Tel: 0121 389 3896. Waterfront Walk. Mediterranean inspired cuisine overlooking Salvage Turn. Open from noon daily. B1 1SN
WAREHOUSE CAFE - Allison Street, Digbeth. Tel: 0121 348 7554. Vegetarian & vegan cafe/restaurant & shop open from 9am Tue-Sat, 10am Sun. B5 5TH
THE WELLINGTON - Bennett's Hill. Tel: 0121 200 3115. *Good Beer Guide* listed real ale mecca between Colmore Row and New Street. Up to fifteen beers on tap. Plates and cutlery and condiments supplied for you to bring your own food. B2 5SN
THE WOODMAN - New Canal Street. Tel: 0121 643 4960. Handsome terracotta street corner pub across the street from the original Curzon Street station. The interior is on CAMRA'S National Inventory. Castle Rock ales. Food served 12-7pm ex Sun. B5 5LG

Shopping
Canallers in a hurry - if that's not an oxymoron - will find convenience stores adjoining the Mailbox, Oozells Loop and Tindal Bridge by Farmer's Bridge Junction. Otherwise you'll find all the facilities of a major city within easy reach of the canal. The Bull Ring markets (located on Edgbaston Street south-east of New Street station) are a famous focal point of midland merchandising. The Bull Ring Shopping Centre has been redeveloped, the landmark Rotunda having escaped by the skin of its Grade II listed teeth, so that it now rubs shoulders with the likes of Kaplicky's shimmering Selfridges store. Grand Central is the city's latest shopping experience located above its revitalised New Street railway station. Un-canal-like sophisticated fashion in The Mailbox.

Things to Do
BACK TO BACKS - Hurst Street. Tel: 0121 666 7671. How Brum's poor used to live. National Trust owned, pre-booking essential. B5 4TE
COFFIN WORKS - Fleet Street. Tel: 0121 233 4790. Tours of Victorian factory embalmed in aspic. B3 1JP
CYCLE CHAIN - Central Sq. Brindley Place. Tel: 0754 758 7050. Bicycle hire/repair from the 1935 Yarwoods butty *Carina*. B1 2HL
LEGOLAND - King Edward's Road. Tel: 0371 222 6937. Canalside visitor attraction. B1 2AA
LIBRARY OF BIRMINGHAM - Centenary Square. Tel: 0121 242 4242. From the Secret Garden on the 7th floor there are bird's eye views over the canals radiating from Old Turn Junction. B1 2ND
MUSEUM & ART GALLERY - Chamberlain Square. Tel: 0121 303 1966. Open daily, admission free. Rivals Manchester in the richness of its Pre-Raphaelite collection. Shop, Edwardian Tea Room. B3 3DH
NATIONAL SEA LIFE CENTRE - Brindley Place. Tel: 0871 423 2110. Turtles, sharks and other non BCN resident maritime species. B1 2HL
PEN MUSEUM - Frederick Street. Tel: 0121 236 9834. Fascinating story of the writing pen trade. B1 3HS
ROUNDHOUSE - Sheepcote Street. NT/CRT redevelopment of circular municipal stables. B16 8AE
SYMPHONY HALL - Broad Street. Tel: 0121 780 3333. Home to Mirga Grazinyte-Tyla's top rank City of Birmingham Symphony Orchestra. B1 2EA
THINKTANK - Curzon Street. Tel: 0121 348 8000. Science for all the family. Contains Watt's Smethwick Engine and Stanier's *City of Birmingham*. B4 7XG

Connections
BUSES - Tel: 0871 200 2233.
TRAINS - Tel: 0345 748 4950.
METRO - Tel: 0345 835 8181.
TAXIS - TOA (black cabs). Tel: 0121 427 8888.

BLUE-BRICKED and tree-grown, the crumbling remains of Duddeston Viaduct span the canal by Bridge 95. Erected out of early railway rivalry, it never carried a paying train. A shame it can't be imaginatively reinvented like New York's High Line, an elevated linear park created along the course of an old railway line on the west side of Manhattan.

Overlooked by the Liverpool Street Bus Depot of 1936 ('Birmingham Corporation Tramway & Omnibus Dept.' remains engraved above the entrance), Bordesley Junction is the point from which the Birmingham & Warwick Junction Canal (aka the 'Saltley Cut') departs beneath a graceful roving bridge cast by Lloyds & Fosters before plunging into the subfusc gloom of an overhanging factory.

If prizes - heaven forbid - were handed out for graffiti, the perpetrators of the 'art' that adorns the environs of Bordesley Junction might well run out of acceptance speeches. Is this depressing vandalism - for however imaginative, it can only be classified as such - policed? Or is it the equivalent of an 'out of bounds'

housing estate where the authorities are powerless to do anything but turn a blind eye. Understandably, the Grand Union Canal appears anxious to extricate itself from Birmingham's nether regions, climbing to the first of three summit sections separating it from London (130 miles away) through the six locks of the Camp Hill flight. They fill rapidly, so don't wander off while lock-wheeling, however tempting the hinterland. Though who, for example, could resist the siren call of the site of Adderley Street Gas Works from whence highly toxic cyanogen was conveyed in tank boats to specialist contractors for crystallisation, prior to being exported to the South African goldfields. And we think that trade is global now! An article concerning the long vanished plant appeared in Issue 61 of the excellent industrial archaeology journal *Archive*. Photographs of the retort house alongside Lock 56 show boats being loaded with containers of coke for the British Small Arms (BSA)

○ **Key**

A Liverpool Street Bus Depot
B site of Adderley Street Gas Works
C former Sampson Road Wharf
D sites of Small Arms Works
E site of Singer motor works
F refuse works
G former Wilmot Breeden works
H former Tyseley Wharf

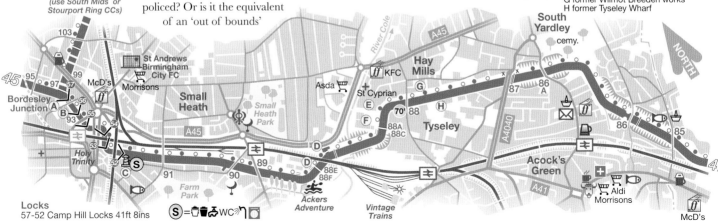

B&WJC to Salford Jnct (use South Mids or Stourport Ring CCs)

Locks
57-52 Camp Hill Locks 41ft 8ins

(S)=🚮♻️🚾⚓🎣📷

works at Small Heath. It is fascinating to see how so many works relied on the canal for short-haul commodities.

Lock 54 has been rebuilt in recent years and the canal realigned to make way for widening of the Bordesley Middleway road. Vaguely reminiscent of King's College Chapel, but woefully neglected, Holy Trinity church (designed by Francis Goodwin in 1822) overlooks the middle of the flight. It gained notoriety in 1880 ('The Bordesley Wafer Case') when the incumbent began to indulge a taste for high church ritualism much to the disapproval of his bishop. Following its closure in 1971, it became an overnight shelter for the homeless. Now it looks as if - sadly notwithstanding its Grade II listed status - it is used for nothing at all. How can civilised society allow buildings of this quality to fester, let alone fall down?

A fine array of lock-up businesses occupy the railway arches by Bridge 91C, part of a viaduct of sixty arches which carry the railway into Birmingham over the valley of the River Rea. Don't be tempted to wait for a train into the city centre at Bordesley's nearby station, it only functions when Birmingham City are playing at home. In any case it may be demolished entirely, or relocated, if proposals for two new chord lines into Moor Street station materialise.

Above the top lock, the canal widens into an L-shaped basin. This was the Grand Union Canal Company's Sampson Road depot, part of which was sub-let to Rugby Portland Cement whose final cargo - from Stockton on Map 52 - arrived here in 1969 aboard the motor *Banstead* and the butty *Tow*. Happily now preserved, *Banstead* 'starred' in the Galton & Simpson 1964 film comedy *The Bargee*, along with Harry H. Corbett, Ronnie Barker and a host of other stalwarts of the British film industry. The depot remains more or less intact, part of it being used as a sofa warehouse. Furthermore, extensive boater facilities are laid on, so that you can have a shower and wash your pyjamas whilst imagining you've just arrived from Limehouse with a cargo of Syrian dates. On the opposite bank of the canal, tucked between the towpath and the railway, stands a four storey warehouse erected by the Great Western Railway using reinforced concrete in 1931: 'Eminently suitable for every class of merchandise' read the

advertising slogans. It's used for self-storage now. Sofas, self-storage! A come down perhaps, but it's good to see these two old transport hubs surviving in one form or another.

Paralleling the former Great Western main line from Birmingham Snow Hill to Paddington, and the dual-carriagewayed A45, which originally led from Birmingham to Felixstowe, the canal runs past the backs of factories reluctant to give any clue of their function. A clock-towered pub and a mosque provide contrasting additions to the skyline in the vicinity of Bridge 90. The adjoining dock belonged to Birmingham Corporation's Public Works Department.

An impressive row of poplar trees accompanies the canal beyond Bridge 89. The Ackers Adventure Centre occupies the basin once used by the Birmingham Small Arms concern, manufacturers of weapons and motorcycles. Nowadays, canoeists and kayakers, climbers and abseilers exude more innocent forms of activity than the production of armaments. As we have seen, refuse collection was another aspect of trade along this length of canal. The Corporation Refuse & Salvage Department operated a fleet of horse-drawn boats collecting rubbish from various points in the city. It was brought out here to the Small Heath tip until 1965. These days the plant belongs to Veolia and is known as an energy recovery facility: 350,000 tonnes of Birmingham rubbish is incinerated annually, producing enough electricity to power 25,000 homes.

Bridge 88 affords pedestrian access to the curious Victorian church of St Cyprian aside the River Cole. 'The nicely eccentric result of some industrial patronage', is how Pevsner put it. Intriguing! Tyseley Wharf was notable for its travelling cranes which coped manfully with some of the heavier commodities bound for Birmingham. A melancholy, no longer glazed concrete canopy, breeze-blocked windows and sealed sliding doors bear witness to busier times, and the site is now utilised by a company dealing in roofing supplies. Nostalgic descriptions of Tyseley Wharf in its pomp appear in Tim Wilkinson's *Hold on a Minute* and David Blagrove's *Bread Upon The Waters*. On the towpath side stood the premises of Wilmot Breeden, the motor accessory engineers.

B RUM'S south-eastern suburbs cling possessively onto the Grand Union, but deep swarthy cuttings disguise their proximity, and the canal - as so often proves the case - socially distances to such a degree that canal explorers have little sense of the pent-up world surrounding them.

By Bridge 84, a builders merchants occupies the site of a wharf which was still receiving timber by boat until 1967. On the opposite bank lived the Birmingham journalist Vivian Bird whose book *By Lock And Pound* is an underated classic of inland waterways literature. Olton Reservoir dates from 1799, having been dug out of marshy ground to feed the summit of the canal, a function it continues to fulfil to this day, though now it's also used for sailing and fishing. The feeder comes in on the off-side between bridges 84 and 83.

Catherine -de-Barnes
Elmdon Heath
Jaguar Land Rover
sports grounds
site of Solihull Wharf
site of Solihull Gas Works
Hob's Moat
Olton ✚
Olton Reservoir

Silhill Brewery
M42 (to M6)
former isolation hospital
River Blythe
B4102 to Solihull
Berry Hall
1: Copt Heath Wharf
M42 (to M5)

Blythe Waters
NORTH
Henwood Hall Farm
Copt Heath
Grimshaw Hall
Grove Farm

78 78A 77 76 75 A/B 75 74 73 72A 79 79A 80 81 82 83 84 46 48 5

The sprawling premises of the Land Rover assembly plant border the canal between bridges 81 and 80. The works can trace its development back to a Second World War 'shadow' factory. Driving 'experiences' can be arranged on the company's test track if you're beginning to find steering a narrowboat all too sedate! Solihull Wharf stood on the towpath side between bridges 80 and 79. Opposite stood Solihull Gas Works, once served by Thomas Clayton tank boats, but closed in 1962. *Gazed at in Awe*, a personal account of life at the works by former employee, Alan J. Sadler, can reasonably easily be acquired via the internet.

Beyond Elmdon Heath open countryside manifests itself, though the canal is under Birmingham Airport's flight-path. Working boatmen knew Catherine-de-Barnes more intimately than most, and were in the habit of calling her 'Kate', though land-based locals have apparently always called the place 'Catney'. This is a popular place for boaters to moor: either to celebrate escaping Birmingham's clutches, or screwing up the nerve to engage it in an arm-wrestle. Near Bridge 77 a former isolation hospital has been redeveloped as housing. The last known victim of smallpox in Britain died here in 1978. Between bridges 77 and 76 an embankment carries the canal over the River Blythe, a tributary of the Tame which it joins near Coleshill.

Catherine-de-Barnes   Map 47

Eating & Drinking

THE BOAT - Bridge 78. Tel: 0121 705 0474. A comfortably furnished Chef & Brewer pub offering a wide choice of food. Open from noon. B91 2TJ

LONGFELLOWS - Bridge 78. Tel: 0121 705 0547. 'English' restaurant est. 1988 specialising in seafood and seasonal game. Open Tue-Fri from noon; Mon and Sat for dinner from 6pm; and Sun lunch. B91 2TJ

Shopping

Spar post office stores. Silhill micro-brewery occupies a unit at nearby Oak Farm - Tel: 0797 744 4564.

Connections

Buses run regularly to Solihull and Coventry.

Knowle   Map 48

A prosperous suburb of Solihull lying approximately ten minutes walking time away from bridges 71-3. Admire the fine Perpendicular church and Chester House, a 15th century timber framed building now housing the library and local history exhibition. John Wyndham, the author, most famously, of *The Day of the Triffids*, was born here in 1903.

Eating & Drinking

ALE ROOMS - High Street. Tel: 01564 400040. *Good Beer Guide* listed micropub housed in what was formerly an undertakers. Pies, and beer from Silhill Brewery at nearby Catherine de Barnes. B93 0LF

BELLA VENEZIA - High Street. Tel: 0788 231 1481. Cosy, family run Italian. B93 0JU

BLACK BOY - canalside Bridge 69. Tel: 01564 772655. Pub which (like others of this name) is thought to be named after the saturnine King Charles II. Nicely furnished within and canalside garden with children's play zone. B94 6JU

JANITO - St John's Close. Tel: 01564 779802. Cosy Mediterranean restaurant. B93 0JU

KING'S ARMS - canalside Bridge 70. Tel: 01564 771177. Vintage Inns pub/restaurant with waterside garden. Accommodation. B93 0EE

LOCH FYNE - High Street. Tel: 01564 732750. Seafood restaurant. B93 0JU

Shopping

Eric Lyons, the family butchers, make their own pork pies and take-away meals in foil containers for heating up at home or, more pertinently, on your boat and The Artisan Bakery is excellent. An Oxfam charity shop specialises in books and music. Away from the High Street there's a small precinct with Tesco Metro.

Connections

TAXIS - A2B. Tel: 0121 744 1111.

Kingswood   Map 48

Eating & Drinking

THE NAVIGATION - Old Warwick Road. Canalside Bridge 65 (Grand Union). Tel: 01564 783337. Pub offering food lunchtimes and evenings. B94 6NA

Shopping

Village shop by railway bridge. Off licence/post office near Bridge 65.

Things to Do

BADDESLEY CLINTON HALL - Rising Lane (access from bridges 65/66). Tel: 01564 783294. 'The perfect late medieval manor house' according to Pevsner. National Trust property hidden in Arden woodland. Shop and restaurant. Open daily from 9am. B93 0DQ

Connections

TRAINS - approx bi-hourly Chiltern Trains service linking with Warwick, Leamington, Birmingham Moor Street/Snow Hill and Marylebone. Tel: 0345 748 4950.

Turner's Green   Map 49

Eating & Drinking

TOM O' THE WOOD - Finwood Road, Rowington (Bridge 63). Tel: 01564 782252. Picturesque country pub named after a former windmill. Open from 11am daily, food served lunchtimes and evenings from 6pm. Greene King IPA and guest beers. CV35 7DH

Shrewley   Map 49

Shrewley's narrow street straddles three eras of transport - canal, railway and motorway - yet remains dreamily oblivious to them all.

Eating & Drinking

THE DURHAM OX - Tel: 01926 842283. Greene King 'Old English Inn' from 11am daily, food served throughout. Breakfasts 9am Sat & Sun. CV35 7AY

Shopping

Post office stores.

Hatton   Map 50

Eating & Drinking

HATTON LOCKS CAFE - canalside adjacent top lock. Tel: 01926 409432. Open daily 9am-5pm. Charming establishment offering a wide range of refreshments, not least 'Full English' for famished lock-workers. Canal Companions on sale! CV35 7JL

HATTON ARMS - Birmingham Road. Access from the canal at Bridge 54. Tel: 01926 492427. Comfortably furnished pub with a wide choice of food, operated by the owners of Hatton Country World. Food served from noon daily. Church Farm, Hook Norton, Purity, Wye Valley & guest ales. CV35 7JJ

Things to Do

HATTON COUNTRY WORLD - Dark Lane. Tel: 01926 843411. Access from canal at bridges 54 (waymarked footpath) or 55 (country road). A shopping village (crafts, clothes, food, jewellery, gifts, toys etc) and adventure farm. Spinning Jenny Restaurant (named after Arkwright, whose descendants own the estate) and Alfies Cafe. Open daily from 10am to 5.30pm. CV35 8XA

REVELLING in delightful Warwickshire countryside, the canal completes its passage of the 11 mile Olton summit and descends, rather dramatically it must be said, through a flight of five locks at Knowle. When it first opened in 1800, this was known as the Warwick & Birmingham Canal, but in 1929 it was absorbed into a new undertaking called the Grand Union. As part of a subsequent rolling programme of modernisation, the locks between Bordesley, on the southern outskirts of Birmingham (Map 46), and Braunston (Map 54), hitherto of narrowbeam dimensions, were broadened. It was intended that a fleet of widebeam barges with a carrying capacity in excess of 60 tons - compared to a narrowboat's maximum of 25 tons - would ply between London and Birmingham, reinvigorating the notion of transport by water. But, apart

from a prototype, somewhat ironically named *Progress*, those barges never materialised, and carrying remained the sole province of narrowboats; though widening of the locks did facilitate the speedier passage of pairs.

The five locks at Knowle replaced six narrow chambers, the remains of which are still to be seen. If these are the first widebeam locks you have encountered, they can be quite intimidating. Furthermore, they 'enjoy' - if that is the right word - a reputation for being hard work. So best allot their operation to the most muscular members of the crew at your disposal!

At Kingswood, a short branch links the Grand Union and Stratford canals, offering a choice of alternative routes and itineraries.

Locks
51 - 47 Knowle Locks 42ft 0ins

for details of facilities at Knowle & Kingswood turn back to page 141

BLISSFULLY lock-free again, the canal traverses an eight mile pound 379ft above sea level. The landscape is unequivocably lovely; part of the old Warwickshire region of Arden which has associations with Shakespeare.

Either side of Bridge 62 at Rowington, the canal negotiates a deep cutting and a high embankment. When the Warwick & Birmingham Canal was being built during the last decade of the 18th century, there were plans for the latter to be a tunnel. Incidentally, the original contractor for this length was dismissed when it emerged that he had resorted to bribery to acquire the tender.

At Shrewley, dusky, echoing cuttings lead to one of those little curiosities which make canal exploration so rewarding. Here the canal builders were forced to tunnel beneath the village, and in doing so provided a bore wide enough for oncoming narrowboats to pass inside. There was, however, no room for a towpath, so the boat horses were led over the hilltop and across the village street, passing through their own short tunnel in the process.

The tunnel's dank approach cuttings are rich in flora and fauna and designated a Site of Special Scientific Interest. Mid Warks Yacht Club, disciples in both sailing and narrowboating, were founded in 1961.

From Hatton's convenient railway station, trains run at fairly regular intervals to the bard's home town, a worthwhile excursion ashore if you have time at your disposal and have no immediate plans to explore the Stratford Canal.

The winding hole between bridges 56 and 55 is concrete lined, part of twenty-six miles of bank protection work done by the Grand Union in the 1930s, when dredging was also undertaken to provide a uniform depth of five and a half feet, a laughable notion now! Given their enthusiasm for superfluous signage, the Canal & River Trust might usefully erect signs at all winding holes stating their maximum current turning length. South of Bridge 55 a by-road bridges the railway - at a point where it is ascending Hatton Bank at a gradient of 1 in 110 - and leads to Hatton Country World, a shopping village and adventure farm.

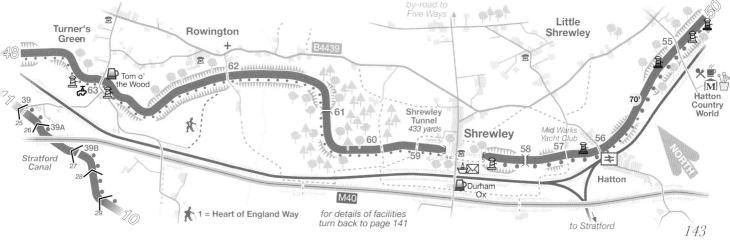

1 = Heart of England Way

for details of facilities turn back to page 141

50 GRAND UNION CANAL Hatton & Warwick 5mls/23lks/5hrs

HATTON Locks leave little to the imagination. They may not grace the record books as Britain's biggest flight numerically - that accolade goes to Tardebigge (Map 17) on the Worcester & Birmingham Canal - but few of its rivals confront the approaching boater with such an intimidating prospect. In its central, most concentrated section, it has the look of an aquatic ski slope, an appearance emphasised by the slalom-like verticals of the encased 'worm & nut' paddle mechanisms. The twenty-one chambers, spread over just two miles, have a combined fall of almost a hundred and fifty feet. At the bottom, the substantial tower of St Mary's church in Warwick provides an encouraging goal to the completion of your labours. If the flight is visibly daunting, it is physically no less so; with heavy mitred gates, and paddle gear which offers few short cuts in operation. The wise boater waits for company; though volunteer 'lockies' are often on hand to provide both moral and physcial support nowadays.

When the new locks at Hatton were opened in 1934, the VIP's cruised aboard the prototype barge *Progress* from Hatton station (Map 49) through the cutting to the top lock, where a tape was cut by Prince George, the fourth son of George V. The Prince, who had served in the Royal Navy, must have felt at home aboard *Progress*. A popular figure with the general public, he had recently been given the title Duke of Kent on his engagement to the Greek-born beauty, Princess Marina. Consequently, a larger crowd than might usually have been expected to witness the opening of a flight of canal locks assembled. It was probably the first time - other than Queen Victoria's opening of the Manchester Ship Canal in 1894 - that royalty had deigned attend a canal event since George III visited Sapperton Tunnel (Maps 39 & 40) on the Thames & Severn Canal in 1788. The Duke of Kent's cutting of the tape at Hatton Top might in retrospect have been seen as a high water mark in his ambassadorial life. In the second half of the Thirties he became regarded as an appeaser with Nazi Germany. In

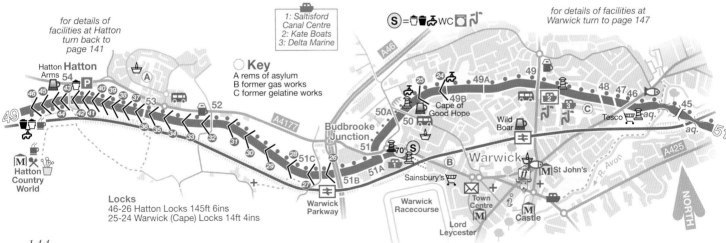

for details of facilities at Hatton turn back to page 141

for details of facilities at Warwick turn to page 147

1: Saltisford Canal Centre
2: Kate Boats
3: Delta Marine

Key
A rems of asylum
B former gas works
C former gelatine works

Hatton Arms 54
Hatton

Budbrooke Junction

Cape of Good Hope

Wild Boar

Warwick

Tesco

Hatton Country World

Locks
46-26 Hatton Locks 145ft 6ins
25-24 Warwick (Cape) Locks 14ft 4ins

Warwick Parkway

Sainsbury's

Warwick Racecourse

Lord Leycester

Town Centre

St John's

Castle

NORTH

144

Coming down Hatton Locks

1942 he was killed in an air crash near Helmsdale on the north-east coast of Scotland whilst undertaking a secret mission to Iceland, the full nature of which has never been satisfactorily explained.

As at Knowle, the original narrowbeam chambers of the Hatton flight have been retained as overflow channels, though it is interesting to note that the old flight was numbered in the opposite direction; No.1 being the top lock. The modernisation scheme cost a million pounds, half of which took the form of a government grant to alleviate the relatively high unemployment prevalent at the time. Most of the thousand men employed came from the local area. Significantly, the adjoining Great Western Railway took the offer of similar Whitehall largesse to quadruple their line north of Lapworth and double the route westwards from Hatton towards Stratford. Incidentally, the railway's corresponding gradient between Warwick and Hatton necessitated the banking of heavy goods trains in steam days. Today's lengthy, diesel-hauled container trains take the climb in their stride, though not without a certain amount of 'thrash'!

Instead of the widebeam barges envisaged, the Grand Union Canal Carrying Company acquired a sizeable fleet of 'pairs' of motor and butty narrowboats. This came into its own during the Second World War when trade on the Grand Union increased considerably. One noticeable facet of operation being the employment of women as boat crews, an activity recorded in several books, notably *Maiden's Trip* by Emma Smith, *Idle Women* by Susan Woolfitt and *The Amateur Boatwomen* by Eily Gayford. Approaching the Hatton 21 before dawn one morning, Emma Smith wrote that 'their full horror was veiled to us in semi-obscurity'! Anything but 'idle', the women will be well into their nineties now, and perplexed, perhaps, to see their former working environs transformed into a tourist attraction. For Hatton is now a honeypot, with a Pay & Display car park by Bridge 54 which brings welcome revenue to the Canal & River Trust's charity coffers. Moreover, the neighbouring workshops are now a centre for heritage skills. It was a joke amongst boaters that they were mad enough, in even attempting the Hatton flight, to gain immediate access to the County Asylum on the adjoining hillside, now replaced by housing.

At Budbrooke Junction the Warwick & Birmingham Canal met its close associate, the Warwick & Napton. The two canals were opened at the turn of the 18th century and together provided Birmingham with a more direct route to London than had hitherto existed. But competition from existing waterways was fierce, and the advent of the railways had both companies in financial straits by the mid-1800s. Eventually they were incorporated within the Grand Union in 1929, and in due course the route established itself as the premier London-Birmingham inland waterway. The actual terminus of the Warwick & Birmingham Canal lay at the end of the Saltisford Arm, closer to the town centre than you can get by boat today. Part of the arm, however, has been restored to provide excellent boating facilities; not least visitor moorings, free of charge for the first night.

Warwick, or Cape Locks - the alternative, more commonly used vernacular inspired by the neighbouring pub - mark the beginning of the 5 mile 'Leamington Pound', the lowest section of the canal between Birmingham and Braunston. A notable tourist destination, Warwick prefers to show its 'better side' to the world, but the canal traveller sees only its posterior! Though, as backsides go, we've seen worse. Kate Boats hire base occupies the site of a former brewery. Delta Marine are based at what was known as Guys Cliff (or Nelson) Wharf. George Nelson had patented the manufacture of gelatine in 1838 and moved his business to Emscote four years later.

Jephson's Farm, Bridge 45

Houses for his employees were erected along Charles Street (Bridge 48) together with a social club. Further along were the Emscote corn mills, their site now occupied by flats. By Bridge 46, where Tesco stands now, there was an early power station (known to the canal fraternity as 'Warwick Light') and a tramway depot. The Leamington & Warwick Electrical Co. operated a short three mile tramway between the two towns of 3ft 6ins gauge. From 1882 the trams were horse-drawn, but between 1905 and the line's closure in 1930 they were electric.

The briefest of rural interludes separates Warwick from Leamington. A sturdy stone aqueduct of three arches spans the Avon. Its setting doesn't really do it justice. But if you picture how it must once have looked, before the watermeadows were inundated by houses, its erstwhile grandeur may be imagined. Steps lead down to the riverbank and a 'Waterside Walk'. They would have been of use to the canoeist, William Bliss, and journalist, poet and 'literary-cricketer' Sir John Squire, who 'slithered down ... sodden slopes' on the offside of the canal to reach the river on a circular tour by canoe from Oxford in 1938 as described in Squire's book *Water Music*. A friend had been roped in to help this challenging portage, and it was only after they had progressed someway downstream on the Avon that they realised he had inadvertently been abandoned on the opposite bank of the canal to the towpath. Look out for him, he may still be there.

Turning a seemingly blind eye to the canal, though apparently still occupied, Jephson's Farm* bucolically abuts Bridge 45 before the canal straddles what used to be the Great Western Railway's main line between London Paddington and Birmingham, a route reinvigorated post privatisation by Chiltern Railways, though Marylebone is the capital's terminus now. Canal travellers may peer down through elegant iron railings onto the roofs of passing trains. Keep an ear out for the Class 68 'Cats' with their trademark throaty bark.

*No connection, that we could trace, with Dr Henry Jephson of Leamington Spa fame: see page 149.

Warwick
Map 50

Warwick's proximity to Stratford-on-Avon guarantees a steady stream of tourists. But, in any case, this is a handsome and historic county town in its own right, and one with a wealth of interesting buildings: the celebrated castle - painted by Canaletto and said, by Sir Walter Scott, to be "the most noble sight in England" - and the stately parish church (a beacon for those engaged in the seemingly never-ending flight of locks at Hatton) being but two examples. Warwick's centre is a mile away from the canal at most points. When you get there, Warwick is compact enough to reconnoitre in an hour or two, but you will want much longer to do it justice. Part of the town easily missed by visitors from the canal lies around the road bridge over the Avon. Here are Mill Street and Bridge End, not to mention the most dramatic view of the castle on its rocky promontory above the Avon.

Eating & Drinking
ART KITCHEN - Swan Street. Tel: 01926 494303. Thai restaurant. Open from noon daily. CV34 4BJ
CAPE OF GOOD HOPE - canalside at Warwick Locks. Tel: 01926 498138. *Good Beer Guide* listed boatmen's pub open from noon daily. Church Farm, Hook Norton and Wye Valley ales. CV34 5DP
TAILORS - Market Place. Tel: 01926 410590. *Good Food Guide* listed restaurant open Wed-Sat for lunch and dinner Tue-Sat from 6.30pm. CV34 4SL

THOMAS OKEN TEA ROOMS - Castle Street. Tel: 01926 499307. Tudoresque refreshments in castle shadows. Open daily 10am-5pm. CV34 4BP
THE WILD BOAR - Lakin Road. Tel: 01926 499968. *GBG* listed taphouse for Slaughterhouse Brewery. Good choice of pub food served 12-3pm and 5-8pm Mon-Sat and 12-6pm Sun. CV34 5BU

Shopping
The town centre is 15 minutes walk from bridges 46, 49, 50 or 51. Frequent buses to/from The Cape. Wide range of shops in centre with emphasis on gifts and antiques. Warwick Books is an excellent independent bookshop in the Market Place. Duncan Allsop's secondhand bookshop is on Smith Street. Also on Smith Street are a beer shop, a tea merchant and a butcher. Antique outlets abound. Market day is Saturday. Large Tesco with its own offside moorings at Bridge 46. Sainsbury's supermarket easily accessed from Saltisford Arm. Useful garages close to bridges 52 and 49 for groceries and fast food. Get Knotted is a traditional fender maker (and other ropes) based at the Cape of Good Hope - Tel: 01926 410588.

Things to Do
TOURIST INFORMATION - Court House, Jury Street. Tel: 01926 492212. CV34 4EW
WARWICK CASTLE - Castle Hill. Open daily, admission charge. Tel: 08701 265 2000. Along with Alton Towers, Warwick Castle is part of the global Merlin Entertainments brand: Wars of Roses re-enactments, dungeon tours et al. CV34 4QU
LORD LEYCESTER HOSPITAL - High Street. Tel: 01926 491422. Open Tue-Sun. Admission charge. Founded in 1571 as a house of rest for poor brethren. Now a delightful place to visit. Coffees, light lunches and teas in the Bretheren's Kitchen during the season. CV34 4BH
MARKET HALL MUSEUM - Market Place. Open daily ex Mons and Winter Suns. Tel: 01926 412501. Displays of local history and natural history. CV34 4SA
ST JOHN'S HOUSE - St Johns. Tel: 01926 412132. Social and military history displays in handsome 17th century Jacobean house. CV34 4NF
ST MARY'S - Church Street. Tel: 01926 403940. Collegiate church dating from 12th century. Beauchamp Chapel, crypt, and access to tower from which there are panoramic views, not least of that other stairway to heaven, Hatton Locks. CV34 4RA
WARWICK BOATS - St Nicholas Park. Tel: 01926 494743. Boat hire on the Avon. CV34 4QY.

Connections
BUSES - Goldline 1 runs every 10 minutes or so from The Cape into central Warwick. Service X68 runs hourly from stops by Bridge 49. Tel: 0871 200 2233.
TRAINS - Chiltern Railways services at both Warwick and Warwick Parkway to/from Leamington and Birmingham Snow Hill and London Marylebone. Tel: 0345 748 4950.
TAXIS - Warwick Taxis. Tel: 01926 499966.

51 GRAND UNION CANAL Royal Leamington Spa 5mls/5lks/3hrs

ANALSIDE Leamington struggles to measure up to expectations of how an inland waterway flowing through a spa town should look. This was always Leamington's seamy side: home to its gas works, a couple of foundries, an engine shed, and tight-knit streets of terraced housing. These days, though, the towpath - overlooked by housing and student flats - is neatly surfaced and provided with copious mooring rings, plus a water point, so plenty of boaters pause here happily overnight, grateful to rest between the lengthy flights of locks that face them in either direction.

East of Footbridge 42, a Morrisons supermarket occupies the site of the Imperial Stove Company works which, after the Second World War, was used by Ford to manufacture agricultural equipment until its closure in 2007. Leamington Priors Gas Company stood on the offside between bridges 41 and 40 until the advent of North Sea gas, in 1964. Its passing brought an end to the use of Thomas Clayton tank boats to carry crude tar, a by-product of the distilling process, to Banbury (in the summer) and Oldbury (in the winter). Clayton boats were named after rivers and, appropriately, the butty *Leam* was used from time to time. Clayton captains reputedly thought of the Oldbury run as a two-day round trip; these days it represents a mind-boggling forty hours cruising; twenty hours a day at the tiller! A faded splash of the Regency architecture, hinting at the splendours of the town centre, exists beside Bridge 40, beyond which the off-side is lined by Rangemaster's cooker factory, established in 1833 as Flavel's Eagle Foundry.

Sydenham's suburbs are soon left astern as the canal parallels the River Leam. Thornley's Radford Hall Brewery stood canalside near Bridge 35 and the canal featured (with some degree of artistic licence) in its advertising material. The brewery closed in 1969 and the site is now occupied by the automotive specialists, Ricardo. At Radford Bottom Lock, southbound travellers commence a 23-lock climb out of the valley of the Avon. A viaduct

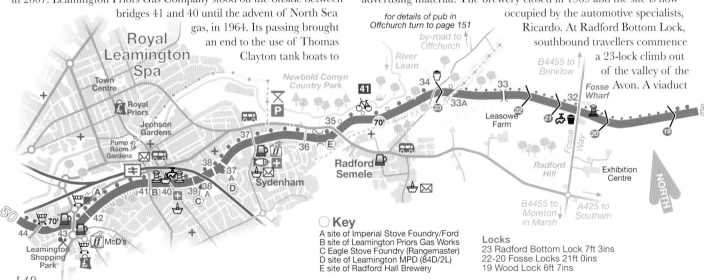

for details of pub in Offchurch turn to page 151

Key

A site of Imperial Stove Foundry/Ford
B site of Leamington Priors Gas Works
C Eagle Stove Foundry (Rangemaster)
D site of Leamington MPD (84D/2L)
E site of Radford Hall Brewery

Locks

23 Radford Bottom Lock 7ft 3ins
22-20 Fosse Locks 21ft 0ins
19 Wood Lock 6ft 7ins

148

carries the old Rugby & Leamington railway across the canal above the bottom lock. Sections of it have been converted for use as a cycle route, though not - disappointingly - across the viaduct itself. This is a shame, because before the high security fencing was erected you could wander on to the viaduct for a photogenic bird's eye view of the lock. From Bridge 34 there's access to the village of Offchurch and its fine church, St Gregory's. Bridge 32 carries the Roman Fosse Way on its way from Lincoln to Exeter, rather busier now than when the Legions tramped it.

East of Leamington the countryside is pleasant, if unspectacular. Reeds have colonised the shallow margins of the canal. Signs of habitation are few and far between. Apart from a cluster of canal cottages at Fosse Wharf, canal users are pretty much left to their own devices - which, of course, is exactly how most canallers, anxious to get away from the 'madding crowd', like it.

Royal Leamington Spa   Map 51

'Do you know that the stucco is peeling?' asked the opening poem of John Betjeman's first volume of poetry, *Mount Zion*, way back in 1932, and some of the buildings look as if they've been losing lumps of plaster ever since; particularly at the rather dowdy canal and railway end of things. But across the river, matters palpably improve, and you find yourself falling for Leamington's Regency elegance and general air of provincial well-being.

Eating & Drinking

FOX & VIVIAN - Clarendon Avenue. Tel: 01926 426559. Pub and steakhouse at the top end of the town. Open from 6-9pm Tue-Fri, Sat 5-9pm & Sun 12.30-4pm. CV32 4RZ

KAYAL - Regent Street. Tel: 01926 314800. Indian restaurant. CV32 5EG

MOMENTI - Regent Place. Tel: 01926 888895. Italian restaurant. CV31 1EH

THE MOORINGS AT MYTON - Myton Road. (Bridge 43). Tel: 01926 425043. Gastro-pub. CV31 3NY

OSCAR'S - Chandos Street. Tel: 01926 452807. French restaurant a worthwhile trek to the far end of town. CV32 4RL

PROCAFFEINATE - Clemens Street (Bridge 40). Tel: 01926 737006. Splendid coffee shop. Open daily from 7.30am (8.30 Sat/9.00 Sun) until 7pm Mon & Tue, 11pm Wed-Sat and 6pm Sun. CV31 2DN

TAME HARE - Warwick Street. Tel: 01926 316191. Small but classy restaurant open for lunch & dinner (from 6.30pm) Wed-Sat and Sun lunch. CV32 4RJ

Shopping

Retail therapy is what brings folk to Leamington now, and the emphasis is on upmarket retailing. Even its House of Fraser store appears to have survived Mike Ashley's takeover. Other chain stores occupy the prestigious Royal Priors shopping mall opened by the Queen in 1988, 150 years after Queen Victoria had granted the town its 'royal' prefix. Two of our more modest favourites are: Berylune on Warwick Street, who bill themselves as 'pint sized department store'; and Presto on neighbouring Park Street, specialists in classical music CDs. An out of town retail development offers a Sainsbury's superstore within easy reach of Bridge 43 for boaters. Easier still is a huge Morrisons on the towpath side. By Bridge 40 on Clemens Street there are a number of useful shops, including a Portuguese deli, pharmacy, Co-op, and cycle shop.

Things to Do

TOURIST INFORMATION - Royal Pump Rooms, The Parade. Tel: 01926 742700. CV32 4AA

ART GALLERY & MUSEUM - Royal Pump Rooms. Admission free. Tel: 01926 742700. CV32 4AA

JEPHSON GARDENS - Parade. Splendid park dating from 1831 and named after the visionary who put the Spa into Leamington Spa. Acres of gorgeously kept gardens, Victorian tea pavilion and boats for hire on the River Leam. The Lakeside Pavilion contains a Temperate House illustrating plant evolution. Rowing and motor boat hire on the Leam from boatyard by suspension bridge - Tel: 01926 889928.

Connections

TRAINS - good Chiltern/Cross Country services to/from Birmingham, Oxford & London Marylebone. Local trains call at Warwick, Hatton and Lapworth, ideal for towpath walking. Tel: 0345 748 4950. TAXIS - Sapphire. Tel: 01926 881313.

Sydenham   Map 51

Suburban shops, fish & chips and a pub called The Fusilier at Bridge 37. Frequent buses to/from Leamington town centre.

Radford Semele   Map 51

Village about ten minutes walk from Bridge 34. St Nicholas church overlooks the canal picturesquely, but is invariably locked in our experience.

Eating & Drinking

WHITE LION - Southam Road. Tel: 01926 885500. Open from 11.30am. Bar & kitchen food. CV31 1TE

Shopping

Well stocked convenience store (and post office) open from 7.30am (9am Sun) to 9pm. Stagecoach service 63 runs to/from Leamington.

52 GRAND UNION CANAL Long Itchington 4mls/15lks/4hrs

BOATERS have to flex their muscles as the Grand Union climbs out of (or descends into) the valley of the Avon. There are flights at Bascote and Stockton and isolated locks elsewhere. A number of the locks are overlooked by pretty tile-hung cottages built when the canal was modernised in the 1930s. Plenty of work, then, but charming countryside provides a stimulating antidote.

Welsh Road Lock recalls the far off days when the adjacent lane was a drover's road, along which cattle were driven on the long trek from Wales to the fattening fields of East Anglia and Smithfield Market in London. The road, which stretched from Brownhills in Staffordshire to Buckingham, is characterised by wide verges. Lofty reeds line the canal bank at intervals, emphasising its other-worldliness, a sense of isolation in the process of being rudely disturbed by the construction of HS2. Whichever camp you fall into - and the scheme does tend to polarise opinion - it is the first significant transport construction project in middle England since the end of the motorway era. A viaduct will carry the line across the canal between bridges 31 and 30, and work had commenced as we went to press.

The four locks at Bascote include a 'staircase' pair which replaced two conventional narrow locks in the 1930s. An embankment carries the canal over the River Itchen and past the attractive village of Long Itchington. Nearby the trackbed of the old Leamington-Weedon branch crosses the canal and the river, the latter upon a substantial viaduct still in situ though inaccessible. Parts of this old railway have been revitalised as National Cycle Route No.41. In *Anderton for Orders*, Tom Foxon described travelling along the line - 'across the night-shrouded Midland plain' - on his journey with John Knill to Braunston, where his working boat career was to begin. Odd, perhaps, to reflect in passing, that a new railway line is being built nearby, sixty years after a former line was abandoned.

Stockton Locks are set in a belt of blue lias limestone in which the fossils of gigantic reptiles have been found. In the commercial heyday of the canal, several lime, cement, brick and tile works flourished in the neighbourhood, providing considerable traffic. Vegetation inevitably hides the sites of most of these undertakings now. Arms extended in both directions to serve a number of sites. Kaye's Arm remains in water and

Locks
18 Welsh Road Lock 6ft 11ins
17-14 Bascote Locks 26ft 9ins
13 Itchington Bottom Lock 6ft 7ins
12-4 Stockton Locks 54ft 7ins

Key
A site of Kaye & Co cement works
B site of Greaves, Bull & Lakin's lime works
C site of Blue Lias lime works (Griffin & Co)

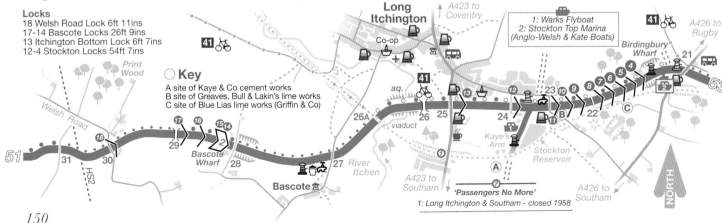

1: Warks Flyboat
2: Stockton Top Marina
(Anglo-Welsh & Kate Boats)

'Passengers No More'
1: Long Itchington & Southam - closed 1958

150

is occupied by a residential community of narrowboat dwellers. Kaye's had their own fleet of narrowboats, some of which were built by Nursers at Braunston. These were later taken over by the Rugby Portland Cement Co. As alluded to on Map 46, it was from their works at the end of the Kaye's Arm that British Waterways' final narrowboat contract was carried in 1969. Beyond the top lock, again overlooked by one of the Grand Union's characterful cottages, the canal penetrates a deepish cutting, before emerging by a busy hire base and welcoming inn.

Offchurch (Map 51)

A pleasant ten minute stroll along a country road north-east from Bridge 34 lies the village of Offchurch, named after Offa, King of Mercia. Charming church of St Gregory with exceptional 'Millennium Window', Saxon stone coffin, and churchyard designated a 'sanctuary for wildlife'.

Eating & Drinking

THE STAG - Welsh Road. Tel: 01926 425801. Thatched country pub under the same ownership as The Moorings in Leamington Spa. Open from noon daily; food lunchtimes and evenings from 6pm. Hook Norton, Purity and St Austell ales. CV33 9AQ

Long Itchington Map 52

The half mile walk up from the canal is amply rewarded by this charming village set beside the little River Itchen, a tributary of the Warwickshire Avon. At the edge of the village is Tudor House where Elizabeth I is reputed to have stayed. A large green then opens out before you, together with a pond that's home to some whopping tench. Further into the quiet heart of the village stands the church, best viewed from the bridge carrying the lane to Bascote over the river. A Blue Plaque commemorates the celebrated inventor of time-travel, Jacob von Hogflume, who lived in the village at one time.

Eating & Drinking

BOAT INN - Birdingbury Wharf (Bridge 21). Tel: 01926 812657. Country pub open from noon daily, food served lunchtimes and evenings from 6pm. CV23 8HQ

Radford 'Bottom'

BLUE LIAS - Bridge 23. Tel: 01926 812249. Popular canalside pub which gains its curious name from the local stone. CV47 8LD

BUCK & BELL - The Green. Tel: 01926 259221. Redbrick pub overlooking village green. CV47 9PH

CUTTLE INN - Bridge 25. Tel: 01926 812314. Canalside pub. CV47 9QZ

DUCK ON THE POND - The Green. Tel: 01926 811333. Charles Wells (of Bedford) pub with a good choice of food. CV47 9QJ.

GREEN MAN - Church Road. Tel: 01926 812208 Local with a beer festival each May. Regular draught ales include London Pride and Mad Goose. CV47 9PW

HARVESTER - village centre. Tel: 01926 812698. Old fashioned, *Good Beer Guide* listed pub run by the same family for over quarter of a century. Hook Norton beers and guests. Food lunchtimes and evenings: pizzas and steaks. CV47 9PE

TWO BOATS - Bridge 25. Tel: 01926 812640. Canalside Charles Wells pub. Food. CV47 9QZ

Shopping

There's a useful little shop (6am-8pm daily, EC Sun) on a housing estate reached via an alley and some lock-up garages from Lock 13. In the village there's a well-stocked Co-op with a cash machine.

Connections

BUSES - Stagecoach service 664 runs to/from Leamington, via the interesting town of Southam. Service 63 calls at stops by the Boat Inn, Bridge 21 for Rugby or Leamington. Tel: 0871 200 2233.

CONVERGING on Napton Junction, from which it shares the route to Braunston (Map 54) with the Oxford Canal, the Grand Union climbs through a trio of locks at Calcutt, completing an ascent of 146ft from the Avon Valley.

Fishing lagoons and scrub covered spoil tips are all that remain of a busy works once famous - in building merchant circles at least - for its 'Celebrated Portland Cement' and bantam cockerel trademark. In their heyday Nelson's operated a fleet of canal boats named after figures in Greek mythology. Three notable steamers were launched in 1885 - *Janus*, *Jason* and *Jupiter*. The cockerel image was incorporated into Nelson's boats livery scheme. The company was bought out by Rugby Portland Cement in 1945 and production transferred to Southam. Willow Wren - once the name carried by a latter-day canal carrying concern - but now tutors of boat-handling skill sets - have restored the arm which led into Nelson's cement works. Near Tomlow Bridge (No.18) the London & North Western Railway's Weedon &

Napton on the Hill (continuation)

1: Ventnor Farm Marina
2: Calcutt Boats
3: Napton Marina (Napton Narrowboats)
4: Wigrams Turn Marina (Black Prince)

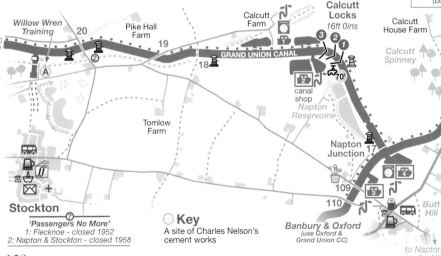

Willow Wren Training

Pike Hall Farm

Calcutt Farm

Calcutt Locks 16ft 0ins

Calcutt House Farm

Calcutt Spinney

GRAND UNION CANAL

OXFORD CANAL

Flecknoe Fields Farm

NORTH

to upper Shuckburgh

Lower Shuckburgh

Tomlow Farm

Napton Reservoirs

canal shop

70'

Napton Junction

Stockton

'Passengers No More'
1: Flecknoe - closed 1952
2: Napton & Stockton - closed 1958

○ **Key**
A site of Charles Nelson's cement works

Banbury & Oxford (use Oxford & Grand Union CC)

Butt Hill

to Napton on the Hill

Leamington branch crossed the canal. When the line opened in 1895 it captured much of the canal traffic in lime and cement centered on the blue lias quarries in the vicinity of Stockton.

Napton Junction once featured a stop lock and toll house. Working boatmen knew this as 'Wigram's Turn'; a name which has resurfaced with one of the relatively new marinas.

The W&N dug a reservoir at Napton in 1800, considering it a more robust and less expensive option than relying on the supply and purchase of water from the Oxford Canal Company. It proved a sound choice, so much so that a second reservoir was opened fourteen years later. The pair still feed the canal, water entering via the marina below the Calcutt flight. Furthermore, the reservoirs are much prized for their coarse fishing under the aegis of Leamington Anglers Association, tench being a notable catch.

East of Napton (that is to the *right* of the map) the shared section of the Oxford and Grand Union routes pursues a lonely course, jostling with the main road between Leamington and Daventry. Where, you may be wondering, are bridges 16 to 1? And the answer is that they were in the Grand Union's imagination. When they acquired control of the Warwick & Napton and Warwick & Birmingham route between Braunston and

Birmingham in 1929 they renumbered the sequence of bridges westwards from Braunston, including those on the Oxford Canal as far as Napton which never actually carried the GUC numbers allocated.

From the picturesque estate village of Lower Shuckburgh, a footpath climbs through parkland inhabited by fallow deer to Upper Shuckburgh. The name is said to mean 'a hill haunted by goblins.' Certainly Beacon Hill, rising to 678 feet, has its spirits. Whilst hunting on the hill, a 17th century member of the Shuckburgh family was reputedly accosted by King Charles I. On his way to the Battle of Edgehill, the King demanded to know how an English gentleman could spare time for country pursuits when his monarch was fighting for his crown. On a clear day it's possible to see westwards as far as the Malverns and the Black Mountains of Wales from the summit of Beacon Hill.

Stockton   Map 53

New housing developments are increasing Stockton's population, but it's the old rows of cement workers cottages which lend it a residual sense of atmosphere.

Eating & Drinking
CROWN - High Street. Tel: 01926 812255. CV47 8JZ
Also, Chinese take-away - Tel: 01926 811266.

Shopping
Post office stores.

Connections
BUSES - Stagecoach servce 63 runs hourly, daily to/from Leamington and Rugby. Tel: 0871 200 2233.

Napton on the Hill   Map 53

Napton (best reached from Bridge 109) basks in the sunshine (or shivers when a gale blows) on its south-facing hill. Ochre stone and thatch characterise the older buildings, brick the infills. Its street pattern takes some fathoming, but there is much green space between the houses and even the seemingly obligatory modern developments dovetail neatly into the whole.

Sheltered in the lee from north-easterlies, the parish church of St Lawrence has a Norman chancel with a sundial. You can climb towards the windmill for a better view, but it is private property.

Eating & Drinking
KING'S HEAD - on A425 south of Bridge 109. Tel: 01926 812202. Hook Norton pub with a good choice of food. Open noon to 3pm and from 5pm Mon-Thur, and from noon onwards Fri-Sun. CV47 8NG
NAPTON KITCHEN - cafe/take-away in village shop.

Shopping
Napton boasts a vibrant post office stores about a quarter of an hour's walk from Bridge 109 (Tel: 01926 812488 - CV47 8LR) open 7am-7pm Mon-Fri; 8am-6pm Sat; and 8am-12pm Sun. They are particularly proud of their locally sourced produce which ranges from honey and preserves to water buffalo burgers, sausages, steaks, cheese and ice cream. Bridge Nursery (adjacent Bridge 109 - Tel: 01926 812737) is open March-Oct, Thur-Sun, 10am-4pm.

Connections
BUSES - service 664 runs to/from Southam and Leamington approximately bi-hourly ex Sun. Tel: 0871 200 2233.
TAXIS - Cardall's of Southam. Tel: 01926 812145.

Lower Shuckburgh   Map 53

The kudos of entry in Simon Jenkins' *England's Thousand Best Churches*, doesn't guarantee an unlocked door at St John the Baptist's canalside church. 'For addicts of Victorian eccentricity', is Jenkins' opening gambit, and it seems that the architect (J. Croft of Islington) was encouraged by the local squire - who had just returned from the Crimea - to incorporate a number of oriental overtones.

Upper Shuckburgh (off the edge of the map) is the location of a stuccoed hall and another church, confusingly also called St John the Baptist. The Shuckburghs have dwelt here since the 12th century and nowadays advertise their otherwise private home as a venue for weddings and corporate hospitality.

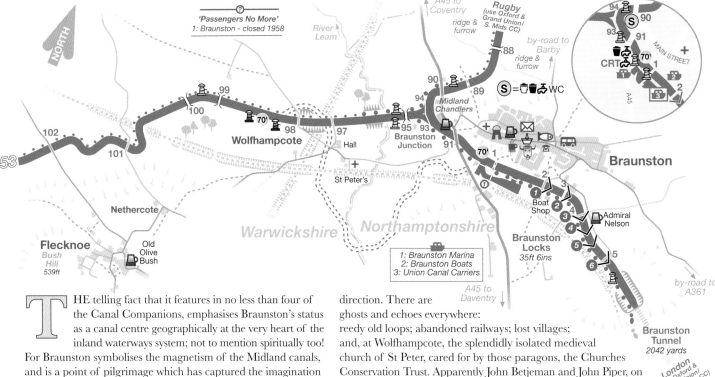

NORTH

'Passengers No More'
1: Braunston - closed 1958

River Leam

A45 to Coventry

Rugby
(use Oxford & Grand Union/ S. Mids CC)

ridge & furrow

by-road to Barby

ridge & furrow

88

99

100

102

101

53

70'

98

97

Wolfhampcote

Hall

St Peter's

+

90

94

Midland Chandlers

95 93

91

Braunston Junction

89

S = WC

CRT

94

93

S

90

91

70'

1

2

3

2

A45

MAIN STREET

+

Braunston

70' 1

Nethercote

Flecknoe
Bush Hill
539ft

Old Olive Bush

Warwickshire Northamptonshire

1: Braunston Marina
2: Braunston Boats
3: Union Canal Carriers

A45 to Daventry

2

1

1

2

3

4

3

4

5

5

6

Boat Shop

Admiral Nelson

Braunston Locks
35ft 6ins

by-road to A361

Braunston Tunnel
2042 yards

London
(use Oxford & Grand Union/ Leicester Line CC)

THE telling fact that it features in no less than four of the Canal Companions, emphasises Braunston's status as a canal centre geographically at the very heart of the inland waterways system; not to mention spiritually too! For Braunston symbolises the magnetism of the Midland canals, and is a point of pilgrimage which has captured the imagination of waterway writers, artists and photographers more than almost any other canal location.

One reaches Braunston from Napton along a thoroughly remote length of canal; the countryside falling flatly away to the north-west, but climbing abruptly to a notable ridge in the opposite direction. There are ghosts and echoes everywhere: reedy old loops; abandoned railways; lost villages; and, at Wolfhampcote, the splendidly isolated medieval church of St Peter, cared for by those paragons, the Churches Conservation Trust. Apparently John Betjeman and John Piper, on a visit circa 1960, accidentally stumbled into the vault in their boyish enthusiasm to explore the church's fabric. Stand in the nave now, and it's easy to imagine Betjeman's giggles emanating from below.

An embankment carries the canal across our old friend the River Leam, which rises west of the village of Hellidon, not far

*figures don't include Braunston Locks

from Daventry; passing from Warwickshire to Northamptonshire in the process. Braunston's triangular junction, with its twin Horseley Iron Works towpath bridges, was not the original meeting point of the Oxford and Grand Junction canals, but dates from improvements undertaken in the 1830s. Prior to that, the Oxford had meandered extravagantly between Braunston and Wolfhampcote, and the junction was in the vicinity of where the marina is today. With the completion of the Grand Junction and Oxford routes, Braunston became the equivalent of one of those out of the way railway junctions of the succeeding transport era; another Melton Constable or Evercreech, where the importance of the junction far transcended the size of the neighbouring community. In this case, the village remained aloof on its ridge, letting canalside Braunston hustle and bustle its way through two centuries of water transport.

Many of the fabled names of canal history went about their business here at one time or another: Pickfords in the early days; then Fellows, Morton & Clayton, whose steamers traded up from London and transhipped into horse-drawn narrowboats at this point. Down the years the roll-call lengthened: Nursers, boatbuilders, and painters of arguably the most sublime 'Roses & Castles' ever seen on the system; Samuel Barlow, coal carriers whose boats were always in the most pristine of condition; then, towards the end, Willow Wren and Blue Line, who kept canal carrying defiantly afloat into the era of the juggernaut. But the working boats have gone, and with them something of Braunston's old magic. An admirable, and justifiably popular Annual Rally of Historic Boats attempts to rekindle such scenes each June, but inevitably, like preserved railways, the essential ingredient of normality cannot be contrived. We can pay lip service to the past, but we can't pin it down. For a visual idea of how Braunston looked, you could do worse than invest in a copy of the late Mike Webb's *The Twilight Years of Narrow Boat Carrying*.

Braunston, nonetheless, is still a flourishing canal centre, home to a hire fleet and a large marina based on former reservoirs, as well as several other canal-orientated businesses. Saunter along the towpath and you'll see new boats being built, old ones restored, and a regular stream of traffic up and down the locks, and it only takes the aroma of a charcoal stove, the beat of a Bolinder, or the rattle of the ratchets in the twilight of an autumn afternoon for the old days to be almost tangibly evoked.

Braunston   Map 54

Village Braunston squats demurely four hundred feet up on the slopes of the Northamptonshire uplands. Enclosed fields, still bearing the pattern of ridge & furrow, distil the spirit of the Middle Ages. Sauntering along the High Street from the village green to the tall crockett-spired church (last resting place of a number of working-boat men and women) one encounters a mixture of stone and brick buildings, including a sail-less windmill and a 17th century manor house. At the foot of a long hill the A45 crosses the canal. This was the Chester turnpike road which became part of Telford's route from London to Holyhead. Now, handsome modern flats overlook the marina, and Braunston must be as busy and as populated as never before.

Eating & Drinking

ADMIRAL NELSON - canalside Bridge 4. Tel: 01788 891900. Refurbished canalside inn. Restaurant and bar meals, attractive garden. NN11 7HJ
THE BOAT HOUSE - canalside Bridge 91. Tel: 01788 891734. Marston's 'Two for One' family pub with customer moorings. NN11 7HB
GONGOOZLER'S REST - Stop House. Tel: 0794 097 3529. Floating cafe open 9am-2pm daily.
OLD OLIVE BUSH - Flecknoe. Tel: 01788 891134. Charming village pub idyllically approached on foot from Braunston via Wolfhampcote or by mooring in the vicinity of bridges 101 or 102 and walking up to Flecknoe, a mile from the canal. CV23 8AT
OLD PLOUGH - High Street. Tel: 01788 878126. Food served lunch and evening (ex Sun eve). NN11 7HS

YOUR CAFE - High Street. Community cafe. Gifts, teas, ice creams and homemade cakes. NN11 7HR

Shopping

Post office stores - open from 6am to 7.30pm (6pm Sun) - who advertise that they are happy to deliver to your boat (Tel: 01788 890334), and an enterprising butcher who additionally deals in hot pies and filled rolls and who also makes his own chutneys and sauces. Fred & Carol Barnes' Boat Shop (Tel: 01788 891310) opens from 8am-8pm throughout the summer season and deals in just about everything from gifts to groceries and friendly local knowledge.

Connections

BUSES - Stagecoach service D2 operates hourly Mon-Sat to/from Rugby and Daventry. Tel: 0871 200 2233.

This Guide

Pearson's Canal Companions are a long established, independently produced series of guide books devoted to the inland waterways and designed to appeal equally to boaters, walkers, cyclists and other, less readily pigeon-holed members of society. Considerable pride is taken to make these guides as up to date, accurate, entertaining and inspirational as possible. A good guide book should fulfil three functions: make you want to go; interpret the lie of the land when you're there; and provide a lasting souvenir of your journeys.

The Maps

There are fifty-four numbered maps whose layout is shown by the Route Planner inside the front cover. Maps 1 to 7 cover the River Avon upstream from Tewkesbury; Maps 8 to 13 cover the Stratford Canal from Stratford to King's Norton; Maps 14 to 20 the Worcester & Birmingham Canal between Birmingham and Worcester; Maps 21 & 22 the Droitwich Canals; Maps 23 to 31 the River Severn downstream from Stourport to Gloucester; Maps 32 to 35 the Gloucester & Sharpness Canal; Maps 36 to 44 the as yet largely unnavigable Cotswold Canals from Saul Junction to the Thames at Lechlade; and Maps 45 the Grand Union Canal between Birmingham and Braunston.

The maps - measured imperially like the waterways they depict, and not being slavishly north-facing - are easily read in either direction. Users will thus find most itineraries progressing smoothly and logically from left to right or vice versa. Figures quoted at the top of each map refer to distance per map, locks per map and average cruising time. An alternative indication of timings from centre to centre can be found on the Route Planner. Obviously, cruising times vary with the nature of your boat and the number of crew at your disposal, so quoted times should be taken only as an estimate. Neither do times quoted take into account

INFORMATION

any delays which might occur at lock flights in high season. Walking and cycling times will depend very much on the state of individual sections of towpath and the stamina of those concerned.

The Text

Each map is accompanied by a route commentary placing the waterway in its historic, social and topographical context. As close to each map as is feasible, gazetteer-like entries are given for places passed through, listing, where appropriate, facilities of

significance to users of this guide. Every effort is made to ensure these details are as up to date as possible, but - especially where pubs/restaurants are concerned - we suggest you telephone ahead if relying upon an entry to provide you with a meal at any given time.

Walking

The simplest way to go canal exploring is on foot along the towpaths originally provided so that horses could 'tow' boats. Walking costs little more than the price of shoe leather and you are free to concentrate on the passing scene; something that boaters, with the responsibilities of navigation thrust upon them, are not always at liberty to do. The maps set out to give some idea of the quality of the towpath on any given section of canal. More of an art than a science to be sure, but at least it reflects our personal experiences, and whilst it does vary from area to area, none of it should prove problematical for anyone inured to the vicissitudes of country walking.

We recommend the use of public transport to facilitate 'one-way' itineraries but stress the advisability of checking up to date details on the telephone numbers quoted, or on the websites of National Rail Enquiries or Traveline for trains and buses respectively.

Walking beside rivers is not always so easy. Over the centuries landowners have appropriated many ancient rights of way, whilst the demise of former ferries has also broken links which once existed. Fortunately, the Avon and the Severn are both accompanied by waymarked long distance paths - Shakespeare's Avon Way and the Severn Way respectively - and both routes are shown on the accompanying maps, though the additional use of an up to date Ordnance Survey Landranger or Explorer sheet is recommended. Should you be considering walking the full length of these paths over several consecutive days, Tourist Information Centres can usually be relied upon to offer accommodation advice.

Cycling

Bicycling along towpaths is an increasingly popular pastime, though one not always equally popular with other waterway users such as boaters, anglers and pedestrians. It is important to remember that you are sharing the towpath with other people out for their own form of enjoyment, and to treat them with the respect and politeness they deserve. A bell is a useful form of diplomacy; failing that, the ability to whistle (not necessarily tunefully) extracts from light operas.

Boating

Boating on inland waterways is an established, though relatively small, facet of the UK tourist industry. It is also, increasingly, a chosen lifestyle. There are approximately 38,000 privately owned boats registered on the canals, but in addition to these, numerous firms offer boats for hire. These range from small operators with half a dozen boats to sizeable fleets run by companies with several bases.

Most hire craft have all the creature comforts you are likely to expect. In the excitement of planning a boating holiday you may give scant thought to the contents of your hire boat, but at the end of a hard day's boating such matters take on more significance, and a well equipped, comfortable boat, large enough to accommodate your crew with something to spare, can make the difference between a good holiday and one which will be shudderingly remembered for the wrong reasons.

Traditionally, hire boats are booked out by the week or fortnight, though many firms now offer more flexible short breaks or extended weeks. All reputable hire firms give newcomers tuition in boat handling and lock working, and first-timers soon find themselves adapting to the pace of things 'on the cut'.

Navigational Advice

Newcomers, hiring a boat on the inland waterways

for the first time, have every right to expect sympathetic and thorough tuition from the company providing their boat. Boat-owners are, by definition, likely to be already adept at navigating. The following, however, may prove useful points of reference.

Locks are part of the charm of canal cruising, but they are potentially dangerous environments for children, pets and careless adults. Use of them should be methodical and unhurried, whilst special care should be exercised in rain, frost and snow when slippery hazards abound.

The locks included in this guide fall into two distinct types: narrow and wide. The narrow locks are to be found on the Stratford, Worcester & Birmingham and Droitwich Junction canals. The wide locks are on the River Avon, Droitwich Barge Canal, and Grand Union Canal. These locks can usually accept narrowbeam craft side by side and it helps save water (not to mention work-load) if they are shared with other boats travelling in the same direction. The locks on the River Severn are large, mechanically-operated and under the control of keepers. Boaters joining the Severn at Stourport, Hawford and Worcester are recommended to telephone ahead to the first lock they will encounter to let the keeper know they're coming.

Finally, it behoves us all to be on our best behaviour at locks. Remember to exercise a little 'give and take'. The use of foul mouths or fists to decide precedence at locks is one canal tradition not worthy of preservation.

Mooring on the canals featured in this guide is per usual practice - ie on the towpath side, away from sharp bends, bridge-holes and narrows. A 'yellow' bollard symbol represents visitor mooring sites; either as designated officially or, in some cases as recommended by our personal experience. Of course, one of the great joys of canal boating has always been the ability to moor wherever (sensibly) you like. In recent years, however, it has become obvious, particularly in urban areas, that there are an increasing number of undesirable locations where mooring is not to be recommended for fear of vandalism, theft or abuse. It would be nice if local authorities would see their way to providing pleasant, secure, overnight facilities for passing boaters who, after all, bring the commerce of tourism in their wake. Few boaters would object to making a small payment in such circumstances, as is the custom on a number of river navigations.

River moorings are not as easily come by as those on canals, mostly because the banks are in private

continued overleaf:

continued from page 157:

ownership. On the Avon and the Severn, therefore, it's wise to plan ahead and identify in advance where you plan to moor for a lunchtime stop or overnight. In addition to the visitor mooring symbols depicted on the maps, many riverside inns also offer mooring facilities for patrons. At busy times designated moorings can quickly fill-up and mooring alongside other boats (with co-operation, obviously) may provide a solution. **Turning** points on the canals are known as 'winding holes'; pronounced as the thing which blows because in the old days the wind was expected to do much of the work rather than the boatman. Winding holes capable of taking a full length boat of around seventy foot length are marked where appropriate on the maps. Winding holes capable of turning shorter craft are marked with the approximate length. It is of course possible to turn boats at junctions and at most boatyards, though in the case of the latter it is considered polite to seek permission before doing so. **Boating facilities** are provided at regular intervals along the inland waterways, and range from a simple water tap or refuse disposal skip, to the provision of sewage disposal, showers and laundry. Such vital features are also obtainable at boatyards and marinas along with repairs and servicing. An alphabetical list of boatyards appears opposite.

Closures (or 'stoppages' in canal parlance) traditionally occur on the inland waterways between November and April, when most of the heavy maintenance work is undertaken. Occasionally, however, an emergency stoppage, or perhaps water restriction, may be imposed at short notice, closing part of the route you intend to use. Up to date details are available on *www.canalrivertrust.org.uk* or from hire bases.

Canal & River Trust

The Canal & River Trust oversee all the canals and river navigations contained within this guide with the exception of the River Avon. Their Head Office is located at: First Floor North, Station House, 500 Elder

Gate, Milton Keynes MK9 1BB *www.canalrivertrust.org.uk* Members of the public can make enquiries at CRT's Customer Service Centre at Cambrian Wharf in Birmingham or their Gloucester office in the docks. Otherwise, the best means of making contact is via the internet or by telephoning: 0303 040 4040.

Avon Navigation Trust

This body oversees the upkeep and maintenance of the River Avon between Tewkesbury and Stratford. Their headquarters are at: Mill Wharf, Wyre Piddle, Pershore, Worcs WR10 2JF. Tel: 01386 552517.

ANT offer an extremely useful 'River Watch' scheme linked to a series of live web cams which provide 'real time' details of water levels, mooring occupancies and weather reports. *www.avonnavigationtrust.org*

Cotswold Canals Trust

The Cotswold Canals Trust have visitor centres at Saul (GL2 7LA - Tel: 0785 402 6504) and Stroud (GL5 3JS - Tel: 0758 228 6636). They operate boat trips and charters at Saul and Ebley - Tel: 0796 082 1642.

Societies

The Inland Waterways Association was founded in 1946 to campaign for the retention of the canal system. Membership details may be obtained from: Inland Waterways Association, Island House, Moor Road, Chesham HP5 1WA. Tel: 01494 783453. *www.waterways.org.uk* Several canals featured in this guide are also supported by individual groups who will advertise their presence locally or on the internet.

Amendments

Updates to current editions can be found on our website: *www.jmpearson.co.uk* Feel free to email us if you spot anything worth notifying others about.

Acknowledgements

Boundless appreciation to team stalwarts Karen Tanguy and Meg Gregory, and to the Short Run Press of Exeter who convert our outpourings into print. Further gratitude to Clive Matthews and Adrian Main of ANT; Gloucester Harbour Trustees; Thompson River Transport; Ralph Barber of H&GCT; the Canal & River Trust at Gloucester; all those invariably helpful River Severn lock-keepers; David Lewis, for coming up with the cricket reference on Map 14; and finally Mrs Jackie Pearson, who undertook to accompany the Chief Compiler on his journeys on the strict understanding that she wouldn't have to go anywhere near ... *water!*

Hire Bases

ABC BOAT HIRE - Alvechurch, Worcester & Birmingham Canal, Map 16; Worcester, Worcester & Birmingham Canal, Maps 20/25. Tel: 0330 333 0590. www.abcboathire.com

ANGLO WELSH WATERWAY HOLIDAYS - Wootton Wawen, Stratford-on-Avon Canal, Map 9; Tardebigge, Worcs & Birmingham Canal, Map 17; Stockton, Grand Union Canal, Map 52. Tel: 0117 304 1112. www.anglowelsh.co.uk

AVON VIEW MARINA - Pershore, River Avon, Map 3. Tel: 01386 641522. www.avonviewmarina.co.uk

BLACK PRINCE HOLIDAYS - Stoke Wharf, Worcester & Birmingham Canal, Map 17, Napton, Grand Union Canal, Map 53. Tel: 01527 575115. www.black-prince.com

BROOK LINE - Oddingley, Worcester & Birming-ham Canal, Map 19. Tel: 01905 773889. www.holidaysonwater.co.uk

CALCUTT BOATS - Stockton, Grand Union Canal, Map 53. Tel: 01926 813757. www.calcuttboats.com

GLOUCESTER NARROWBOATS - Slimbridge, Gloucester & Sharpness Canal, Map 34. Tel: 0777 446 4555. www.gloucesternarrowboats.co.uk

KATE BOATS - Warwick, Grand Union Canal, Map 50; Stockton, GU Canal, Map 52. Tel: 01926 492968. www.kateboats.co.uk

NAPTON NARROWBOATS - Napton, Oxford Canal, Map 53. Tel: 01926 813644. www.napton-marina.co.uk

STARLINE - Stourport, River Severn, Map 23. Tel: 01531 632003. www.starlinenarrowboats.co.uk

UNION CANAL CARRIERS - Braunston, Grand Union Canal, Map 54. Tel: 01788 890784. www.unioncanalcarriers.co.uk

Boatyards

ANGLO WELSH - Wootton Wawen, Stratford Canal, Map 9. Tel: 01564 793427. B95 6BZ

ANGLO WELSH - Tardebigge, Worcs & Birmingham Canal, Map 17. Tel: 01527 87389.8 B60 1LR

ALVECHURCH MARINA - Alvechurch, Worcester & Birmingham Canal, Map 16. Tel: 0121 4451133. B48 7SQ

AVON VIEW MARINA - Pershore, River Avon, Map 3. Tel: 01386 641522. WR10 3BX

BIDFORD BOAT SERVICES - Bidford, River Avon, Map 6. Tel: 0779 652 0825. B50 4JJ (day boat hire)

BOATING DIRECTORY

BLACK PRINCE Stoke Wharf, Worcester & B'ham Canal. Map 17. Tel: 01527 575115. B60 4LA

BRAUNSTON BOATS - Braunston, Grand Union Canal, Map 54. Tel: 01788 891079. NN11 7HJ

BRAUNSTON MARINA - Braunston, Grand Union Canal, Map 54. Tel: 01788 891373 NN11 7JH

BREDON MARINA - Bredon, River Avon, Map 1. Tel: 01684 773166. GL20 3XZ

BROOK LINE - Oddingley, W & B Canal, Map 19. Tel: 01905 773889. WR9 7JX

CALCUTT BOATS - Stockton, Grand Union Canal, Map 53. Tel: 01926 813757. CV47 8HX

COPT HEATH WHARF - Copt Heath, Grand Union Canal, Map 47. Tel: 0121 704 4464. B91 2SX (day boat hire)

CRAFTED BOATS -Worcester & B'ham Canal, Stoke Prior, Map 17. Tel: 01527 876438. B60 4JZ

R. W. DAVIS & SON - Saul, Gloucester & Sharpness Canal, Map 33. Tel: 01452 740233. GL2 7LA

DEFFORD QUAY MARINA - River Avon, Map 2. Tel: 0797 104 1461. WR8 9BU

DELTA MARINE - Warwick, GU Canal, Map 50. Tel: 01926 499337. CV34 5JB

DIGLIS MARINA - Worcester & Birmingham Canal, Map 20. Tel: 01905 356314. WR5 3BW

DROITWICH SPA MARINA - Droitwich Canals, Map 22. Tel: 0797 062 6807. WR9 7DU

EVESHAM MARINA - Evesham, River Avon, Map 4. Tel: 01386 768500. WR11 3XZ

HILL FARM MARINA - Wootton Wawen, Stratford Canal, Map 9. Tel: 01564 627280. B95 6DE

KATE BOATS - Warwick, GU Canal, Map 50. Tel: 01926 492968. CV34 5JB

KNOWLE HILL WHARF - Knowle, Grand Union Canal, Map 48. Tel: 01564 778210. B93 0JJ

LIMEKILN CHANDLERS - Stourport, Staffs & Worcs Canal, Map23. Tel: 01299 821111. DY13 9EL

FRANK LYONS - Warstock, Stratford-on-Avon Canal, Map 13. Tel: 0121 474 4977. B14 4SP

SALTISFORD CANAL CENTRE - Warwick, GU Canal, Map 50. Tel: 01926 490006. CV34 5RJ

SANKEY MARINE - Evesham, River Avon, Map 4. Tel: 01386 442338. WR11 4TA

SAUL JUNCTION MARINA - Saul, Gloucester & Sharpness Canal, Map 33. Tel: 01452 740043. GL2 7JY

SHARPNESS MARINE - Sharpness, Gloucester & Sharpness, Map 35. Tel: 01453 811476. GL13 9UN

STARLINE MARINE - Stourport, Staffs & Worcs Canal, Map 23. Tel: 01531 632003. DY13 9EP

STOCKTON TOP MARINA - Stockton, GU Canal, Map 52. Tel: 01926 492968. CV47 8HN

STOURPORT MARINA - Stourport, River Severn, Map 23. Tel: 01299 827082. DY13 9QF

STRENSHAM MILL - Strensham, River Avon, Map 2. Tel: 01684 274244. WR8 9LB

SWALLOW CRUISERS - Hockley Heath, Stratford-on-Avon Canal, Map 11. Tel: 01564 783442. B94 5NR

TEWKESBURY MARINA - Tewkesbury, River Avon, Map 1. Tel: 01684 293737. GL20 5BY

UPTON MARINA - Upton-on-Severn, River Severn, Map 28. Tel: 01684 594287. WR8 0PB

VENTOR FARM MARINA - Calcutt, GU Canal, Map 53. Tel: 01926 815023. CV23 8HY

WARINGS GREEN WHARF - Illshaw Heath, Stratford Canal, Map 12. Tel: 0744 457 946.9 B94 6BU

WARKS FLYBOAT - Stockton, GU Canal, Map 52. Tel: 01926 812093. CV47 8LD

WELFORD BOAT STATION - Welford, River Avon, Map 6. Tel: 01789 750878. CV37 8PP

WIGRAMS TURN MARINA - Napton, Oxford Canal, Map 53. Tel: 01926 817175. CV47 8NL

WORCESTER MARINA - Lowesmoor Wharf, Worcester, Map 20. Tel: 01905 734160. WR1 2RS

WYRE BOATYARD - Wyre Piddle, River Avon. Map 3. Tel: 0775 436 2567. WR10 2JF

THE TEN CANAL COMPANIONS

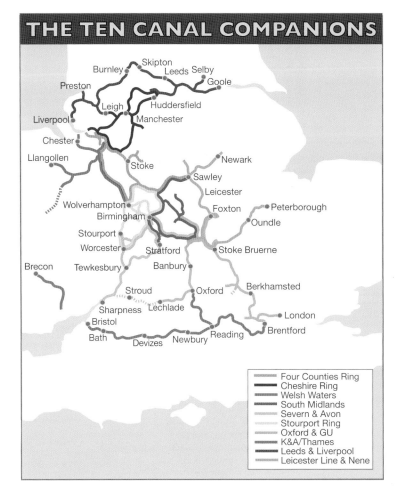

- Four Counties Ring
- Cheshire Ring
- Welsh Waters
- South Midlands
- Severn & Avon
- Stourport Ring
- Oxford & GU
- K&A/Thames
- Leeds & Liverpool
- Leicester Line & Nene